THE POSTAL AGE

WITHDRAWN

DAVID M. HENKIN

THE POSTAL AGE

THE EMERGENCE OF

MODERN COMMUNICATIONS IN

NINETEENTH-CENTURY

AMERICA

THE UNIVERSITY OF CHICAGO PRESS • CHICAGO AND LONDON

The University of Chicago Press, Chicago 60637
The University of Chicago Press, Ltd., London
© 2006 by The University of Chicago
All rights reserved. Published 2006
Paperback edition 2007
Printed in the United States of America

16 15 14 13 12 11 10 09 08 07   2 3 4 5 6

ISBN-13: 978-0-226-32721-1 (paper)
ISBN-10: 0-226-32721-3 (paper)

Library of Congress Cataloging-in-Publication Data

Henkin, David M.
    The postal age : the emergence of modern communications in nineteenth-century
America / David M. Henkin.
        p.   cm.
    Includes bibliographical references and index.
    ISBN-13: 978-0-226-32720-4 (hardcover : alk. paper)
    ISBN-10: 0-226-32720-5 (hardcover : alk. paper)
    1. Postal service—United States—History—19th century.   2. Communication—Social
aspects—United States.   I. Title.
HE6371.H46   2006
383'.497309034—dc22

2006013710

For R. S., friend and correspondent

CONTENTS

PREFACE

It has become commonplace—almost to the point of being unfashion-able—to describe electronic mail, faxes, video conferences, automated banking, and other communications media of recent vintage as agents in a millennial refashioning of current sensibility and subjectivity. New technologies, we often observe, have altered our experiences of time and space and unsettled the boundaries separating persons, communities, and nations. Against the backdrop of this particular strand of cultural self-consciousness, older forms of communication can appear quaint and even reassuring. The traditional posted and stamped letter—what enthusiasts of the new media call "snail mail"—seems so slow, so heavy, and so material by current technological standards that it is sometimes hard to remember that we still rely on the U.S. Postal Service for much of our daily business and many of our daily pleasures. Even in an age of digital information, the postal system remains a central and almost won-drous institution. For a very small fee, an elaborate national bureaucracy comes to our homes and workplaces and delivers objects of our choos-ing virtually anywhere in the country and to countless foreign locales. Linking distant individuals in a web of regular exchanges and tethering them to networks of institutional power, the postal system fulfills several of the cultural functions attributed to newer media, if at a significantly slower pace. If the posted letter appears in the role of dinosaur in many dramatic accounts of global social change, it nonetheless continues to play an intensely modern function in everyday life.

The following chapters push this claim further. A postal network that became popular during the middle of the nineteenth century laid the cultural foundation, as I hope to demonstrate, for the experiences of interconnectedness that are the hallmarks of the brave new world of telecommunications. What is most odd about this argument is probably not that it anchors current phenomena in the bygone antebellum era. Apart from the fact that historians are always in the habit of pressing paternity suits for newborn social arrangements against the periods of their own expertise, the nineteenth century—the age of industrialization and urbanization—is conventionally regarded as the point of origin for much of what we regard as modern. We have come to accept without blinking suggestions that the railroads introduced modern notions of time or that the telegraph was "the Victorian Internet." What is unlikely about the particular genealogy that I propose in this book is that the mid-nineteenth-century post was not, by any conventional standard, a new medium at all. The post would appear to be an ancient institution—as old as writing itself—and mail service in mid-nineteenth-century America dwells in the popular imagination somewhere in the *longue durée* that stretches from Herodotus's swift couriers working the gloom-of-night shift up to the Pony Express (1860–61). In a recent study of the "social history of the media," the accompanying chronology of events in media history (broadly enough conceived to include the first typewriter in 1829, the 1850 debut of *Harper's New Monthly*, the introduction of the bicycle in 1870, and the Athens Olympic Games of 1896 among hundreds of entries) lists only one development in the history of the nineteenth-century post, and none from the United States.

Yet despite the absence of a flashy new machine or a celebrated turning point, a new set of practices and expectations was emerging at this time. Before telephones, before recorded sound, before the transcontinental railroad, and even before the spread of commercial telegraphy, postal exchanges began habituating large groups of Americans to new expectations of contact with distant places. Mail delivery, which had served for most Americans in the early national and Jacksonian periods as their primary contact with an expanding federal government, came to mark during the 1840s, '50s, and '60s the dominant moment of connection with what was being reconstituted as an outside world. *The Postal Age* explores the social practices and cultural stakes that developed around that moment of connection and around the new forms of intimacy and alienation that it came to represent. Seen from the perspective of ordinary people, what may have been most remarkable about the middle decades of the nineteenth century was the novel experience of being accessed and addressed by a system of mass communication.

The full sociological and psychological implications of the changes described here undoubtedly varied, spilling beyond the borders of any meaningful historical generalization. Especially hard to assess is the role of the post in the cultivation of those habits of mind that are cited by scholars and cultural commentators to contrast traditional communities with modern impersonal societies. As with the new communications media that have proliferated in recent years, the spread of mail facilitated new patterns and forms of intimacy while simultaneously promoting and institutionalizing diverse and dizzying possibilities of anonymous exchange. In both historical developments, the interesting story is not so much how a medium cements or severs meaningful social relations but how users adapt their understanding of the world they inhabit to changing social expectations, norms, and desires. What follows, in any event, is an interpretive account of how, at an earlier moment in American history, ordinary people negotiated a modern communications network.

ACKNOWLEDGMENTS

To its impatient author, this publication feels a long time in coming. It humbles me to imagine how much longer it would have taken without the generous collaboration of so many people and one large institution. The institutional debt is easy to acknowledge, if not to discharge. The University of California has been a wonderful employer, not least in providing the material assistance that made it possible to write a book. A fellowship from Berkeley's Townsend Humanities Center in 1998–99 helped launch the project, while sabbatical leaves (funded in part by Humanities Research Grants) and a University of California President's Research Fellowship in the Humanities effectively underwrote much of the research and writing that appear here. Significant funding from the Hellman Faculty Fellowship and numerous smaller awards from the Committee on Research supported archival visits, helped me to acquire research materials (including numerous nineteenth-century letters on eBay), and mustered the army of research assistants without whom an attack on the vast subject of postal culture would have been unthinkable. Again, all of this support came from the public university where I am fortunate and honored to work.

My debts to people are harder to reckon, simply because they are so numerous and varied. Over the past few years countless friends, colleagues, readers, auditors at conference presentations, and even casual acquaintances have suggested sources, forwarded citations, offered encouraging and provocative thoughts, or simply asked curious questions that got me thinking in some new way about my subject. That I now recall the contributions (intended or not) of Jill Anderson, Tom Augst, Dorrie Beam, Cathy Carson, Kon Dierks, Paul Erickson, Paula Fass, Kathy Frydl, Jon Gjerde, Amy Greenberg, Mark Healey, Leon Jackson, Kerwin Klein, Erika Kreger, Susan Lepselter, Sharon Marcus, Lori Merish, Sam Otter, Leah Price, Jennifer Spear, Richard Stillson, Rabbi Joseph Telushkin, Tamara Plakins Thornton, and James Vernon probably covers a very modest fraction of the variety and volume of informal assistance that came from such encounters.

My research assistants contributed in more sustained and systematic ways and deserve more than this paragraph. Listing them alphabetically diminishes the nature of their work by concealing the variety of roles they played—scouring newspapers and digital databases, translating secondary literature, analyzing architectural plans, reading legal cases, securing publication permissions, deciphering handwritten correspondence, and photocopying dead-letter lists. At different points along the way (and in some cases for long periods of time), Corey Brooks, Jen Dibara, Kathryn Eigen, Carlton Evans, Phil Gruen, Katherine Hijar, Sarah Jackson, Eric Klocko, Karen McNeill, Ana Vohryzek-Griest, Bill Wagner, and Aaron Wunsch climbed aboard this project and performed at least one of those valuable services. In a different academic discipline, a few of those names would have appeared on the title page.

Though my contacts with them were far more fleeting, staff members at libraries and archives in San Francisco, Berkeley, Chicago, Chapel Hill, Washington, D.C., Philadelphia, New York, New Haven, Worcester, and Cambridge were uniformly helpful. Timothy Carr at the National Postal Museum Library took time to discuss my project and pointed me to several useful sources. Later in the process, two kind anonymous reviewers for the Press helped me reorganize some of the material presented here and pushed me to clarify some of my claims and investments. Later still, Nicholas Murray labored mightily to improve the prose and tame the morass of documentation that follows in the endnotes. I am grateful for all of their help.

In the course of writing this book I met two people (both Chicagoans) who went beyond the call of their respective positions to enrich my work. Richard R. John's generous engagement with me as I worked in the field that he had cleared and cultivated will come as no surprise to those familiar with his professional dedication and his deep passion for the postal system. But such explanations do not even begin to account for the energy he invested, the materials he shared, and the broad-mindedness with which he engaged an interpretive approach to postal history that he surely found odd and exasperating at times. While he is obviously acquitted of any complicity in the arguments I put forward here, I trust he won't resent my thinking of him as a collaborator. The other collaborator can hardly be surprised by the designation. From our first discussion, Robert Devens has helped me to understand the book I was writing, and, throughout the process, his has been the advice I have been most likely to follow. He is a conscientious reader and an exemplary editor.

Finally, I acknowledge my parents, whose lives continue to remind me to write often and to read deeply, and my brothers, who have shared (in different ways) the burden and the blessing of that injunction. And then there are lots of friends who buffeted this project along and helped me figure out why I cared about the mail and the social worlds that develop around it. Some, like James Vernon and Sharon Marcus, are colleagues with whom I explicitly discussed the book. But most are lay people who conducted this conversation with me in oblique and displaced ways. Maybe it need not or should not be expressed, or maybe it cannot be expressed, but it strikes me that for some or all of the past seven years Alexandra Weathers Smith, Carlton Evans, and Jennifer Elias lived with this book. It is hard to tell the story of how I wrote about the post without reflecting on their very daily, decidedly nonpostal presence in my life in San Francisco. Other, older friends, including the one to whom this book is dedicated, reaffirm my faith in the endurance of ties of a different sort.

INTRODUCTION

Immediately following his dramatic recapture in 1854, the fugitive slave Anthony Burns was forcibly returned to a life of legal bondage in Virginia, where he languished for four months in the solitary confinement of a cramped and fetid Richmond jail cell. Handcuffed and fettered for much of his stay, Burns struggled heroically to maintain human contacts, boring a hole in the floor with a stolen spoon so that he could communicate with other prisoners. More remarkably, Burns also succeeded in communicating with people at far greater distances. Having managed to conceal stationery, procure ink, and break off pieces of the cell's brick walls, Burns would wait for a black person to pass below his cell and drop a letter (paper fastened to rock) through the window bars. From the depths of his solitary confinement, six letters composed by Burns's manacled hands made their way out the window, to the post office, inside a U.S. mailbag, and ultimately to destinations as far away as Massachusetts, where one of them reached his lawyer, Richard Henry Dana.[1]

Narrating this moral triumph of the unbroken spirit—and the written word—over physical incarceration, Burns's contemporary abolitionist biographer Charles Emery Stevens emphasized the irony that a slave such as Burns could expect no reply to his letters, as "none would have reached him had they been written."[2] A letter addressed to a slave and bearing a postmark from the North, Stevens noted ruefully, would be withheld from its addressee and turned over to his or her master. But while this rupture in postal transmission outraged Stevens, modern readers are more apt to be struck by the fact that Burns was successfully using the post at all. A man whose status as chattel under the law of Virginia had just been reaffirmed by the United States government (at considerable financial cost and with armed force) managed to use the facilities of the federal postal system, including those housed in Virginia, to engage in confidential correspondence with his abolitionist lawyer in Boston. However compromised and selective the U.S. mail appeared (quite justifiably) to critics of slavery in the United States, there was room within its impersonal network for someone like Anthony Burns at a time when all of his other petitions for inclusion were denied and all his other attempts at mobility thwarted.

Though his unlikely acquisition of writing materials and the laborious process of passing letters out of a locked cell endow Burns with a mythic quality in Stevens's hagiographical text, there was in other respects nothing extraordinary or fortuitous about his use of the post. Burns's success depended not only on his ingenuity and courage, but also on a broadly shared awareness of the existence and accessibility of a national postal network. Burns's African-American accomplice passing below was "in all probability an entire stranger, as well as a person unable to read." Nonetheless, as Stevens noted, the prisoner assumed, "not unreasonably, that his wishes would be rightly interpreted, and that his letters would reach the post-office."[3] Even an illiterate slave, both Stevens and Burns imagined, could recognize mail and know what to do with it. The safe arrival of the letter in Dana's hands (after a brief delay caused by its misdelivery to a distant relative with the same surname) vindicated this assumption.

Nowadays, in an age when envelopes, stamps, standardized mailboxes, uniformed letter carriers, and distinctive mail vehicles are ubiquitous and recognizable, the faith of Burns and Stevens may seem commonplace. In 1854, however, this signaled a remarkable cultural transformation. During the middle decades of the nineteenth century, ordinary Americans began participating in a regular network of long-distance communication, engaging in relationships with people they did not see. The change was not the direct result of any scientific breakthrough in what we customarily think of as communications technology, nor was it entirely the product of a particular political or entrepreneurial vision. It is even tempting to argue that the spread of postal practices was not really an event in the conventional sense; rather, like many far-reaching changes in daily life, it was protracted and uneven. The best evidence suggests, however, that in 1820 most Americans did not engage directly in any form of interactive, long-distance communications network, while by 1870 most of them did. In the long historical view, this appears as a powerful rupture and a fundamental divide.

For convenience, one might date the crux of the change around the years 1845 and 1851, when Congress enacted substantial reductions in the cost of sending a letter, thus bringing an expanding system of post roads and mail carriers within the grasp of millions. These acts are compelling signs of the revolution that was taking place, but they do not entirely explain it. On the one hand, postage reductions were passed on the strength of new expectations that masses of people would in fact use the post, and thus these reforms reflected changes in American society that were already visible. On the other hand, it would take several years for the opportunities presented by cheap postage to be absorbed into the rhythms of ordinary life. The dates 1845 and 1851 thus stand at the center of a revolutionary era in nineteenth-century U.S. history, when a critical mass of Americans began reorganizing their perceptions of time, space, and community around the existence of the post.

It is possible to quantify the changes that took place in the middle decades of the century. From 1840 to 1860 the number of letters carried annually by the U.S. Post Office increased from about 27 million to about 161 million. Per capita, the yearly total more than tripled, from 1.61 to 5.15.[4] These figures do not tell the whole story, however. What changed was not simply the volume of correspondence or the number of correspondents but the expectation of contact and the perception of access. During the middle of the century, it became increasingly common to describe postal access as a fundamental condition of modern life. Postal agent James Holbrook found it "impossible to conceive" in 1855 how society could exist without "the regular delivery of letters": "Imagine a town without a post office! a community without letters! 'friends, Romans, countrymen, and lovers,' particularly the lovers, cut off from correspondence, bereft of newspapers, buried alive from the light of intelligence, and the busy stir of the great world! What an appalling picture!"[5] A speaker at a public meeting in Minnesota in 1859 proclaimed proudly that the "American citizen is not willing to live beyond the reach of a post office" and "takes too much interest in the world's progress to be content with anything less than a semi-weekly mail."[6] Junius H. Browne, in an 1869 guide to New York, asserted that postal correspondence was universal in the United States. "The man who has not received a letter has not been discovered, though, if he exists, he lives in the interior of Arkansas or the Eastern part of Louisiana."[7] Earlier, in an 1826 epistolary guide, a professor of French at a Connecticut military academy had insisted that "every person, in the course of his life, finds it necessary to write a letter." By 1869, a composition book could expand the claim considerably: "By far the largest part of all that most people write, or have occasion to write, consists of letters."[8] Thoreau's classic dismissal of correspondence in *Walden*, where he boasted that he "could easily do without the post-office," confirmed the status of the post as a pillar of modern sociability—a universal obsession renounced by a defiant and secluded individual.[9]

Such assertions about the indispensable nature of mail service reflected various motivations and suggested different investments in the institution of the post. Epistolary guides can hardly be trusted to provide reliable testimonials about the universal use of the mails, and commercial boosters in Minnesota were far less interested in personal correspondence than in the frequent arrival of newspapers. But the plausibility of all of these paeans to the post rested on a growing self-consciousness among Americans of various social situations about their dependence on postal communication. Most dramatically, Americans began to turn expectantly to the post, calibrating their perceptions of connectedness to the regular schedules of the U.S. mail.

This sense of expectation was especially acute among those who were separated from their homes or their loved ones for what they thought of as a protracted but temporary period—itself an increasingly common condition in antebellum America. In an 1846 letter to her husband, an officer fighting in the Mexican War, Frances Webster testified that the "mail is the barometer by which my spirits are elevated or depressed; if it comes without the expected letter from you (and *once* a week at least I look for one) I am completely disconsolate." For Susan Folger Gardner, whose husband Charles had joined the California Gold Rush, daily life back in Nantucket in 1852 meant continual attendance to the regular arrivals of boats from the mainland. "Ah I live in hope about the next mail," she admitted in her diary.[10] Charlotte Forten, a young African American from Massachusetts who spent part of the Civil War in South Carolina, recorded in a diary some of her frustrations with this anxious dependence:

> This morn. Mr. R[uggles] beaming with delight informed me that there was a large mail in by the "Star of the South." I'm afraid I answered somewhat impatiently that I was disgusted with mails, and that I wasn't going to expect any more. I had been so often disappointed. Nevertheless, I *did* expect, despite myself. I did hope for those letters this time. And when we heard that there were letters for us at The Oaks, we at once despatched our trusty Cupid there. With what a beating heart did I await his coming. Calm outwardly, but what a flutter of expectation within. I never sh'ld have thought that I sh'ld become so *insane* about letters.[11]

Not every American suffered the same "flutter of expectation" at the announcement of a mail delivery. Webster, Gardner, and Forten found themselves in unusual situations created by wars and spectacular migrations. But their turn to the post office involved them in everyday rituals and habits. Though a mail steamer or stagecoach might embody an absent parent, lover, or business partner in the imagination of a displaced correspondent, it also came to represent a system of circulation whose regular openings and transmissions rendered absent people always in some sense accessible. Posted letters were not simply individual utterances sent through a specifically appointed messenger; they were the content of a continuous stream of messages passing through a network of communication channels that ran whether or not any particular person had something to say. "Remember the mail is always open," advised an 1852 article in *Godey's Lady's Book*, whose author wished to reassure readers that a prompt response to a letter was better than a complete one.[12] The postal system was becoming, in other words, a network in the most modern sense.

Studies of postal service in nineteenth-century America have emphasized how technological innovations and administrative interventions extended the reach of an impressive federal bureaucracy into all areas of economic and political life. Postal records provide a compelling picture of the growth of government, the geography of capital, and the migration of people during this era. Debates about postal patronage, finance, protocols, and schedules also illuminate the central political dilemmas and conflicts of the antebellum era. But to understand what mail meant to *users* requires a more sustained look at American life in the 1840s, '50s, and '60s. What did it mean for different groups of Americans to interact with absent friends and relatives or to transact business with invisible parties? How did Americans come to expect regular contact with an outside world and to turn to the institution of the post office as their point of access to that world? How did they cultivate particular kinds of intimacy and detachment suitable to the forms of exchange that the post facilitated? These inquiries inevitably lead us beyond the confines of an institutional history of the Post Office Department into the world of everyday experience and belief—to a diffuse *culture* of the post.[13]

Describing the changes that took place during the middle of the nineteenth century as the emergence of a new postal culture does not imply that those changes took place exclusively in the realm of ideas or that the history of the post is best glimpsed through the study of works of art or symbolic representation. Nor should the word *culture* be misunderstood to suggest that the impact of the mail was determined largely by features of the American national character or by those entrenched systems of belief that historians sometimes have in mind when they characterize their interpretations as cultural. The new postal culture was a cluster of new practices, attitudes, norms, discussions, and, crucially, habits—of communication, inquiry, and expectation—that grew up around a modern postal system.

It is of course more difficult to locate and assess evidence for changes in these realms of human experience than to document the proliferation of mail routes, but the culture of the post is hardly beyond the reach of the historical record. Published accounts of the practices associated with the mail surfaced throughout the daily and periodical press at mid-century and contributed to the emergence of a public discourse about the post, much as the culture of information technology in our own time is simultaneously documented and constructed in newspapers and magazines. Novels, short stories, political essays, and travel literature also provide, both intentionally and inadvertently, clues to the way Americans experienced the post. A striking number of mail users recorded their postal habits and anxieties in diaries and personal recollections, genres whose popularity blossomed in tandem with the general increase in correspondence. Finally, letters themselves provide an invaluable source for understanding what the spread of the post meant to the lives of everyday people. Despite the exaggerated aura of secrecy and privacy that surrounds personal correspondence (and despite the flimsy materials, ephemeral purposes, and unheeded wishes for self-destruction that attended so much epistolary contact), an extraordinary number of letters have survived, filling historical societies, manuscript collections, and private attics throughout the country. The sheer volume and diversity of this archive is daunting—and potentially confusing—but there is no better repository of information concerning the uses to which Americans put their increasingly accessible postal network and the expectations they brought to it. Historians have relied upon this source base, perhaps more than any other, to reconstruct everything from diplomatic negotiations to courtship rites, from slaveholding practices to immigration patterns, often with the underexamined assumption that letters provide unusually transparent windows into the sincere beliefs or private lives of their authors. In most of these accounts, however, letters are read with minimal critical attunement to their construction and with little interest in the material and cultural conditions of their transmission. We have, in other words, barely begun to study the modern posted letter as its own distinctive historical practice. A comprehensive study of nineteenth-century correspondence lies beyond the limitations of this book, but an understanding of the implications of letter-writing in this era requires rereading some of these documents within the context of postal history. As sources, letters are most instructive not so much as samples of epistolary practice (variations in style, content, and context limit the sorts of generalizations one can draw from such an enormous archive) but as commentaries on the medium, as special sites where public perceptions of the post are both absorbed and elaborated. Letters, as this book will argue, reflected and reinforced emerging beliefs about the possibility and meaning of interacting with absent parties.

The diffuse character of the new postal culture documented in this wide array of sources calls for a study of straining and unlikely breadth. Such a history would appear to fly in the face of decades of accumulated historical research and insight. The more we know about the United States during the nineteenth century, the harder it is to sustain a narrative (or even a single claim) about what that society was like as a whole—the harder it is to speak, in other words, with any confidence or coherence about Americans as a collective entity. As historians locate new sources, attend to neglected voices and perspectives, pose new questions, and constitute new aspects of everyday life as subjects of scholarly inquiry, the heterogeneity of historical experience becomes the increasingly salient fact about the American past. This is not an unwelcome development. Far from impoverishing public dialogue about the past, recognition of divergent experiences, distinct subcultures, contradictory perspectives, and mutually indifferent pursuits enriches our relationship to history by helping us to see in earlier periods the contrasts, variations, and continuities that we recognize in the societies we currently inhabit. There is no reason why the study of the past needs to produce grand syntheses of eras or generalized claims about nations or other collective entities.

Nonetheless, there are collective stories that can and should be told. Expanded research agendas ought to enable rather than impede inquiries into the collective features and dimensions of everyday life and into moments when otherwise unconnected people become newly entangled around an event, a social practice, or a perception of a shared border. The history of the first half of the nineteenth century in the United States is especially rich in examples of new institutions and rituals through which masses of American people became aware of their interconnections and interdependencies. Many of the hallmark developments of the era—market expansion, participatory democracy, class formation, rail transportation, fixed-route urban transit, mass commercial entertainment, mass publishing, mass literacy, public schooling, cheap daily newspapers—conform to this model. Though these developments, taken together, did not collapse social differences or create a unified national culture, they were nonetheless crucial (not least in fostering many of the cultural preconditions for modern thinking about unity and difference in historical experience). The emergence of a postal culture is part of this history and counts as another new medium through which people who lived very different lives came to imagine continuities and connections with one another. For that reason, the story of how America became a postal society traverses the boundaries that typically define studies of social experience during this period.

To say that the postal system was a mass institution or a medium of collective consciousness is not to pretend that mail meant the same thing to all people. As the first chapter explains, the extent and nature of postal participation varied wildly. The experience of a clerk copying dozens of letters in a mercantile office differed markedly from that of Anthony Burns bound in a Virginia jail cell. Different Americans used the post differently during the 1840s, '50s, and '60s, much as different Americans today put their mailboxes, televisions, telephones, and computers to a broad array of uses. Ultimately, a fuller history of the nineteenth-century post must consider separately the impact of the nineteenth-century postal revolution from the perspectives of city dwellers, Native Americans, college students, upcountry Southern farmers, illiterate German-speaking immigrants, employees of the federal government, Jews, unmarried adult women, slaveholders, and many other groups with distinctive relationships to the mail. The place to begin, however, is with an account of the revolution itself, an account that is by definition and necessity extremely broad. A new culture of national (and, in specific ways, international) connectedness emerged in the nineteenth century around a cheap and comprehensive postal system. Without making any assumptions about the unity of that culture or its homogenizing powers, the chapters that follow explore the post as a discrete historical phenomenon.

As a starting point, then, the first chapter offers a brief history of the transitional moment in American history when a remarkably broad range of new users joined the postal network. While outlining the changes that took place and making a case for their significance, the chapter also proposes understanding the spread of the post within the context of a number of historical developments in nineteenth-century U.S. society—most crucially, the extraordinary demographic mobility of mid-century Americans.

Calling the mid-century proliferation of postal use revolutionary may raise eyebrows among historians, especially those familiar with Richard R. John's groundbreaking study of the American postal system in the early national and Jacksonian eras. John demonstrates convincingly that with the Post Office Act of 1792 the United States began creating a network of vast proportions that would by the 1830s come to symbolize national connectedness in several important respects. Advocates of postal expansion during the 1820s and '30s frequently celebrated the capacity of the new network to bridge distances and erode differences, to annihilate time and space. But although the infrastructure of such a network had been laid in the preceding decades, its penetration to the level of popular experience remained significantly limited before 1840. Only with time, habituation, social changes, and crucial institutional reforms did ordinary users gain full access to the post.

In part, the revolution of the middle decades amounted to a democratization of the postal system that the Founding Fathers had designed and a realization of its most radical implications for long-distance communication in everyday life. In addition, the 1840s and '50s witnessed a fundamental shift in the nature of postal business. Chapter 2 charts the transformation from a post organized around the circulation of newspapers to one organized around the exchange of mail in the modern sense. Though the United States Post Office had mapped routes, built branch offices, and introduced a federal bureaucracy into the lives of most Americans, it did so for the purpose (and with the effect) of promoting a particular kind of national print culture. The posting of handwritten letters and material objects from one user to another was, through the first third of the century, a distinctly secondary and largely undeveloped feature of the system. Much of what was revolutionary about this era in postal history involved popular reappropriations and adaptations of what was primarily a news medium for the diverse purposes we now associate with the mail. One index of this diversity of purpose can be found in the variety of objects that new users posted during the middle decades of the century. Popular items of postal exchange, including money, daguerreotypes, seeds, and autographs, registered contemporary fascination with new possibilities of mail and shaped popular understanding of the post as a medium of long-distance communication involving more than just epistolary correspondence.

Mid-century Americans circulated unprecedented volumes of objects and messages across great distances, but participation in these exchanges brought them into contact with their neighbors as well. With cheap postage, the post office became the focus of new kinds of attention and interest for new mail users, a phenomenon that was particularly conspicuous in the nation's growing cities. Chapter 3 turns to some of the public settings in which the postal revolution unfolded. Especially before 1863 (when the United States inaugurated free home delivery in large cities), urban post offices were uniquely public spaces, places where letters, correspondents, and expectant users of the mail all came into contact. While they were highly visible symbols of an abstract communications network, post offices also facilitated various (and sometimes unsettling) forms of face-to-face interaction in local communities. They became classic sites of public life and evocative models of heterogeneous and promiscuous intermingling.

The second half of the book considers what this revolutionary transformation in America's postal network meant for social relations. Looking back from an age when holograph letters seem strikingly engaged and intimate to many users of faster telecommunication devices, it is tempting to see the proliferation of mail exchange simply as an event in the history of emotional life. But the experiences of intimate connection in and around the post were complex, and they emerged as a part of a new postal culture, both in daily rituals and practices and in public discussion of their meaning. Much of this new culture did, of course, relate to written correspondence and to the forms of intimacy associated with the personal letter. Chapter 4 considers the practice of personal letter-writing from the perspective of new users. As increasing numbers of people were able and inclined to send letters in the public post, they adjusted to shifting expectations of contact, formulated new models of correspondence, and wrestled with slippery notions of confidentiality. Taking a closer look at the epistolary texts of everyday life, this chapter examines the forms and conceptions of intimacy that grew up around the personal letter. Letter-writing was (and is) simultaneously celebrated as an art and a uniquely authentic form of self-expression. But writing letters was a novel mode of interaction in the experience of most Americans, who had to master stylistic codes and formulaic expressions that made personal correspondence recognizable and appropriate. How did new correspondents from different classes and social positions master these codes and formulas, and in what forms and contexts were they elaborated? While educating themselves in the ways of the post, new letter-writers also brought to their correspondence expectations and fantasies of privacy and publicity, proximity and distance, that arose from the particular set of historical circumstances in which they wrote and the novelty of the postal culture that was emerging around them. These expectations and fantasies, which were incorporated into the texts of personal correspondence, appeared frequently in public discussions of the mail, and surfaced in a number of interesting public scandals in which intimate letters were presented in the press as conclusive evidence of the private thoughts and desires of their authors.

A mythology of epistolary intimacy spread along with the post, as new users applied old motifs in the history of letter-writing to their regular correspondence. The idea that letters allowed absent parties to achieve a special sort of closeness (both modeled on and in some ways exceeding face-to-face communication) had deep roots in Western culture, but some new conditions in antebellum America gave the familiar ideology a novel spin. Chapter 5 describes how mail came to assume a particular burden in the maintenance of long-term relationships that were threatened (or simply structured) by physical separation, especially of family members. This burden assumed dramatic proportions in the context of the two most publicized internal mobilizations of this period in American history—the California Gold Rush and the Civil War—when large numbers of Americans, mostly (though by no means exclusively) men, left their homes for what they hoped or insisted was a short period of time, expecting in the interim to maintain some symbolic presence within those homes. These two events created communities on both sides of a postal divide where the daily rituals of mail delivery assumed especially high stakes, habituating new groups of Americans to the postal culture and dramatizing scenes of mail call for a national readership. At the same time, the dramatic public spectacle of separated kin using the post to perform family obligations and affirm family intimacy helped shape the meaning of mail in American culture.

But although mail was constructed as a kind of intimate communication, many of the postal practices that spread during the middle of the century conjure a different picture. A suggestive symbol of some of the other dimensions of mid-century postal culture appeared every February 14 in the form of the St. Valentine's Day greeting, which emerged at the same time as cheap postage and became the central artifact of what was essentially a new, modern holiday. Valentine's Day, one of the centerpieces of chapter 6, celebrated features of the new postal culture that studies of letter-writing often overlook. People mailed valentines anonymously, typically to many recipients, and the greetings deviated in several ways from the model of epistolary intimacy described in earlier chapters. During the rest of the year, a broad range of print circulars, solicitations, and junk mail filled the letter bags by mid-century, reminding new users that the post was not simply an instrument for conducting personal relations at a distance but was crucially (and paradoxically) anonymous. While the spread of the post transformed the individual name into a legitimate site—an operational address—in the new communications network, the nature of postal communication lent itself to various forms of concealment, confusion, and miscommunication in the use of personal names. Nowhere was this clearer than in the institution of the Dead Letter Office, which became an object of widespread fascination by mid-century. As a compelling public monument to the mail system, the spectacle of undelivered letters offered some conflicting evidence about the meaning of the post. Mass participation in an interactive communications network marked both the construction of new kinds of personal contact in the face of dislocation and transience and the cultivation of new forms of impersonal contact that reinforced the impact of dislocation and transience.

By the 1870s, postal use in the United States had become the locus and the focus of familiar modern dilemmas about the possibilities and limitations of intimate connection in a world where large numbers of people are partially, potentially accessible to us. Thus, while the story of America's postal age ends in that decade (in part because, as the epilogue suggests, the role of the post in everyday life would shift thereafter in the wake of various administrative, political, and technological changes), the period covered in this book belongs, in a broader sense, to a chapter in the history of communication that is decidedly unfinished.

PART

1

Joining a Network

ONE

BECOMING POSTAL

A COMMUNICATIONS REVOLUTION
IN ANTEBELLUM AMERICA

Not all shifts in the popular experience of space and time during the nineteenth century took the historical stage amid fanfare and pageantry. Compared to the laying of a transoceanic cable or the first journey of a steam-powered train, the spread of mail practices and mail culture unfolded discreetly in countless scenes that barely obtrude upon the historical record. Sitting in Charleston, South Carolina, on a Tuesday in 1856, Caroline Pettigrew addressed her mother, located on a plantation in the northwest corner of the state, with the confidence that "if I write to you by today's post the letter will be received on Friday."[1] Though a young woman of some means, Pettigrew was not alone in imagining that she enjoyed relatively direct and predictable access to people who lived at a distance. By mid-century ordinary men and women throughout the United States made similar, deceptively simple recalculations of how they might regularly communicate with people they did not see.

Conventionally, the history of communications has been understood as a series of disruptive, technology-driven increases in the speed at which people can transmit information. From this perspective, the importance of the 1840s to communications history lies in the introduction of the electromagnetic telegraph or perhaps in the spread of railroad service— not in postal service as such. Dan Headrick, in his study of the history of information, points out that this technological bias in most accounts of the origins of what we like to call telecommunications obscures earlier, less flashy breakthroughs in information exchange, such as the optical telegraph systems of the eighteenth century, which did not rely on new forms of power.[2] But the limitation of standard definitions of telecommunications is more fundamental. From the perspective of everyday life (as opposed to scientific experimentation), it is difficult to establish a trans-historical criterion by which to distinguish modern telecommunication from long-distance communication more generally. Although there may be a clear difference between modes of contact that appear to users as instantaneous (smoke signals, telegraphs, telephones, electronic mail) and those that involve a perceptible time lag (carrier pigeon, bike messenger, DHL air courier), any other dividing line runs the risk of being arbitrary. The ability of locomotive trains or optical telegraph relays to carry information faster than the "speed of a galloping horse or the fastest sailing ship"[3] (which might be a reasonable threshold for those interested in the history of technical solutions to social problems) did not produce instantaneous communication, nor did the invention of jet airplanes. If we are interested in the cultural impact of long-distance communication systems, we must assess the significance of something like the railroad in terms of the ways in which new expectations of contact and feelings of proximity emerged around rail transport, not whether the railroad dispensed with animal fuel or exceeded allegedly natural rates of movement. The same standard applies to all forms of long-distance contact.

For social, cultural, and political history, the important question is not how fast information travels in absolute terms or relative to previous records for land speed, but how new media connect physically separated parties within a shared temporal framework. Whether or not surpassing the gallop of a horse creates new experiences of contemporaneity and proximity will obviously vary with historical context and can only be determined by sustained inquiries into local practices and sources. The galloping post riders of the Persian Empire may well deserve a more important place in the cultural history of what we call telecommunications than do faster conveyances in other times and places that did not have as profound an impact on the spread of imperial authority or on ordinary experience of contemporary events.[4] Popular confusion over the significance of the Pony Express (which was a short-lived publicity venture by a private firm that postdated the use of steam railroads) reflects in part the widespread assumption that the crucial threshold of telecommunications was crossed when horses were replaced by machines. But to figure out the kind of communications world that Americans inhabited during the middle of the nineteenth century, we must suspend these assumptions. And the relative importance of the post, the railroad, and the telegraph to the experiences of distance in that world cannot be reduced to measures of speed. We would need to know, first, how accessible different systems were and to which uses they were put. The large claims made in this chapter for the mid-century post as a modern communications network rest on such considerations of access and use.

Before the advent of cheap postage, mail was not a regular feature of everyday life for most Americans. It was not that the institution was insignificant. On the contrary, during the early national period the Post Office functioned for most Americans as the principal embodiment of the federal government and a powerful symbol of national connected-ness. In the Jacksonian era, as Richard R. John has demonstrated, the post lay at the center of major political debates about political patronage, slavery, evangelical Protestantism, the marketplace, sectional conflict, federal power, and moral responsibility. In addition, the government's commitment to postal service formed part of the foundation for com-mercial growth. But the political and economic significance of the mail did not translate into a widespread postal culture. Throughout the first third of the century, most Americans (with the significant exception of merchants) neither exchanged mail nor organized their daily lives around the expectation of postal contact.[5]

During the early decades of the history of the U.S. Post Office, mail was relatively slow, and systems of collection and retrieval were highly irregular. Receiving a letter was, for most Americans, an event rather than a feature of ordinary experience. Personal correspondence might therefore travel along a variety of informal circuits, as illustrated by the experience of Abner Sanger, a New Hampshire farmer and day laborer in 1794. Having been informed (presumably by a personal acquaintance) at some point in early June that a letter from his brother in northern Vermont was waiting for him in the Boston post office, Sanger asked a local storekeeper to pick it up for him when he next visited the city. In the meantime, however, Sanger's wife's cousin had seen the letter and picked it up. At this point Sanger knew that the letter was headed for the town of Keene, ten miles away from where he was currently farming, but it was not until July 27 that he arrived in Keene to inquire (unsuccessfully) in all of the public houses and streets for the whereabouts of the elusive epistle. Another ten days passed before Sanger's own son appeared with the letter, having received it from the brother of the storekeeper whom Sanger assigned the task of retrieving it. Historian Richard D. Brown cites the two-month odyssey of this fraternal correspondence to demon-strate the importance attached to letters in the early national era, but this compelling anecdote also suggests how poorly prepared most Americans were for the exchange of mail. Sanger's frustrations say nothing about the slowness of the mails as such (since the letter may have arrived at its official destination in the Boston post office with great dispatch); rather, they reflect a society in which postal correspondence took place without what later generations would regard as adequate supplemental circuits of information. To put it another way, letter-writing was not yet common enough to warrant daily habits of inquiry and delivery.[6]

Whether or not letters lay unretrieved in post offices or circulated hap-hazardly along networks of personal acquaintance, the time lag involved in transmitting mail at the beginning of the century was too great to encourage regular correspondence over great distances. A letter's round-trip journey between Portland, Maine, and Savannah, Georgia, typically spanned forty days in 1799. Even a shorter journey, say between New York City and Canandaigua (near the Finger Lakes), took twenty days. Over the next ten years, improved roads and conveyances cut those rates substantially (to twenty-seven and twelve days respectively), but mail still traveled at a slow pace by the standards of just a couple of decades later.[7] Even on short and well-worn routes, winter conditions often disrupted service well into the 1830s. Relatively lengthy and often unpredictable delays between sending a letter and receiving a response tended to underscore the distance between absent correspondents, many of whom wrote without expectation of a timely reply.[8]

Others avoided the post altogether, preferring to communicate through individual travelers. In the 1780s, for example, Virginia physician Charles Mortimer relied upon informal and irregular modes of conveyance in order to correspond with his son Jack, an apprentice in Philadelphia. "You are in my debt several letters now," Mortimer admonished Jack in 1785, "and must watch out for families of Gentlemen coming here, and have your letters ready to go by them." The Mortimers' letters depended on the unpredictable mobility of particular persons and followed their trajectories. And, far from riding the impersonal waves of an open postal system, Jack's access to his father was mediated by forms of class privilege.[9]

By far the most serious obstacle to widespread use of the mail before 1845, perhaps even for those with social access to "families of Gentlemen," was financial. Letter postage, which was assessed based on distance and the number of sheets enclosed, could be extremely costly (typically to the addressee, who most often bore the burden of postage prior to 1851). From 1816 to 1845, for example, the postage on a single-sheet letter traveling more than four hundred miles (say between Albany and Pittsburgh) would be twenty-five cents, or between one-quarter and one-third of the average daily wage of a nonfarm laborer. The postage on a letter from New York City to Troy in 1843 was more than 50 percent higher than the price of shipping a barrel of flour over the same route.[10] (Letters sent outside the country were of course far more expensive and entailed multiple charges for the various stages of their journey.)[11] There were, to be sure, plenty of correspondents who could afford such costs. Merchants depended on the transmission of orders and remittances through the mail, and the potential profits of long-range transactions could easily absorb the postage. Wealthy individuals might not even bother to make such calculations of costs and benefits. John Pintard, the prosperous East India trader who founded many of New York's leading philanthropic and cultural institutions, corresponded frequently with his daughter in New Orleans from 1816 to 1833, paying both high postage rates and surcharges to penny posts for special delivery privileges.[12]

Others managed to cut expenses. Anna Briggs Bentley, who migrated from Maryland to Ohio in 1826 and spent much of the century writing to her family, used various economizing strategies in the early decades of her correspondence, including crossing her letters—inscribing the second half of the letter at a ninety-degree angle between the lines of the first half in order to avoid paying postage for an additional sheet. Whenever possible, she would send letters outside the post, indulging her desire to exceed the ordinary limits upon epistolary communication. "This I expect will be forwarded by a private conveyance and save you the postage," she explained at the start of an especially lengthy 1826 letter back to Maryland.[13] Bentley was also able to take advantage of the franking privileges of relatives working in the Post Office. In 1827 she promised to write more frequently now that her brother-in-law James Stabler had become the postmaster of Sandy Spring, near the family estate. Attaching a long missive to the entire family to a short note to Stabler, Bentley predicted that "James's kindness will remove the greatest barrier (the postage) to my writing very often."[14] Franking privileges could not always be used without restraint, however. Bentley's husband Joseph became postmaster in 1828, but she cautioned her relatives against exploiting this opportunity. "As this is a newly established post office and very little business done," she wrote, "Joseph feels some scruple about so many free letters yet awhile; for there is seldom anything goes or comes but to and from us, and he fears it will appear altogether a matter of self-interest in soliciting for the office." Separate letters from "the dear children," Bentley maintained, would be a frivolous luxury that might arouse suspicion, especially in an era when personal correspondence was relatively infrequent.[15]

For those without wealth or access to special franking privileges, there was a great temptation to seek a way around the high postal tariffs. Since postage between Roxana Watts's home in Peacham, Vermont, and that of her daughter and son-in-law in Jackson, Michigan, ran twenty-five cents per sheet in 1843, Watts sent a box and a letter through a man traveling to Detroit, who would deposit them in the post office. The letter advised her Michigan relatives to confirm receipt of the package by "mail[ing] a Paper and send[ing] it with some mark that we my [sic] know that they have got there."[16] The practice of mailing a marked paper at the considerably lower newspaper rate of one cent, as discussed in the next chapter, was sufficiently common to provoke specific regulations and heightened vigilance on the part of the Post Office Department. Alternatively, letters might be smuggled by some other means into the addressee's post office, where they would be assessed at the drop letter rate of one cent—the fee for mail that entered and exited the same office. In the early decades of the nineteenth century, for example, New Yorkers would pay ship captains to carry letters to the Albany post office, which explains the high number of surviving letters from that period bearing Albany postmarks and New York datelines.[17]

Wealthy customers, business exigencies, franking privileges, and clever subterfuges all contributed to the steady increase in American correspondence between 1790 and 1845, but the effects of high letter rates were nonetheless powerful. Compared to Great Britain, as advocates of cheap postage were fond of pointing out in the 1840s, people in the United States hardly mailed letters at all. And when they did, the complex and incremental pricing system tended to reinforce their sense that long-distance communication was for special occasions. The correspondence of the Callaghan siblings, who grew up in Virginia in the early part of the nineteenth century, reveals some of the strain of using the post to maintain family ties under conditions of high geographical mobility. Though one of the brothers was a postmaster (and thus could frank letters), the others were forced to pay high prices to stay in touch with one another as parts of the family moved to Missouri with the westward migration of slaveholders during the antebellum era. Not many of their twenty-five-cent letters between Virginia and Missouri survive, and those that do suggest a modest standard for family correspondence. "Your letter of the 25th. April came safe to hand a longtime after its date," wrote Oliver in Virginia to William in Missouri in a communication composed in late July of 1833 and posted in early August. The following June, Oliver wrote to William again. "I have rec'd your letter of the 13th, Nov. last a long time after its date, & have omitted to reply to it for sometime." None of the Callaghan siblings complained about the postage. Still, the leisurely pace of their correspondence was not unusual in an era when everyone understood that personal letters were luxury items.[18]

Under these circumstances, most Americans tended to use the mail, if at all, for shorter distances or special occasions when the high price of sending a letter would mark the significance of the gesture. An 1856 article in the *Ladies' Repository* claimed that "no tax can be prohibitory" on familiar letters between kin and speculated that "a poor solitary woman whose husband is on the other side of the globe" would go begging door-to-door rather than forgo correspondence.[19] Such a rosy picture of the appeal of letters was possible in 1856; a decade or two earlier, the tax on letter writing was, for most Americans, prohibitory indeed. Elizabeth Keckley's autobiographical account of her rise from slave to presidential seamstress notes that when she joined her master Hugh Garland in St. Louis in 1847 (after the first reduction in postage, but before the second and prior to the requirement of prepayment), he was "so poor that he was unable to pay the dues on a letter advertised as in the post office for him."[20] In Keckley's retrospective view, this was indeed a mark of serious penury. From a more distant vantage point, the phenomenon of a slaveholder (and a lawyer who, incidentally, would successfully represent the interests of Dred Scott's putative owners in denying Scott's 1852 petition for freedom) who could not afford to collect his mail appears as an episode from a very distant era in the history of communication.

Letters were priced beyond the reach of most Americans, not because technological developments had yet to lower the costs of transmitting the mail, but because letters were expected to finance the main business of the post. From its creation, the U.S. Post Office was committed principally to facilitating the wide circulation of political news, allowing an informed citizenry to live far from the metropolitan centers of government while remaining active in its affairs. Individual letter-writers, typically merchants, were depended upon to absorb the costs of this political commitment by subsidizing an extremely low rate on newspapers.[21] To later users of the post, the preponderance of newspapers in the mail might appear as a vestige of an antiquated and unjust privilege, but in the early republic the link between the press and the post made perfect sense. To be sure, not everyone shared the view that the only proper function of a post was to circulate printed newspapers and subsidize political communication. In the early decades of the nineteenth century, many celebrants of the federal postal system, especially from the Northeast, emphasized other and larger applications and implications of widespread use of the mail. As more letters passed in the mails, postal reformers took aim at what they saw as a short-sighted rate policy. Correspondence itself was in the nation's political and economic interest, advocates of cheap letter postage insisted, and a combination of lowered rates and improved service could induce a high enough volume of mail to cover the costs (largely fixed) of the expanded system. This shift in thinking was more than simply a new approach to financing the post or a refusal to prioritize political speech over economic intercourse (though it certainly was both of those things). Proponents of cheap letter rates and mass participation were articulating a new relationship between the post and the state. Ancient and medieval posts had been mouthpieces of the state, and well into the modern era governments had used their monopoly over postal transmission to facilitate and legitimate particular types of political speech. Postal reformers envisioned a mail system in which the state simply encouraged and regulated high volumes of unspecified exchange between customers.[22]

The American ratification of this new model began in 1845, when Congress revamped the postage scale. Letters would now be charged on the basis of weight at a radically reduced rate of five cents per half ounce for a distance up to three hundred miles and ten cents per half ounce for greater distances. Six years later, the Postal Act of 1851 set the basic rate at only five cents for any half-ounce letter traveling up to three thousand miles within the United States, effectively eliminating distance as a determinant of cost. The 1851 law also introduced a 40 percent discount for prepaid postage, allowing half-ounce letters to travel virtually throughout the country for three cents. Four years later, the Post Office began requiring prepayment, and by 1856 such payment had to take the form of postage stamps (which had been introduced in 1847) or stamped envelopes. While lowering and standardizing the costs of sending letters, Congress enacted a series of newspaper rates that were differentiated according to distance (and generally raised). Though some of the newspaper provisions were soon rescinded, the major reorientation of the post office had been accomplished. Thereafter, the primary category of mail would consist of letters—a homogeneous class of prepaid correspondence—circulating without restriction within a postal network. Sending a letter had been transformed into a fundamentally affordable activity.[23]

A complete history of the postal reductions of 1845 and 1851 has yet to be written, and it is not the intention here to provide one. It is worth thinking briefly, however, about the larger historical context in which these reforms took place and the role that cheap postage played in the expanded use of the postal system. Histories of the nineteenth century take it almost for granted that any turning point in the development of long-distance communication in the United States revolves around new technologies—especially in transportation. The key players in most such accounts—steamboats, canals, railroads—certainly did facilitate the expansion of the post and the proliferation of mail, as did the introduction of the telegraph in 1844, just one year before the first major reform. All of these advances and innovations helped reduce the time lags in mail transmission (though improved roads were at least as important along many routes). Canals and railroad lines also helped bring more people and more places into regular contact with (and lasting dependence upon) the market economy—and consequently fostered greater need for postal access. Technological developments also played an important role in the increasing geographical mobility of Americans and thus in the greater likelihood that Americans would live at a distance from friends and family. Railroads and (even more immediately) telegraphs also contributed to a striking shift in experiences of simultaneity among distant places and people.[24] By 1849, for example, telegraphed results of the boxing match between Tom Hyer and Yankee Sullivan on a desolate island off the coast of Maryland created a sense of instantaneous connection among boxing fans gathered at bars and newspaper offices throughout urban America.[25] Americans who imagined that they were living in the same moment as fellow sports enthusiasts in another city were also more likely to turn to the post to conduct ongoing relationships with people they did not see. Other inventions and innovations figured in this history as well, including the steam-powered printing press, new techniques in paper production, and the greater availability of corrective lenses. It would be a mistake, though, to simplify the causal role of these innovations in the mid-century postal revolution. Technology does not explain the transformation, though it is hard to imagine a mass postal network without these technological developments.

An equally necessary precondition for widespread participation in the post, of course, was mass literacy in the United States. Without the presumption that ordinary Americans could write letters, reformers would have been hard-pressed to make a convincing economic case for reducing postage. It is also significant that the drive for cheap postage coincided roughly with other efforts at promoting literate habits among the American masses, such as the common school movement, and that many of the loudest voices for cheap postage echoed from the same northeastern, middle-class, evangelical, Whig circles from which educational reforms drew their strongest support. Economic, political, social, and religious investments in the power of writing and print underwrote many reformist interventions during the antebellum era, and cheap postage can persuasively be numbered among them.[26]

The precise relationship between reductions in the letter rate and high rates of literacy in mid-century America is hard to identify, however. The best evidence suggests that the United States was a broadly literate society well before 1845, and a general political commitment to promoting reading had in all likelihood been part of the charge of the post office from the 1790s onward. The ability to read and write does not (and did not) translate in any straightforward way into epistolary practices or postal habits. What is clear, though, is that mass participation in the postal system reinforced the skills and desires that reformers were counting upon in the first place. As with the proliferation of so many artifacts of the expanding antebellum print culture (including newspapers, novels, political pamphlets, urban signage, and fashion magazines), the increasing availability and affordability of the post encouraged the acquisition, cultivation, and maintenance of literacy.[27] Former slave and Baptist minister Elijah P. Marrs recalled the central role of the mail in his attempts to teach himself how to read as a boy in Kentucky. "[T]he white people would send me daily to the post-office," he explained, where he "would read the address of the letters."[28] More commonly, letter-writers spoke of correspondence as an occasion for developing or showcasing their skills in composition and penmanship. Parents and older siblings often cited correspondence as both the reward and the litmus test for learning how to write, and letters were routinely evaluated by their addressees for evidence of progress in this regard.[29] In a nonposted letter entered into a family book in the decade before postal reform, a young Quaker girl named Jane Elfreth offered her younger brother a standard bit of sisterly encouragement: "Thee cant read my letter now but perhaps thee will be able to some years hence if thee learns to write." Jane's advice was in keeping with the explicit function of the letter book, which her father had purchased, according to another family member, so "that we may improve in our writing," a phrase that recurs often in nineteenth-century correspondence.[30] Thomas Watkins, a Mississippi plantation owner, wrote in 1848 to his thirteen-year-old daughter (away at school in Tennessee) that "[y]ou have improved in letter writing & I am glad of it. Still there may be corrections made in your letters." The girl's mother offered some faint praise along the same lines two months later: "You wrote to know if I did not think you have improved in writing. I think you have improved a little." In one of her many letters to her Gold Rush husband, Mary Wingate coaxed a brief, penciled contribution from her young daughter Lucy: "I want you to come home as soon as you can for we are very lonely without you. I hope I shall learn to write soon so that mother wont have to hold my hand next time I want to write to you. From your own Lucy." Ten months later, Mary reported that "Lucy says she means to learn to write next summer so that she can write you a letter. She is so nervous I am afraid it will be some time before she can do [it]." Such pedagogical attention to interpersonal correspondence formed a crucial part of the cultural construction of letter-writing as a particular kind of performance (as it had in the early national era as well).[31] On a simpler level, though, the striking recurrence of these admonitions and assessments provides a useful reminder of how mail habits and writing skills were mutually reinforcing during the period when Congress redefined the post as an affordable medium of mass communication.

The perception, ideology, and reality of mass literacy enabled most Americans to imagine the post as a broadly inclusive network. For enslaved African Americans, a majority of whom did not read or write, the post was far less accessible, but it is not clear that illiteracy among them was either a necessary or a sufficient obstacle to postal participation. Slaveholders had various means other than restricting literacy for regulating slaves' use of the mail. And even illiterate slaves managed to send and receive letters, often relying upon amanuenses and readers, both white and black. (Illiterate whites dictated letters as well, especially immigrants seeking to correspond with distant families.)[32] Among slaves, plantation discipline was often more important than literacy in constraining access to the post. Lucy Skipwith, an enslaved woman in Hopewell, Alabama, encountered white resistance to her letter-writing, even when she was corresponding with her absentee master John Cocke. "I hope to write more sattisfactory than I have done heretofore," she apologized in an 1863 letter. "[T]he white people who have stayed on the plantation are always opposed to my writeing to you & always want to see my letters."[33] Similarly, an 1854 letter from an illiterate slave to his brother began with the explanation that "I have obtained the consent of my master to get a friend to write these lines to you."[34] Solomon Northup's 1853 slave narrative described his own frustrated efforts at "getting a letter secretly into the post-office" and testified directly about the larger obstacle of postmasters who would refuse to mail letters composed by slaves without written authorization from their owners.[35] Literacy, in such cases, was not the crucial variable.

For illiterate postal users, there were risks, of course, associated with reliance upon literate intermediaries, as a fugitive slave from Louisiana discovered in 1841 when he posted a letter to an illiterate friend back home upon crossing the Ohio River into Cincinnati. Because he could not read, the addressee showed the letter to a white man who proceeded to share its contents with the fugitive's master. Ultimately the letter was published in the local newspaper and reprinted in the New Orleans *Picayune* under the headline "CAUTION TO SLAVE-OWNERS."[36] Though even the letters of fully literate correspondents were often shared among unintended readers (and sometimes, as a later chapter notes, had an unfortunate afterlife on the pages of the daily newspaper), African Americans, both free and enslaved, were especially vulnerable to postal interference, which may have provided a further incentive to master the epistolary arts. A black sergeant in the 55th Massachusetts Infantry during the Civil War noted proudly in his diary that several in the regiment "who, although never having been slaves, [had been] unable to write their names," were now "applying themselves assiduously with spelling book, pen, ink, and paper." Alluding vaguely to the perils of dictation and mediation, the author explained that "a year's experience in the army has shown most of them the disadvantage of being dependent upon others to do their writing and reading of letters."[37]

Illiteracy, in other words, compromised but did not preclude participation in America's postal network. A fascinating correspondence between absentee slaveholder William S. Pettigrew and the enslaved foremen on his two North Carolina plantations illustrates this crucial point nicely. During an extended convalescence at Healing Springs in Virginia, Pettigrew sought to manage his business affairs by corresponding with Moses and Henry, the two illiterate overseers, relying upon a white intermediary. "Thinking you would be glad to hear from me," Pettigrew wrote to Moses in 1856, "I have concluded to write you a few lines and will enclose them to Mr. White who will read them to you." Though Malica J. White's own skills were quite rough, he dutifully transcribed the replies of three different slaves, and a detailed correspondence ensued, dealing with countless details of crop production, workplace discipline, and plantation life. Pettigrew always addressed Moses and Henry directly, and they responded in kind. Upon receiving their replies, Pettigrew offered paternalistic congratulation to Moses for his "succe[ss] as a letter-writer," proudly showed the letter to a friend, and instructed Moses to "writ[e] more frequently," de-emphasizing White's mediation. The relationship between dictation and transcription, as Pettigrew imagined it in a letter addressed to Moses and read to him by White, could be somewhat complex:

> I wish you to send me a letter every other week & Henry every other week—which will enable me to hear from home *every week*. Perhaps Mr. White, who will be good enough to write for you, would prefer writing Saturdays; it will be immaterial to me on what day the letter is written so that one is sent every week. When it is Henry's time, he can ride out to Belgrade & Mr. White will write as he may request him. He will inform me of all that is worth reporting to me at Belgrade as well as Magnolia; and when you write, you will, in like manner, send me a report of what Henry says, as to his affairs at Magnolia as well as your own report.[38]

But if the multiple reports and competing claims of White, Moses, and Henry to the status of letter-writer require some disentangling in

Pettigrew's instructions, the larger correspondence makes clear that it was the illiterate foremen (who had authority to make business decisions) and not their more literate white secretary who were engaged in an epistolary exchange with the slaveholder. Pettigrew's faith in the capacity of the mail to extend his monitory presence over distant plantations is itself a noteworthy artifact of the antebellum postal culture. But what is equally remarkable is that his use of the post did not depend on the literacy of his correspondents.[39]

While the histories of transportation, print technology, and literacy figure prominently in the spread of the post, they cannot adequately explain the shift toward mass participation that was signaled and encouraged by the postal legislation of 1845 and 1851. Among the various social forces that contributed to the move toward cheap postage, the most powerful were demographic. Antebellum Americans were far more likely to patronize the post than their early national ancestors and counterparts because they were even more mobile and had more economic and social ties to people who lived at a distance.[40]

Famously, the middle third of the nineteenth century was a time of extraordinary mobility in the United States. Much of it involved individual shifts in residence that show up in rough aggregate form on census reports. American cities, both old and new, were conspicuous showcases of this demographic transience during the antebellum era, but residential mobility was not restricted to urban areas.[41] The frontier town of Sugar Creek, Illinois, for example, saw two-thirds of its families turn over in the space of ten years, and even in the much older community of Sturbridge, Massachusetts, more than one-third of the families recorded in one decennial census had moved by the next. Urbanization and westward migration were especially and poignantly apparent from the vantage point of the rural New England counties from which so many mobile Americans hailed. By mid-century more than half of the living persons who had been born in Vermont resided elsewhere. Meanwhile, in Ohio, a major destination for transplanted Yankees, more than half of the population in 1850 had been born beyond state borders.[42]

There were, of course, particular patterns to the individual moves: planters and slaves left Virginia and North Carolina for Arkansas and Texas, for example, while young men and women from New England farms migrated to New York, and farmers from Indiana and Illinois (themselves one generation removed from coastal states) relocated to Missouri, Iowa, and across the overland trail to California and Oregon. Some movements even took the form of collective migrations, such as those of Irish families crossing the Atlantic during the potato famine or Cherokees marching along the Trail of Tears at gunpoint. Other mass movements involved temporary dislocations, such as those created by war in 1846 and 1861 and by the discovery of gold at mid-century. All of this meant that America's modern postal culture emerged during a time when the relationship between persons and places in the United States was remarkably fluid.

Images of a perpetually mobile population, which dominated visitors' accounts of U.S. society before the Civil War, loomed large in the arguments of postal reformers for making mail service more broadly accessible. Advocates of cheap postage cited mobility as a basis for their sanguine predictions of a nation of letter-writers and insisted that America's exceptional demographics made the case for rate reductions and uniformity especially urgent. Elsewhere, members of the same family "live and die at their native homestead, or within a few miles of the spot where they were born," argued the *New Englander* in 1843. "The American, on the other hand, is born for migration," and families routinely scatter "hundreds of miles apart." As the members of New England households moved to Illinois, Wisconsin, and Iowa, the evangelical magazine proceeded to imagine, countless impulses for long-distance communication would inevitably arise in "hearts that warm toward their kindred here."

> There is the teacher whose trials would be lightened, and his heart cheered, if he could freely communicate by letter with those who were once his instructors or his companions in study. There is the minister of the Gospel, the home missionary, to whose self-denying work free communication with friends, brethren and helpers far away, is of the greatest moment. There is the young man, exposed to strong temptations, whom a free and frequent correspondence with his mother, or his sisters, or with another friend still dearer to his hopes, might keep from falling. There is the anxious wife or mother, who sees the health of some dear one in the family beginning to fail, and who would like to get one word from the old family physician. There are the planters of new towns and villages, laying the foundations civil, ecclesiastical and literary, who would love sometimes to get a short answer to one short question from the judge, the 'squire, the minister, the schoolmaster, or the deacon, whom they knew in old Connecticut or in the old Bay State. But how, in that new country, can they raise the half dollar to pay the post-office tax upon a single question?[43]

While following the lead of Great Britain, the United States entered the new postal era with a distinctive set of expectations about how the mail might function as a mass medium. In addition to facilitating commerce, fostering inter-regional ties, and promoting contact between a republican government and its dispersed citizenry, the post would serve the needs of what the great postal reformer Pliny Miles called "our large floating population."[44] Mobility and postal reform were thus mutually reinforcing historical developments. Population dispersal encouraged reformers to imagine the post as a medium of regular communication for ordinary people, while cheap and uniform postage encouraged Americans to imagine that they might travel (and even relocate) without severing their existing social and familial ties. For Americans who wished to communicate with friends and family in homelands outside the nation's postal zone, of course, reductions in postage did not always make correspondence affordable, though in 1845 the Post Office Department also began subsidizing foreign mail transport and pursuing international postal treaties.[45] But reformers were primarily concerned with internal migrants. An advocate of postal reform observed in 1820 that in the recent past a man would hesitate to form new settlements out of fear that "the grave might for months have entombed his most endeared friends, before he could become acquainted even with the decay of their health." Letter-writing, he announced, was eroding these fears.[46] In a letter back to her family in Maryland shortly after her arrival in Ohio, Anna Briggs Bentley instructed her correspondents to provide steady streams of mundane detail in the mail "so that as I am journeying on through time in my distant habitation I may keep up a kind of acquaintance and not feel like a stranger in my own dear native land, if ever I should visit it again."[47]

Not all Americans were mobile, and not all who did move used the post to forge or maintain connections to the people and places they left behind. It would be a mistake to exaggerate or oversimplify the relationship between migration and correspondence. Nations with lower rates of mobility also shifted to cheap letter rates and also promoted popular participation in the post during the nineteenth century.[48] Nonetheless, a simple point is worth stressing. Increased mobility enhanced the appeal, utility, and economic viability of a medium that would be redefined in the United States around the desire of ordinary people to communicate with those who lived elsewhere. In 1800, far fewer Americans would have wanted to maintain correspondence, even if they had access to the franking privileges of a postmaster or a Congressman. By mid-century a demographic foundation for popular participation in the postal system had been laid.

The massive mobilization of Americans—male and female, black and white, rich and poor, immigrant and native—was a development rather than a sudden occurrence, though a number of dramatic events (such as those examined in chapter 5) helped facilitate and broadcast this ongoing phenomenon as something distinct and momentous. Migrations, mobilizations, and dislocations belong to the history of the postal revolution; they were effects as well as causes of the transformation of the mail into a mass ritual. As more and more people relocated from the communities in which they had been born, the desire to correspond with absent friends, family members, and business associates intensified. The post, in turn, reinforced migratory patterns and itinerant impulses.

However implicated in large historical developments, the Congressional Acts of 1845 and 1851 were, at the same time, political and administrative reforms born amid a set of specific constraints and concerns. Congress elected to tap the perceived potential popularity of correspondence in the face of private competition, widespread criticism, and foreign example. Rival private carriers such as Adams Express, Harnden Express, and Wells Fargo flourished during the early and mid-1840s in response to increased business demands, often providing delivery service and expedited access as well as cheaper letter rates. The larger express firms made good use of the new railroad lines connecting major urban centers and enjoyed a significant price advantage over the Post Office, since they did not have to ask letter-writers to subsidize newspaper transmission.[49] Other, smaller operations simply undercut the U.S. mail by collecting letters headed for the same destination and sending them through the post at a package rate.[50] Private posts encouraged letter-writing (primarily among businessmen), popularized important new business models (including uniform postage and home delivery), put enormous economic pressure on the Post Office Department, and even called into open question the government's monopoly on the mail. An 1844 broadside for Lysander Spooner's American Letter Mail Company asserted the intention of his intercity post to use its success "to agitate the question, and test the constitutional right of free competition in the business of carrying letters."[51] Instead of conceding its monopoly, the government responded by reforming its operations.

In seeking to meet the challenge posed by the express firms, Congress turned to the model that had been instituted in Great Britain five years earlier under the direction of postal reformer Rowland Hill, who had published in 1837 a major treatise on post office reform after several ventures into other reform causes. Hill advocated a cheap, uniform rate of postage that would encourage a significant increase in the use of the mails. He also called for prepayment through the use of stamped letter sheets or small adhesive stamps. If postage were reduced to one penny prepaid, Hill argued, the post would enjoy a net gain in revenue. After substantial agitation and initial hesitation, Parliament enacted these proposals in 1839, providing a major boost to postal reformers across the Atlantic. Other governments followed (the cantons of Zurich, Geneva, and Basel in the early 1840s; Brazil around the same time; the United States in 1845; and Belgium and France by the end of the decade, followed by Spain, Denmark, Holland, and Luxemburg), collectively creating the modern postal system.[52]

How immediately decisive the legislative reforms of 1845 and 1851 were in facilitating widespread postal participation in the United States is a difficult question. As was true in Great Britain, cheaper postage did not entirely and instantaneously fulfill reformers' bold predictions.[53] Yet it is clear that uniformity, prepayment, and affordability did spark a considerable increase in the volume of mail in postal circulation. In the first decade following the 1845 act, the number of letters mailed in the United States more than tripled, reaching 132 million in 1855. This figure did not necessarily represent the sudden birth of a nation of avid correspondents. Letter-writing remained a disproportionately urban activity in an overwhelmingly rural society (in 1856 New Yorkers sent thirty letters per capita, more than six times the national average), and commercial mail undoubtedly accounted for a majority of the total volume. Moreover, some of the increase may have come from the shift of patronage from private express companies to the government post.[54] Nonetheless, the slashing of rates to less than one-fourth (in many cases) of their former level had a major material and symbolic effect on the practice of writing letters.

Who exactly used the post in the 1840s, '50s, and '60s is impossible to determine, but a few crucial divisions within the new postal nation are clear enough. Northerners sent more mail than Southerners—more than twice as much per capita in both urban and rural areas—in large part a reflection of higher rates of literacy, long-distance commercial activity, and urbanization.[55] City residents posted far more letters than those who lived on farms or in small towns. In 1852, for example, 28 percent of all letters mailed in the United States were posted in one of six cities (the five largest and San Francisco). Two years later the number of letters sent per capita in the six largest U.S. cities was more than six times the total for the rest of the country. Two years after that, Manhattan alone accounted for 10 percent of the nation's posted correspondence, more than any entire state on the Gulf of Mexico.[56] Such high rates of urban participation suggest an undeniable link between the mail and the market economy, but it would be a mistake to attribute the entire imbalance to business mail. Whether or not they were merchants, city people were far more prone to post letters than their rural counterparts. At mid-century, most adult residents of large American cities had been born elsewhere and were likely to have friends and family living at a distance. The disproportionately urban character of the nineteenth-century postal network went beyond the numbers of letters sent. Residents in more densely settled areas enjoyed a different kind of access to the mail than those whose location forced them to wait as much as a week between deliveries or collections. In Caroline Kirkland's semifictional account of frontier life in Michigan in the late 1830s, weekly mail service appears both as a major adjustment and as an unexpected delight. "I have learned to pity most sincerely those who get their letters and papers at all sorts of unexpected and irregular times," she announced, deprecating the bustling, haphazard character of the seaboard post she had left behind. As the volume and variety of mail increased, however, what Kirkland found precious others came to regard as a frustrating inconvenience. As late as 1876, an Alabama Congressman complained that many of his constituents received mail only once a week and that he himself had "but three mails a week from the railroad to the town in which I live."[57] Americans living in the rural hinterland used the post in increasing numbers during the middle third of the century, but they timed their compositions and inquiries to the slower rhythms of their mail service and thus remained in some respects at the margins of an emerging postal culture dominated by city people.[58]

Other disparities are a bit harder to track, but were probably even more significant. The relationship between male and female participation in the post was a subject of much interest in the antebellum period, as it had been earlier and as it remains today. In the emerging postal culture, women's use of the mail figured prominently in an ongoing construction of letter-writing as an intimate activity. Certain observers celebrated women's superior capacity for correspondence, while critics mocked the loquacious, disorganized, and transgressive excesses of women's epistolary practices. Both of these tropes and all of this attention tended to identify women with personal letters (an identification that has survived in mystified form in numerous current discourses, both popular and scholarly) and to obscure the point that the typical user of the post was male. Men dominate images and accounts of mid-century post office life, and lists of addressees for uncollected mail (the famous "dead letter lists" that appeared regularly in nineteenth-century newspapers) usually included a preponderance of male names. The postage reforms narrowed the gap a bit, but did not eliminate it. Both men and women used the post after 1845, though not at the same rates.[59]

Race was also a significant divide in the American postal network, largely because the majority of African Americans living in the United States were illiterate, poor, and subject to severe legal (and other) restrictions. Still, both slaves and free blacks used the post to a striking degree. Slaves wrote, dictated, and posted letters to masters, former masters, friends, family, abolitionist allies, and even to famous strangers.[60] The access of enslaved men and women in the South to the post office varied widely. In some cases, delivering or collecting mail was a menial duty assigned specifically to slaves.[61] In other situations and under different circumstances, slaves could encounter serious obstacles to their participation in the postal network. When interviewed by an antislavery minister shortly before the Civil War, former slave Louisa Picquet spoke of learning a special procedure for corresponding with her enslaved mother. "There is a kink about mailing a letter, so as to have it reach a slave, that we never dreamed of," the minister noted, "but Mrs. P. does not wish it published."[62]

However mediated, regulated, and compromised, the mail could prove a valuable resource to slaves in difficult situations, as the dramatic example of Anthony Burns's letter illustrates (see the introduction). In her famous autobiography, Harriet Jacobs narrates a comparably impressive but strikingly different use of the post. Hiding out from her master, Dr. Flint, in a nearby house, Jacobs deceived him into believing that she had escaped to New York by having a letter delivered up North and then mailed back to Flint bearing a New York postmark. Unable to appear in public in her home town, Jacobs nonetheless managed to orchestrate and time the movements of a letter along a round-trip journey between North Carolina and New York and throw her pursuers off the trail by means of an impersonal and authoritative postmark.[63] Whereas Burns's correspondence fulfilled the classic promise of a postal system to transport distant speakers and incarnate absent bodies, Jacobs's ruse underscored other, more modern, features of the post that could prove useful to fugitives from the law.

For other slaves, the role of the post in the quest for freedom was more direct. Traveling with his master in New York in the mid-1840s, John S. Jacob announced his flight from slavery in a letter, which he dictated to a literate friend and dropped in the post office. Jacob stayed on the job through the evening, knowing that the following day he would be on his way to Massachusetts while his master would receive the following letter: "Sir—I have left you, not to return; when I have got settled, I will give you further satisfaction. No longer yours, John S. Jacob."[64] Certainly the best-known and most remarkable use of the post by a person seeking to escape legal bondage took place in 1849, when Henry "Box" Brown successfully mailed himself by shipping crate from Richmond to Philadelphia. Brown's crate, which a white accomplice addressed and marked "this side up," was conveyed by one of the private express companies and was mistaken by observers for a box of mail.[65] Well-publicized uses of the post by fugitive slaves reinforced the symbolic link between literacy and freedom among African Americans, but they offered a more specific lesson as well. The postal network, though dominated by prosperous merchants, could also accommodate the enslaved, the transient, the dislocated, and the dispossessed. The epistolary archives of the mid-nineteenth century are filled with contributions from Norwegian immigrants, rural Midwestern teenagers, and black artisans, as well as Philadelphia dry goods dealers and New England poets.

Users of the mail network acknowledged the revolutionary changes of the 1840s and 1850s through a complex range of responses and adjustments. Perhaps out of tact, or perhaps because it did not require excessive emphasis, most American correspondents passed over the postal reforms largely in silence. Occasionally, however, a letter might refer playfully to the new possibilities presented by cheaper postage. Writing to her cousin Joseph in Connecticut just after the new law was passed, Catherine Huntington inquired how "the P.O. reformation suit[s] you." Catherine, who had intended "to have a heap of letters ready to send, as soon as July came in," extended her "heartfelt thanks to the first mover of this reform," and teased Joseph about his own epistolary habits. "Maybe the letters will come pouring in upon you in such multitudes that you'll wish for the old rates of postage." Six years later, on the eve of the second reduction, Mary Wingate of Meriden, Connecticut, informed her husband in San Francisco that "when the new postage law takes effect I shall be selfish enough to want to hear from you by every Steamer."[66] Lower rates also made it easier for letter-writers to be magnanimous in bearing the costs of transmission. A year after the first reduction, medical student Charles Hentz mailed a letter to a young woman who had sent him a newspaper, "obeying I suppose," he noted in his diary, "the rules of etiquette by paying the postage." Around mid-century, *Godey's Lady's Book* encouraged its readers to observe this practice as a rule. "At the present rates this may seem a small item. At so much cheaper price, then, do you purchase the reputation of a gentleman." Especially during the early 1850s, when prepayment of postage was encouraged but not mandated, a new set of calculations of value and interest entered into the postal protocols of American letter writers.[67]

Explicit discussions and assessments of the relative costs and benefits of personal mail were most likely to appear in exchanges between
correspondents negotiating unfamiliar postage situations, as in the case
of international mail or of letters posted to and from California during
the Gold Rush.[68] A gold-seeker in Sierra County informed his sister in
1856 that since the arrival of an official post office at his location, postage
to the rest of the United States was now ten cents, instead of one to
two dollars, "so you need not think that you will brake us by writing
if you should write all the time." According to another dislocated New
Englander writing from San Francisco in 1849, his sister's "rather dry"
letter was "hardly worth 40¢." The editor of a California newspaper, who
liked to compare the value of a letter to its postage due, reassured one of
his correspondents that he "need not be alarmed about heaping postage
on me. That is nothing. Why, dear fellow, I would do it a thousand
times."[69] In the case of international mail, which was charged different
rates depending on specific treaties and conventions between the United
States and the country of destination, correspondents often discussed
costs, though here the significance of the 1845 and 1851 reforms was less
uniform. As a Norwegian immigrant explained to his parents in 1863,
a decade before a postal convention would establish cheap letter rates
to Norway based on prepayment and weight, "When I work one day I
am able to pay for 2 or 3 letters, so now you will realize that we receive
any letter we may have with pleasure. But do not send white paper but
write the page full, for it costs as much in postage whether there are
many or few lines on the page." Another Norwegian immigrant, writing
home around the same time, expressed concern that if she wrote without
constraint, her "letters would cost too much by the time they reach you."
"Incidentally," she added, "it would be interesting to know what you
actually do have to pay for postage."[70] Martin Weitz, a German immigrant living in Astoria, New York, encouraged his father to write back
without prepaying the postage. "Letters cost 22 cents here," he noted in
1854, "that's 36 kreuzers in German money." Twenty years later another
German immigrant pressed his family for correspondence. "You'll write
to me soon, won't you? A letter costs five cents = 7 1/2 kreuzer."[71]

On other occasions, discussions of postage focused on ways to be more
cost-efficient in using the mail. Confederate Congressman Warren Akin
gave detailed postal instructions to his absent wife in an 1864 letter, asking
her to "mail letters to me tuesday evening, wednesday evening and friday
evening, and *make* some of the children write to me every time you do, so
each one will write every week, and put their letters in the same envelope
with yours and postage will be saved." After the 1845 law switched the

cost basis from sheets to weight, the practice of enclosing multiple letters in the same envelope appears to have become widespread, especially for correspondents writing to several friends and family in the same home community.[72] Letter-writers adjusted to the new postal laws in other ways as well, reducing the size of their stationery and becoming slightly less obsessed with cramming as many words as possible onto a single sheet.[73]

To be sure, old habits and expectations were not instantly eliminated by the new postal economics. The Cincinnati *Atlas* complained in 1851 that "even now-a-days when the postage is only three cents, pre-paid, correspondents often consign their letters to a private hand instead of the Government conveyance." Such misplaced and obsolete concessions to thrift were "bad economy and worse politeness," the *Atlas* charged, since in all likelihood the personal messenger would "rather pay the postage himself than be troubled with attending to its delivery." In an age when the government carried mail faster, more safely, and "almost for nothing," the metropolitan press pointed out, there was no longer any reason to send letters outside the post.[74] After the second postage reduction, such advice was both new and necessary.

Other features of the reform required equally dramatic shifts in popular practice, especially outside major cities. The *Illustrated Magazine of Art* announced in 1853 that "the stamp system is now becoming generally used in the United States," and that close to 80 percent of the letters posted in New York bore stamps. But in other parts of the country, the magazine noted with surprise, "there seems to be a sort of reluctance to make use of . . . this easy, simple process."[75] In Philadelphia, at least, some initial reluctance to adopt this innovation may have reflected ignorance about the proper use of stamps. Two separate letters to the *Public Ledger* in September of 1851 referred to popular complaints about "postage Stamps not adhering." (Both observers saw fit to point out that stamps adhere better when properly moistened.)[76] During that same pivotal year, the same Philadelphia newspaper had to admonish readers who had gotten carried away with the spirit of postal reform, imagining that the new cheap and uniform rates applied as well to international letters. "Many letters are dropped into the Post-office in this city, intended for the continent of Europe," ran an August, 1851 article, "upon which the U.S. three-cent stamps are affixed."[77]

It is hardly surprising that the transition to prepaid mail and adhesive stamps occasioned some reticence and confusion. What is more remarkable is how quickly the new approach to the mail took hold. The earliest stamps, issued by individual postmasters to encourage prepayment in the two years after the reduction of 1845, introduced novel practices as well as novel artifacts. One surviving Vermont letter bearing one of these "postmaster provisionals" (as they are designated in philatelic parlance) includes the note "I pay this just to shew the stamp. It is against my principles you know."[78] Old principles about the mail were rapidly eroding, however. In January, 1852, Emily Wharton Sinkler of South Carolina reported to her father in Philadelphia that "stamps appear to be universally used," at least in her elite circles. "In all my numerous correspondence I have received but two letters unstamped since July" of the previous year.[79] By the time of the Civil War, just over a decade after the introduction of federally issued postage stamps and only a few years after prepayment became mandatory, Union soldiers clamored for stamps as a basic necessity of military life. William A. Clark of Indiana requisitioned his parents continually, explaining that although he could get his captain to frank letters so that they would arrive home postage due, this was not a palatable option. Perhaps relatives could be imposed upon in this way, "but to others it would be funny."[80]

In a very short period of time, stamps had become indispensable instruments of correspondence and objects of broadly acknowledged utility in everyday life. Throughout the state-banking era (before the Treasury Department began issuing currency in 1863), stamps were the only pieces of paper authorized by the federal government to circulate at a set value throughout the country. During the war, when specie was rare and banknotes depreciated, stamps became useful as money, and stores in cities would give them as change. The first national paper money issue, in fact, was a fractional currency known as "postage currency." Though their suitability for this purpose reflected special problems and possibilities brought about by economic crisis and a diverse, unstable, and deregulated money supply, postage stamps were an administrative innovation that quickly and palpably came to dramatize the popularity of the post in mid-century America.[81]

Beyond the somewhat unique case of stamps, a large body of postal materials flooded the American home and workplace during the middle decades of the century. Prestamped envelopes, which provided a popular alternative for prepaying postage, first appeared in 1853, and were available in thirteen different denominations, ranging from one to forty cents. In the first year of their issue, five million three- and six-cent envelopes were distributed to post offices all over the country, and a decade later the annual purchases of the Wells Fargo Express company alone included over two million envelopes bearing three-cent postage. By the time of the Civil War, the Post Office Department was also offering newspaper wrappers with prepaid (one-cent) postage and prestamped letter sheets that could be folded and mailed—though the latter proved far less popular than the envelopes.[82] Envelopes emblazoned with distinctive mottoes and images, a phenomenon described in a later chapter, also proliferated during the war. But even earlier, private printers had begun to cater to the rising interest in new types of mass-produced stationery and postal paraphernalia. Beginning in 1840, Americans composed letters on paper promoting the campaigns of presidential candidates.[83] In the 1850s, California printers did unprecedented business selling letter sheets, envelopes, and corner-cards (a part of an envelope devoted to advertising a product or a company) to those who had emigrated to San Francisco and the Sierras in search of gold.[84]

While new users adjusted unevenly to the novel opportunities and unfamiliar products that emerged during the advent of cheap postage, subtler shifts in the experience of communications were also taking place. As the mail system grew into a popular, participatory network in the 1840s and 1850s, Americans registered their integration into the new postal culture in their everyday epistolary practices, as they confidently scheduled and anticipated correspondence with family members, social contacts, and commercial partners. In imagining such access, Americans were not simply observing technological, political, and economic changes in the U.S. postal service. They were also responding to and participating in a new way of life that we now take for granted. With the arrival of cheap, standardized, prepaid letter postage, mail was redefined as a popular network that embraced in principle anyone who could be expected to visit a post office.

This network, as much as other, more celebrated developments in nineteenth-century America, became the site and the engine of revolutionary changes in everyday experience. The significance of those changes, of course, would depend on how Americans used their newly inclusive post and on how they imagined those uses. At its conceptual core, though, the postal network of the mid-nineteenth century introduced a radical innovation in the mapping of the United States that was at once abstractly ubiquitous in its reach and tethered, albeit imperfectly, to the personal identities of its users. In contrast to the Cartesian grids through which American statesmen and planners in the early national period had defined geographical space as a set of repeatable and interchangeable rectilinear units, the world of the post was oddly nonspatial. By 1851 the nation as a whole constituted a single postal zone within which individual post offices and mail routes formed the only significant spatial coordinates. There was no uniform field of spatial reference;

names of persons and localities were special entities produced by contingent historical circumstances. Unlike lots on a Western land map or blocks on a municipal plan, names and addresses (which consisted at mid-century simply of post office locations) were irreducible to constitutive components and were not easily assembled into larger units.[85]

Instead of mapping American space in orderly, geometric terms, the new postal cartography conjured an ill-defined, vaporous outside world through which or within which individual people could be located and accessed. How this new picture informed ordinary Americans' perceptions and experiences of being in the world is impossible to say with any precision. Some postal users may well have conceived of letters as messages tossed upon the seas, washing up miraculously at their intended destination. Correspondents of a literary bent certainly indulged such thoughts. "I know not whereabouts this letter will find thee," Nathaniel Hawthorne wrote to his fiancée Sophia Peabody in 1840, "but I throw it upon the winds." Thomas Carlyle evoked a related image in a transoceanic letter to Emerson, whose location was more or less known, but so far away that Carlyle wondered if it did not seem "a beneficent miracle that messages can arrive at all; that a little slip of paper will skim over all these weltering floods, and other inextricable confusions; and come at last, in the hand of the Twopenny Postman, safe to your lurking-place, like green leaf in the bill of Noah's Dove?" The comparison to Noah was a tellingly imprecise way to imagine the successful transmission of letters between the two literati, since the biblical dove was no carrier pigeon; she returned with a leaf collected from the soggy world beyond the ark— not from an intentional, personal correspondent. Fanny Fern's popular mid-century novel *Ruth Hall* also captures the modernity of that ancient mail call, mobilizing the story of the aftermath of the Flood to describe her protagonist's state of mind as she posted an important letter—at once heart-wrenching and savvy, both business and personal—to an editor whom she had never met but who was holding out the prospect of financial rescue. "Ruth carried her letter to the post-office; dropping it into the letter-box with more hopeful feelings than Noah probably experienced when he sent forth the dove from the ark for the third time."[86] From the perspective of many nineteenth-century postal users, letters did not necessarily bear the inimitable traces of other known individuals; they arrived from and departed for a vaguely defined and thickly veiled outside world.

Several contemporary sources made sense of this mode of communication by analogy to the supernatural. In "Song of Myself" (1855), Walt Whitman evoked the image of regular postal service and voluminous correspondence to describe his own experience of the divine imprint on everyday life: "I find letters from God dropt in the street, and every one is sign'd by God's name / And I leave them where they are, for I know that wheresoe'er I go / Others will punctually come for ever and ever."[87] More commonly, though, observers compared mail to prayer. In *The Post-office; or, An Illustration of Prayer*, a London publication put out in revised form in 1844 by the Massachusetts Sabbath School Society, a mother explains to her curious young son Henry the workings of the postal system. Asking how is it possible for his mother to have such faith that the words she writes will reach their destination ("[H]ow do you know that they will take care of your letter? [A]nd how do you know just what time they will bring the letters?"), the innocent boy articulates an understandable wonder at the complex web of faith undergirding postal relationships. Having laid out in didactic detail for her son—and for the book's readers—the principles, policies, and infrastructure of the modern post, the mother segues into a discourse about an analogous subject, "still more important than sending letters by the post...." Every day, she notes, there are "affairs of the greatest consequence to carry on, about which I must send far beyond this world," and her faith in the audibility and efficacy of those postings is no more remarkable, she points out, than her confidence in the mail.

> Now, Henry, when I put a letter in the post, I have four reasons for expecting that it will safely reach the person to whom it is directed: because I send it in the regular, appointed way; because every thing necessary is provided at the different places for sending letters in that way; because I know that every day hundreds and thousands of letters go safely in that manner; and because I have myself received many letters in the same way.
>
> The very same reasons encourage me to hope and expect that I shall receive the blessing I need in answer to prayer."[88]

Literary outpourings from the California Gold Rush, which (as chapter 5 demonstrates) endowed the conduct of postal correspondence with an aura of sanctity, similarly linked letter writing to supernatural communication. In Reverend John Steele's account of the Coloma post office in 1853, letter recipients are easily moved by the singing of hymns. "The effect was inspiring," Steele recalled, "and made me feel that God was not only present but considering our individual interests."[89]

Despite its evident modernity and its association with mundane commercial transactions, observers could find something otherworldly about the postal system in the middle of the nineteenth century. Much as in a particular gothic tale published in 1860, where the ghost of a falsely convicted man communicates with the living through the mail, ordinary letters collected at the post office could spark fantasies about relationships that exceeded the ordinary bounds of space, time, and social possibility.[90] The habituation of hundreds of thousands of mid-century Americans to the practices and expectations that such ordinary letters represented marked a momentous shift in those bounds.

TWO

MAILABLE MATTERS
FROM NEWS TO MAIL

Though cheap uniform postage and adhesive prepaid stamps were major innovations in postal service, in most respects the institutional framework of the U.S. Post Office Department had been in place for decades by the middle of the nineteenth century. What was revolutionary about the spread of postal practices and the rise of postal culture was not the invention of a new bureaucracy or the construction of a new mode of communication. These had been invented and constructed in bold strokes at the beginning of the nation's history.[1] Instead, the postal revolution amounted to a complex conversion of an already powerful state institution into a network of popular exchange and sociability. This involved not only the radical opening up of the network to mass participation described in the previous chapter, but also a fundamental redefinition of the basic function of the post. Whereas an earlier generation of Americans had experienced the post as a kind of broadcast medium, postal users in the antebellum era joined a far more interactive network, employing the older bureaucratic apparatus for a new set of recognizably modern purposes. Central to this transformation was the shifting status of printed newspapers within the postal system. As popular experience of the post disentangled from the press it supported, a new relationship to mail emerged.

From the early years of U.S. mail service, newspapers were the staple item of postal exchange. Encouraged by low rates, the practice of mailing newspapers seized upon the basic premises of the 1792 postal legislation, which linked the spread of the post to the diffuse circulation of the press. For the next half century, large numbers of Americans subscribed to nonlocal journals, and newsprint flooded every post office in the country, comprising the bulk of what Americans called the mail. To most observers, this preponderance must have made a good deal of sense. The extraordinary significance of the post in American public life from the 1790s at least until the 1830s lay precisely in this special relationship to the periodical press, whose rhythms it mirrored and reinforced.

The post and the press were deeply intertwined and mutually supportive cultural institutions; their claims to overcome barriers of time and space by bringing news from afar (typically at regular weekly intervals) were essentially one and the same. Americans during the first third of the century valued the post, in other words, for the same reasons they valued the weekly newspaper, not because it allowed them to maintain regular contact with people they did not see.

To those who worked at the post office or watched mailbags being loaded onto carts, the privileged place of the newspaper in the early national post was unmistakable. Sixteen million newspapers passed through the mail in 1830 (not including those exchanged postage-free by editors), and by the end of the decade, the figure had increased by close to ten million. The two to three thousand people who lived in the small Illinois city of Jacksonville in 1831 maintained at least 486 subscriptions to newspapers that came in the mail. In the postal records kept for the small town of New Market, Virginia, for the period 1830–33, more than 40 different newspaper titles appear. And during one three-month period in 1841, the post office in the small town of Marion, Alabama received 6,829 newspapers, a rate of almost 7 for each resident.[2]

Subscriptions accounted for only a portion of the postal traffic in newspapers. Individual mail users put newspapers into the mail, sharing their contents with distant relatives and friends, especially those who had migrated from their homes. "Transient newspapers," as postal authorities called journals posted by someone other than their publisher, offered a reader a source of information, identification, or entertainment without the cost or commitment of subscribing, but the popularity of these papers transcended such practical considerations. Part of the appeal of the transient newspaper was that it served as a souvenir of a distant place—somewhat like a postcard, except that it ordinarily hailed from a familiar locale. In his famous travel narrative, *Two Years Before the Mast* (1840), Richard Henry Dana recalled the power of seeing a Boston newspaper when he had been traveling in California almost a decade earlier. "No one has ever been on distant voyages," he mused, "and after a long absence received a newspaper from home, who cannot understand the delight that they give one." Even classified advertisements and auction listings evoke home, Dana remarked. "Nothing carries you so entirely to a place, and makes you feel so perfectly at home, as a newspaper." Charlotte Forten, homesick for New England during her Civil War service at St. Helena Island, was similarly moved by the arrival of William Lloyd Garrison's *The Liberator*. "It is familiar and delightful to look upon as the face of an old friend," she wrote in her diary. Papers could transport a

displaced person back to his or her home, and, as in the case of the abolitionist *Liberator*, they could reaffirm the values of a reader's upbringing.
Emily Wharton Sinkler, having moved from Philadelphia to South Carolina in 1842, clamored for copies of her favorite metropolitan weekly
papers. "Any thing of the kind is an excessive treat in the country."[3]

Posted papers were even more treasured as tokens of affection and gestures of attentiveness between correspondents. Because it was so much
cheaper to send a newspaper than a letter before 1845 (a one-sheet letter
traveling five hundred miles cost almost seventeen times as much to mail
as an entire newspaper), the exchange of papers was an affordable sub-
stitute for epistolary contact, providing an interesting model for what it
might mean to stay in touch. Letters and diaries from the period immediately preceding the 1845 postage reductions are filled with references to
transient newspapers and reflections on the value of these papers as correspondence. Samuel Kempton of Baltimore sent newspapers regularly
to Anna Briggs Bentley and her family after they moved to Ohio in 1826.
Bentley reported proudly to her mother that Kempton sent five or six
papers every week. "Though he don't take them himself," she explained,
"yet he takes the trouble to collect them of his friends, seal them up, and
send them every week." She wrote often of this gesture, acknowledging
to her friends in 1831 with pride and gratitude that Kempton and his wife
wrote letters "very often" and had been sending them newspapers "every
week for nearly three years." Three years later she cited the fact that the
Kemptons had sent "5 or 6 newspapers every week for 6 years, folding,
sealing, and directing them," to illustrate their "many acts of affectionate
kindness."[4] Hiram Abiff Whittington, who left Boston for Arkansas in
1826, regularly sent copies of the Arkansas *Gazette* to his family. When
they did not respond as often as he would have liked, he pointed out that
he considered "the sending of a newspaper the same thing as if I wrote a
letter."[5] Whittington had mailed the *Gazette* not simply to let his family
know what the world looked like from Arkansas; he had been engaging
in a postal relationship—and he expected reciprocity. The *New Orleans
Picayune* picked up this theme in 1840, when it urged readers to consider
the "new and neat idea" of giving subscriptions to "distant friends" in
fulfillment of the novel and growing practice of Christmas gift-giving.
"To those negligent of epistolary correspondence," the paper suggested,
"this idea offers another inducement, for while you send your friend all
the news in a printed journal you have a very fair excuse for being lazy
with your pen."[6] However self-serving, the *Picayune's* pitch relied on the
proposition that sending a newspaper could count as a form of letter-
writing, allowing those without energy or resources to form postal ties.

Newspapers may have sought to sell gift subscriptions by advertising them as an easy way to correspond, but for many Americans it was the discrete and deliberate posting of individual transient papers (a practice newspaper editors may have wished to discourage) that constituted or approximated letter-writing. Edward Jenner Carpenter, an apprentice cabinetmaker from Massachusetts who began keeping a journal in 1843 at the age of eighteen, regularly used newspapers in this manner. Carpenter's diary offers a rare glimpse of the way aspiring postal users conceived of and related to their news-letters. Frequent entries refer to receiving papers from distant friends, usually without identifying the name of the journal. On May 7, 1844, for example, Carpenter "received a paper today from Eliza A. Whitney also one from L. W. Benton. I sent him one to-night." The exchange of papers was a moment of social contact and an occasion for thinking about an absent friend or relative. Carpenter writes, "I received a paper this morning from S. W. Dickinson, an apprentice that left here a little more than a year ago, he is now working in North Adams," and "I received a paper today from my brother Tim, who lives with Mr. P. L. Cushman in Bernardston." Like a letter, a newspaper brought with it some implicit news of the sender's whereabouts, if not his or her condition. "I received a paper this morning from Eliza A. Whitney dated at New Orleans," Carpenter noted in November, 1844. "I cannot hardly believe she is there, but I suppose I must." A posted newspaper also implied the same obligations to reciprocate as those that attended personal letters. The day after Whitney's paper arrived from New Orleans, Carpenter mailed one to her "in answer." A few months later he recorded the receipt of "a paper from Jane Slate this week" and observed that he "must send her one in return." Some of these exchanges became quite regular. After receiving his second monthly issue of the "Despatch" (one of two papers to which he mentions subscribing) in July of 1844, Carpenter decided to make a regular habit of sending this paper to James M. Lyons. In a twelve-month period ending in March of 1845 (when Congress enacted the postage reform), Carpenter recorded monthly paper exchanges with Lyons. The name of the paper Carpenter received in return is never mentioned (let alone its contents); what is important to the diarist is simply that the two men are maintaining a correspondence.[7] Ritual exchanges of newspapers through the mail were quite common in the years leading up to 1845, and must be understood as early forms of postal contact and not simply as symptoms of America's attachment to the press.

But were posted newspapers the same as letters? New postal users were not so sure, and they routinely classified letters and papers separately (both before and after 1845) in reporting their mail activities. Richard Henry Dana took the position that newspapers were superior to letters, at least insofar as a paper "carries you back to the spot, better than anything else." For others, newspapers were simply more informative, as Elizabeth Lee wrote to her husband in the Union Army in 1861, by way of explaining her own practice of sending him papers on a daily basis: "[N]o letters can keep one posted like the papers."[8] Many recipients felt differently. "Had some newspapers, but no letters," Charlotte Forten confided in her diary in 1862, "which disappoints me greatly." Away at a New Hampshire school in 1857, Anna May maintained the same invidious distinction, but gave papers their due as a form of correspondence. One day in February she reported that she had "expected a paper from mother today, but did not receive one. Perhaps she forgot to send it. I should like to have heard from her by a paper even."[9]

Though no one conflated the two categories, the relationship between transient papers and personal correspondence was closer than later generations might imagine. Writing to his aunt in 1840, Princeton undergraduate Theodore Cuyler expressed the familiar dilemma of pre-1845 correspondents. "I have waited some time to collect a budget of news before I commenced my long promised letter," he explained with a certain amount of defensiveness, "and now I think that a sufficient supply is received to warrant me in making an attempt." Efficient use of the post, Cuyler suggested, required postponing letters until they resembled newspapers. "In the mean time," Cuyler reminded her, he had "despatched a sufficient no. of newspapers to convince you of my continual remembrance of your wants & my desire to furnish you with reading material in your retired situation." In the absence of something better, his letter seems to suggest, newspapers could serve many of the same purposes as letter-writing, providing literary evidence of personal concern. Whether Cuyler's aunt accepted his newspaper offerings as substitutes for deferred letters we do not know. Like most postal users, she probably regarded a posted paper as something resembling but not equaling a letter. Forty-niner John Ingalls shared this common view of transient papers as an inferior grade of interpersonal mail. Berating his foster brother Jonathan Trumbull Smith for not writing more than one letter in five months, Ingalls clung to the hope of "hearing from you again" and begged not to be forgotten by Smith "in this land of strangers." Reemphasizing the neglect of his Eastern friends and family, Ingalls complained about not having "heard a word from Hartford for more than five months . . . except through the Courant you are so kind to send me." A Hartford newspaper brought word from home, but apparently did not acquit the members of the Smith family of their responsibilities to attend to a relative in a distant land.[10]

Despite their shortcomings as media of interpersonal expression, transient newspapers in the pre-1845 era were temptingly inexpensive stand-ins for costly letters. The difference in price was sufficient to induce many postal users to see how far they might stretch the epistolary powers of a printed journal. A common, illegal practice of marking newspapers with personal information reflected popular perceptions of both the suitability and the limitations of newspapers as correspondence and called into open question the purposes of the nation's growing postal system.

Already in 1825, Congress sought to suppress the habit of writing on newspapers by subjecting such papers to letter postage (typically paid by the addressee) and imposing a fine (on the sender) for the attempted evasion of the law. Prohibitions notwithstanding, the practice persisted. Roxana Watts's instruction to her daughter, mentioned earlier, that she mark a newspaper to indicate receipt of a package, was not an isolated occurrence.[11] By the early 1840s, references to this practice were common. An 1841 communiqué from the Post Office Department cited "increasing attempts to violate the law and defraud the revenue" by writing on newspapers. Americans, the postal administration alleged, were "enclosing memoranda or other things within" newspapers, as well as "underscoring, or pricking letters or words" in order to avoid paying letter rates for their mail. In the view of the postmaster general in 1842, the "practice of carrying on a business or friendly correspondence, by writing on the margin of newspapers" had become "extensive." A Baltimore paper reminded readers in 1843 of the postal regulations on this subject and reprinted an official directive that postmasters remove newspaper wrappers, since "frauds are very often attempted by concealing letters or memoranda in these articles." That same year, the *New Englander* magazine spoke of the frequent habit of communicating through "some cabalistic mark on the margin or the wrapper of a newspaper."[12]

"Cabalistic" concealment could take several forms. James Holbrook, a special agent of the Post Office assigned to investigate fraud and theft of a more serious variety, recalled in 1855 how "before the adoption of the present rates of postage," patrons would cross out portions of transient newspapers so that "the letters left legible conveyed the meaning which the operator intended." Holbrook took evident delight in the ease with which "pugnacious editorials were converted into epistles of the mildest and most affectionate description, and public news of an important character not unfrequently contracted into a channel for the conveyance of domestic intelligence." The *New Orleans Picayune* reported an incident in which a milliner sent a paper from New York to Boston addressed to John Garigo Smith. The fictitious middle name, the *Picayune* explained, was an acronym for "Goods All Received in Good Order." Other codes were even more elaborate. According to an 1842 memorandum from the Post Office Department, a man who wished to communicate with his father without paying letter rates would pencil into the margins of a paper a drawing of an awl pointing to a well. This part of the rebus was fairly straightforward (all was well, the son was announcing), though an additional depiction of a bucket facing upward, which reportedly signified an intended visit, would probably have required greater familiarity or ingenuity to decipher.[13]

Other efforts at communication were simple and involved less subterfuge, but they too risked the ire of the law. Edward Carpenter referred in his diary to "doing up" the papers he mailed to friends, which presumably entailed, at the very least, identifying himself as the sender. (When Eliza Whitney mailed a newspaper from an unlikely location, for instance, Carpenter could tell that it came from her.) Even this apparently innocent amount of writing turned a newspaper into a letter, according to Postmaster General Charles Wickliffe. Any writing that "conveyed an idea to the person to whom the paper was sent, or informed him of any distinct fact" was subject to letter postage, as Wickliffe advised a confused postal user from Kentucky who had been sending newspapers to his son bearing a handwritten address.

> If A write his name on the margin of a paper, and send that to a friend by mail, he conveys to him several distinct ideas and facts: 1st. that he is still alive; 2d. that he was well enough to write; 3d. that he remembers him, though distant; 4th. that he has sent him by mail the very newspaper upon which he has written his name, or caused it to be done; and 5th. he tells his friend where he is.... The only true and safe principle is, does the writing on the paper convey to the person to whom it is sent a fact, any intelligence, or idea, from the person sending it?[14]

By 1842, the Post Office was adopting an extremely strict interpretation of the prohibition against writing on printed newspapers. Wickliffe's concern that a hand-addressed envelope communicates "several distinct ideas and facts" about the sender acknowledged the way transient papers functioned as correspondence and also pointed to the difficulties of protecting the newspaper rate against stowaways. Still, this hard-line position was upheld by the courts in the 1843 case of *U.S. v. Elder*. The U.S. District Court ruled that a printed paper bearing the words "From Elder, Gelston & Co., Baltimore" warranted the assessment of letter postage and a fine for the sender.[15] Pushed with regulatory vigilance to its logical conclusion, the Post Office's long-standing commitment to the newspaper had reached an impasse. By the 1840s, the newspaper's status and value as an object of postal exchange was, paradoxically, uncertain.

Though the glaring disparity between newspaper and letter rates was as old as the U.S. Post Office itself, and though the prohibitions against supplementing papers with personal memoranda had been on the books since 1825, the bulk of the evidence for this practice comes from the period 1840–45. During the final years of expensive letter postage, public awareness of the temptation to disguise letters as newspapers had come to a sudden crescendo. Exactly how rampant the actual subterfuge was is impossible to deduce from the public discussion, but the chronological coincidence is striking, as is the fact that Charles Wickliffe himself presented to Congress the draft of the reforms that went into effect on the last day of his tenure in office. The decision to dismantle the differential rate system was made during a critical moment when both the federal bureaucracy and the public were aware of the threat posed by popular epistolary impulses. A nation of postal free riders was, among other things, a nation desperate to correspond.

Transient newspapers continued to flow through the mails after the reductions of 1845, but not in the same proportions and not with the same function.[16] Edward Carpenter's diary ends just as the new laws took effect, leaving us to speculate as to how he maintained relationships with James Lyons and Eliza Whitney in the new postal world. An 1847 law raised the rates on transient papers to 3 cents, thus closing the period when scrawled marginalia booked secret passage on the ship of American print culture.

In demoting the newspaper from its long-standing place of privilege in the mail system, postal reformers of the 1840s were in part reinforcing changes in the press that were well under way. Already in the 1830s, the link between newspapers and the post was attenuated by the arrival of cheap dailies in large cities that circumvented the mail altogether. Hawked in city streets, sold by the issue, attuned to sensational stories about the cities in which they were published, and priced within the reach of ordinary people, the new model of a big-city newspaper did not emphasize the bridging of distant populations; increasingly the metropolitan press became a local enterprise more dependent on urban growth than on postal subsidies. Unprecedentedly popular and increasingly powerful, these daily newspapers were no longer designed to travel and could no longer serve as models of postal circulation.[17]

Weekly newspapers, on the other hand, continued to cater to a dispersed readership, and reductions in newspaper rates in 1851 and 1852 were important to the phenomenal growth of a national periodical press during the decade before the Civil War. Printed newspapers did continue to travel by mail, and postal subsidies still played a role in shaping the news industry, but the identification of the post with the press had become disrupted. Post offices were no longer newsstands, and letters were no longer expensive guests on conveyances meant to transmit the news.

To be sure, displaced Americans might still romanticize a beloved newspaper as a symbol of home or an affirmation of continuity, but they were far less likely to ask for it to be sent. The case of Hiram Rumfield, a postal official stationed in Utah during the 1860s, illustrates this point. Rumfield's letters home to his wife show us much concern for his favorite paper (the *New York Tribune*, which was sent to him through the mail) as any correspondence from earlier in the century, but he never asks her to mail him issues as a form of epistolary contact. Far from requesting newspapers as surrogates for physical presence, Rumfield neatly (and perversely) reverses the relationship, citing his concern for the preservation of his *Tribunes* as an argument against her traveling to Utah. Among such arguments, Rumfield ranked as a "consideration of the gravest moment" the possibility that "during your absence, my Tribunes will be in danger of being lost or misplaced, by being taken from the post office by persons who will too lightly esteem their value and the great care I bestow in their preservation."[18] Few readers of the new urban dailies, which were light, easily disposable, and perishable by design, shared Rumfield's obsessive attitude toward their "preservation," but his assumption that letters, rather than newspapers, provided the best way to maintain contact with his wife was broadly shared by the second half of the century.

As letter-writing became more common and as newspapers evolved, Americans began to think differently about the mail. With increasing frequency during the early decades of the century, postal panegyrics emphasized the social and interpersonal ties cultivated in the mail, often citing examples of communication among friends and family rather than informed citizens and government officials. A contributor to an Albany agricultural newspaper in 1820 celebrated the power of the post office as a steady source of news and an agent of economic growth. But the most important function of the mail, according to this advocate of increased government expenditure on the post, was its tendency to diminish the psychological costs of moving away from home. The spread of the post was reducing "distance . . . almost to contiguity," by allowing "a transcript of our dearest friend's mind" to pass quickly over what might otherwise seem like a vast spatial divide.[19] Nine years later, Unitarian minister William Ellery Channing, whose deep faith in the national benefits of a broadly participatory post drew on traditional Protestant optimism about the power of reading and writing, argued that the post office "binds the whole country in a chain of sympathies" but offered, alongside more predictable observations about economic growth and national governance, some strikingly nonpolitical illustrations. "It perpetuates friendships between those who are never to meet again," Channing remarked. "It binds the family in the new settlement and the half-cleared forest to the cultivated spot from which it emigrated."[20] In an epistolary guide for children first published in 1834, the popular author Mrs. John Farrar has her fictional wise adult wax poetic on the importance of letters. Leaving aside its effects on commerce and public affairs, the kindly gentleman asks his nephew to imagine a world without a post, and to consider "for a moment what a doleful change . . . in all our intercourse with our fellow beings" would be entailed. Would the young boy even have known enough about his cousins, the uncle wondered, to choose to visit them?[21] Even as news remained the core content of postal transmissions, a number of critics were beginning to stress the larger social applications and implications of widespread use of the mails.

In a sense, transient newspapers both enabled and underscored this shifting approach to the post. In taking advantage of the federal subsidy of the press, Americans were demonstrating social uses of the mail that had little to do with the printing industry or with the contact between constituents and their elected representatives. One might even say that transient newspapers were elementary items of mail exchange through which ordinary Americans acquired many of the postal habits that would underwrite the revolutionary changes of the 1840s and 1850s. For postal users who exchanged papers, the post office was no longer simply a newsstand. It was, instead, a point of access to a world of social relations that required special gestures of solicitation and inquiry. From this point of view, however, the privileged status of the printed paper no longer made much sense. In its place emerged a capacious and heterogeneous category of mailable matter for which the impersonal print document was not necessarily a compelling paradigm. After 1845, most mail was measured by the indifferent criterion of weight, rather than by an assessment of the kind of text it was or the number of pages it comprised.[22] Mail was defined, simply and influentially, as a package of objects— potentially different in kind but measurable on a uniform scale—which one person selects, prepares, and pays to send to another. According to this definition, mail could be anything and need not have a particular character associated with news. What was crucial was the act of address and not the content. Still, the particular objects that postal patrons saw fit to mail during the middle decades of the century revealed a great deal about popular perceptions of the newly inclusive postal network.

"A bunch of keys, a specimen of wheat, bottles, sugar samples, hanks of yarn, a bed quilt, a rattlesnake skin, two diamond ornaments, an old hat." Examining the curious collections of posted objects at the Dead Letter Office in 1852, the *Albany Register* offered a remarkable inventory of the sorts of objects that traveled (and in this case remained) in the U.S. mails at mid-century. For newspaper readers, these inventories of uncollected mail offered a glimpse of a fascinating new world of correspondence. For historians, they provide a useful reminder that the expanding postal network facilitated more than just the exchange of personal words. Then, as now, the U.S. Post Office was in the business of transporting material artifacts. Correspondence, as accounts and descriptions of undelivered letters attested, came in all shapes and sizes and involved frequent enclosures, especially after 1845 when the Post Office shifted to a rate system that charged letters on the basis of weight. In order to understand how new users experienced the post as it was transformed into a medium of mass participation, it is essential to consider the kinds of objects they sent and received. The new letter rate appeared to embrace and encourage all kinds of enclosures, and catalogues of lost postal property emphasized the endless diversity of items in the mail. After the legislative changes of 1851, the *New York Times* remarked that "the public mail has become a kind of package, parcel, and express line, for the conveyance of all sorts of goods and chattels, ... anything, in short, under the size and weight of cooking stoves or cotton gins." Still, certain objects were particularly common at mid-century, reflecting and informing the expectations Americans brought to the post and helping to shape the new postal culture.

For most Americans, and certainly for the Post Office Department, the enclosure that attracted the most interest was money. In an era before personal checking accounts and before money orders (which were introduced by the Post Office in 1864), Americans relied on the mails to conduct financial transactions. Though some businessmen might exchange letters of credit or bank drafts, a great deal of the money passing through the post consisted of paper currency, typically in the form of state-issued banknotes. Merchants had been posting large sums of money in this manner from before the period of the postal reforms (the need to transfer a large sum could make the high postage rates seem relatively insignificant), and this practice increased as markets expanded and economies grew. James Holbrook's 1855 account of his work investigating theft for the Post Office documented the heavy dependence of American businesses on the mail system for their quotidian financial transactions. Holbrook described a typical process by which a company (in this case a firm in upstate New York "extensively engaged in manufacturing and real estate operations") gained confidence in the post. "For a long time they confined themselves to the use of drafts, checks, and other representatives of money, but as everything went on smoothly for years, they finally remitted money itself...without bestowing a thought upon the insecurity or danger of such a course."[23]

By the year of Holbrook's publication, one hundred million dollars in cash passed through the mail each year, much of it presumably sent by merchants.[24] Ordinary people also needed to move money across distances, and they too came to rely upon the post. Before 1845, sending cash in the mail could be costly, since each dollar bill counted as a separate sheet for purposes of assessing postage. As one advocate of cheap postage argued, "the apprentice boy who . . . wants to send a dollar to his widowed mother . . . must be taxed not for his letter only, but to the amount of from six to twenty-five *per cent.* on his poor paper dollar."[25] When larger sums were involved, the risks of loss or theft might seem daunting. Like merchants, new postal users took time to grow accustomed to placing significant sums of uninsured cash in the hands of mail carriers. When she first arrived in Ohio in 1826, Anna Briggs Bentley wrote to her father in Maryland asking him to send money by mail. As a precaution, she instructed him to "procure as large notes as thee can, in United States or Baltimore notes, cut them in half, send one half and retain the other till thou hears from us, keeping a particular description of them and the half of but 1 note at a time."[26] Whether they conducted this elaborate experiment is hard to determine (though there is evidence that others resorted to similar tactics),[27] but within a short time banknotes were flowing freely and without undue anxiety between Bentley and her correspondents. When she received, in 1829, twenty dollars in the mail from a man she did not know, only the generosity of the gift caught her special attention.[28] As postal correspondence proliferated during the middle decades, ordinary people in various circumstances found frequent occasion to send money—as gifts, reimbursements, payment for services, or shared earnings. One mid-century correspondent felt the need to inscribe the following disclaimer on the outside of his letter:

> Robber, shouldst thou seize this letter,
> Break it not; there's nothing in't,
> Nought for which thou wouldst be better:
> Note of bank, or coin from mint.[29]

The playful gesture, a grandiloquent version of the advisory to would-be thieves that would appear in the windows of parked cars in New York City toward the end of the twentieth century, registered a general awareness that ordinary letters might well be lucrative booty. By 1870, the Dead Letter Office was reporting more than twenty-two thousand undelivered letters a year containing money "in sums of one dollar and upward" as well as a slightly higher number of letters bearing amounts less than a dollar. Presumably the hundred thousand dollars in banknotes that washed up in Washington that year (more than three-quarters of it uninsured) represented but a tiny fraction of the total volume of money that Americans posted to one another, much of it in small portions and denominations.[30]

Apart from making the post a tempting target for thieves and a convenient medium for fraudulent solicitations, the popular practice of enclosing money in letters highlighted particular affinities between paper currency and mail. Though the state banknote system was far more heterogeneous, chaotic, and unstable than the federal post, the explosive growth of paper money and the post during the antebellum period reflected and reinforced the mobility of persons, the extensive reach of commercial relations, and the increasing interconnectedness of society's disparate elements. Americans used the post to maintain relations with people they could not see and in some cases to forge relations with people they did not really know. Light and easily transferable, banknotes served both of those purposes quite well. They were classic examples of mailable matter. And to the extent that participation in the postal network became in principle universal, mail could provide a model for a basic form of paper currency. In criticizing Congress for not mandating the use of prepaid stamps in the 1845 reform legislation, the *National Intelligencer* seized upon this possibility, citing "the convenience which such stamp affords for the payment of small amounts of money to correspondents at a distance, . . . furnishing a universal circulating medium of small change, of *par* value in all parts of the Union." Though this suggestion was not adopted, postage stamps did serve as money in times when specie was in short supply. In 1870, 45,457 dead letters had postage stamps enclosed in them.[31]

Banknotes and postage stamps did not travel alone, however. Impersonal, transferable, paper currency was enclosed in personal letters, typically composed and addressed by hand. Personal letters, even when they bore printed enclosures, were material artifacts whose meaning was connected to the very personal act of writing.

Post Office regulations from the pre-1845 period had reaffirmed in a radical way the distinction between written and printed mail. This opposition was by no means coextensive with the much-discussed dichotomy between business and personal correspondence, both of which were usually handwritten (typewriters were not widely used among businesses until the last quarter of the century). Yet it was a culturally loaded distinction. As Michael Warner has explored in his study of the late colonial and early national periods, the cultural status of print in the United States was founded on the proposition that printed documents bracketed the personal identities of their authors. Handwritten documents, by contrast, relied upon the expression of that identity for their authority. By the nineteenth century, Tamara Plakins Thornton emphasizes, popular interest in handwriting hinged on the ideological equation of writing and selfhood, and the inherited notion that what distinguished writing from print was its distinctive and foregrounded relationship to the human body.[32] Of course penalties against handwritten marks on posted newspapers were designed to prevent the appropriation of special privileges intended solely for newspaper publishers. But the effect of such penalties was to reinforce a widespread perception of handwriting as the essence of personal correspondence.

Letter-writers frequently focused on the impact and significance of handwriting, pulling a metonymic string that linked chirography to hand to bodily presence. "To see the handwriting of my dear parents, after this long separation, filled me with too much emotion," one young woman wrote to her parents in 1820. Several decades later, a Confederate soldier opened a letter to his wife with the self-assurance that she must be "delighted to see my handwriting in ink once more, something like myself." In part this perceived resemblance between a person and his or her handwriting rested on a growing association between handwriting and mail, as well as on the more straightforward fact that recognizable penmanship on a sealed sheet or envelope offered the first indication of the origin of a letter. Theodore Tilton wrote to his wife, "Oh, how my heart bounds at the sight of your handwriting!" This reaction was not simply based on familiarity. A few weeks, later Tilton articulated the larger significance of handwriting: "There is something in the exchange of letters that ranks next to the greeting of palm to palm. When I receive one of your letters the sheet seems to contain more than you were writing; it is something which has been touched by your hand, which has caught a pulse of your feeling, and which represents more than the words can possibly say." Handwritten letters bore the trace of physical contact and not simply the recognizable imprimatur of individual identity. "Oh, how I could have blessed the paper your hand had travelled over," a forty-niner exclaimed to his wife from a mining camp near Stockton. James H. Hammond Jr., courting his future wife in 1859, put the point more provocatively. His letter, he writes, "is mine now, in my hands, but day after tomorrow it will be yours, and will tremble and bend in those little fingers."[33]

Among chirographic traces, the most valued and fetishized tokens of personal presence were autographs, especially those of famous people. Supported by widespread beliefs in the power and meaning of handwriting and new interest in the phenomenon of celebrity, the hobby of collecting signatures became popular during the middle third of the nineteenth century.[34] In two important ways, this phenomenon was part of the postal revolution. First, the proliferation of regular postal contacts and far-flung postal relationships meant that many people were acquiring the habit of associating handwriting with absent correspondents. Second, and on a more practical level, the postal system provided a means for soliciting and obtaining autographs. Charlotte Forten, away at school in 1858, wrote to antislavery leaders William Lloyd Garrison and Charles Sumner to request their autographs. A few days later, she announced in her diary "a day to be marked with a *white stone*." Upon returning from school, "weary and sad, as usual," Forten found waiting for her two pieces of mail from Sumner, one containing his own signature and the other "filled with other valuable autographs,—of the Duchess of Sutherland, the Duchess of Argyle, the Earl of Shaftsbury [*sic*], Longfellow, W. H. Furness, Sen. Blair, Jared Sparks, and Lady Napier, the lady of the British Minister at Washington." Lucia Alden, a Massachusetts schoolgirl, justified an unsolicited postal overture to the poet Henry Wadsworth Longfellow in 1858 with the explanation that "all the great girls that I go to school with here at the Academy, are getting Autographs." In her memoir of growing up in San Francisco during the postbellum era, Harriet Lane Levy recalled using the post to procure autographs from various celebrities, writing to them "as to a friend." To her fondly remembered satisfaction, "nobody failed to answer."[35] Every postal reply contained a signature, something Josephine Clifford noted wistfully in her survey of the remains at the Dead Letter Office. "It was always with a sigh of regret," she observed "that letters signed by such names as Bancroft, Whittier, Grant, Greeley, were returned to their rightful owners" and not kept for their autographs.[36]

As signatures became celebrated tokens of physical presence in the expanding postal culture, a newer mode of representing absent persons entered the mail. When Louis Daguerre announced his successful experiments with photography in 1839, the popular applications of the new technique were by no means clear. Daguerre himself had imagined that the camera would be suitable for depicting still-life scenes and landscapes. Personal portraits seemed an especially unpromising use of the daguerreotype, given long exposure requirements and generally unflattering results (verisimilitude, early photographic pioneers understood, was not necessarily an advantage in human portraiture). But over the next decade daguerreotype portraits became immensely popular in the United States. In a mobile and transient society concerned with preserving stable images of personal identity, a photographic likeness, however awkward and inelegant, held a powerful appeal. By mid-century there were a hundred daguerreotype studios in New York City alone, conducting a flourishing business and securing photography a lasting place in American culture.[37]

Daguerreotype portraits entered American life during the period of postal reform and quickly became a staple item of postal exchange. Photographs appeared in large quantities in dead letter inventories (thousands per year, often accounting for most of the "valuable letter" category) and are referred to frequently in the correspondence of Americans from all classes.[38] Daguerreotypes appealed to many of the same impulses that were prompting increased correspondence more generally. As a later chapter explores in detail, letters and photographs were related—and mutually reinforcing—elements of postal contact during the Gold Rush and the Civil War, as well as in other circumstances when Americans wished to assert continuity and contiguity during what they hoped would be a temporary separation. Forty-niners were unusually fond of posting and receiving daguerreotypes, and they felt fortunate to have this novel technique of visual representation available. "Thanks to the inventor who brings yourself in imagination present with me," Jonathan Locke wrote to his wife in 1850.[39]

To new postal users, for whom both long-distance correspondence and photography were still unfamiliar, daguerreotypes appeared to make good on the promise of handwritten letters to incarnate absent friends and family. Upon receiving his son's "likeness" in the mail, Iowan J. H. Williams went so far as to pronounce it "as good as a short visit." Sabrina Swain of Ohio, while writing to her husband that she regretted having consented to his trek to California, took some comfort upon receiving his photograph. "I think I never saw anything but life look more natural," she told him in an 1849 letter, and related the response of their young child: "I showed it to Little Cub, and to my astonishment and pleasure she appeared to recognize it. She put her finger on it, looked up at me and laughed, put her face down to yours, and kissed it several times in succession. Every time it comes in her sight she will cry after it." Projected onto her daughter, Swain's own substitution of the daguerreotype for the husband reads as an equivocal mix of satisfaction and frustration, and thus represents broader patterns of response to mail that the posted (and fetishized) photograph brought into relief.[40]

The claim of photographic portraits to represent the bodies of absent correspondents was enhanced before 1851 by the fact that the daguerreotype was not mechanically reproducible from a negative but was a unique image of a particular moment. Posted photographs were therefore more like signed holograph letters and less like printed documents than they would later become, once the face recorded on film could be endlessly duplicated and promiscuously circulated. Daguerreotype portraits could more convincingly be read as personal gestures of communication. "Its silence speaks words of love to me which the rest do not understand," Mary Wingate wrote of her husband's daguerreotype mailed from California, "and when I look at it I step forward in imagination to that time when I shall see your own dear self not *through a glass*."[41] The unique daguerreotype image was both a bodily relic, resembling in many respects the locks of hair that were frequently enclosed in letters, and an intimate epistle in its own right.[42]

To be sure, not all correspondents treated photographic portraits as magical incarnations or even as reliable representations of their subjects. Elizabeth Tilton received her husband's photograph in 1867 with grave disappointment: "Did you have revenge in your heart when you sat for that picture?" she wondered. "It is a false representation of my beloved." Forty-niner Franklin Buck's picture faced similar criticism when he sent it to his sister in Vermont in 1853. "However repulsive it may appear to you," he responded, "I think it a good likeness and I flatter myself that there are worse looking men, at least there are here." But if forced to choose between his appearance and the fidelity of the new medium, he would surely give way on the latter. "My friends say it looks rather older than the original," he wrote of the daguerreotype. "Perhaps I can give you a better description. I am five feet eleven, weigh 175 lbs., well-proportioned, perfectly straight with a graceful and dignified carriage."[43] There were clearly advantages to more prosaic forms of self-presentation.

Photographs could have the effect of accentuating the distance between correspondents rather than erasing it. William Allen of San Francisco showed his brother Charles a photograph of their other brother that had arrived that day in the mail, but Charles did not recognize him.

"I should not have known if it had not been in your letter," William confessed.[44] Other postal users assumed an ironic stance with respect to the romantic mystique of the photograph. Ellen Horton of Connecticut enclosed her picture in a letter to her husband in the Union Army, adding that "I guess you wont say enney more about my getting annother chap for you will see by this that I hav grone so homly that a fellow must be a fool to hav enney thing to say to me when there are so menney better locking ones around."[45]

Historians have largely ignored the historical connection between photography and the mail, but the roughly contemporaneous emergence of daguerreotype portraiture and cheap postage is striking, especially given the affinity between these two forms of paper representation. The frequency with which postal users sent photographs by mid-century would have been impossible before 1845, when a daguerreotype enclosure would have doubled the already discouraging price of personal correspondence. After the first reform, the cost of adding a daguerreotype to a letter was reduced in most cases to nothing, barring of course the unlikely event that it pushed the weight of the letter over the one-ounce threshold. In other words, photographic portraits could travel basically for free throughout the United States. In his important and influential study of the history of photography in the United States, Alan Trachtenberg characterizes the striking use of personal portraits by ordinary people in the late antebellum era as "memorial," emphasizing the value Americans attributed to the daguerreotype as a bulwark against the vagaries of personal history and the ravages of time. But patrons of the new art also appreciated portraits for their ability to traverse large spatial divides. A traveling likeness, as the phenomenally successful daguerreotypists of the Gold Rush understood, was valued for its wings and not just its durability.[46]

If new postal rates enhanced the appeal of daguerreotypes, the availability of cheap mechanical likenesses added an inducement to correspond, at least for those who inhabited or visited cities. Photography introduced a visual dimension to postal self-representation. "I will send you my likeness," Aaron Stevens of Cedar County, Iowa, wrote to his brother in Minnesota. "[I]t is not a very good one, but then you see how I look somewhat. I wish you would send me yours."[47] In the grand scheme of the postal revolution, the possibility of sending photographs was surely a relatively minor factor (in Great Britain, for example, cheap postage and the proliferation of correspondence predated widespread purchasing of daguerreotype portraits). Still, to many Americans, photographs were a central feature and a favorite option of the transformed postal medium. Instead of having to encode newspapers with hidden traces of personality and identity, they could transmit their own distinct and recognizable images.

By sending daguerreotypes (and, later, wet-plate collodion photographs, from which multiple prints could be produced from a negative) to absent friends and family, mid-century correspondents sought to negotiate the vast distances that frequently defined a postal relationship. Photographic images in a letter emphasized the mobility of persons and encouraged the fantasy of instantaneous transportation that was central to the appeal of mail (even when delivery was irregular, uncertain, or subject to delay). Other commonly posted objects expressed a different sort of fascination with the possibilities of long-distance communication. Surpassed only (though by some distance) by money and photographs, the next most popular enclosures in mid-century letters may have been agricultural samples—typically in the form of seeds. References to the posting of seeds and (to a lesser extent) flowers appear throughout the epistolary archives, in the letters of both women and men, from genteel Easterners to military personnel in Mexico and rugged migrants along the overland trail.[48] From the Oregon Territory, Abigail Malick wrote back to her daughter in Illinois requesting "musk-mellone, greap, cabage, parcely, and flour seades," among others, and announced her intention "to Get some seades sent from pennsylvania." Annette Kolodny has suggested that women on the overland trail were especially eager to transport and transplant seeds from their native regions as a way of reimagining and refashioning their new homes in the West as familiar, cultivated gardens. But the appeal of posting seeds extended to both sexes and to both sides of the continent. John Everett of Kansas instructed his sister back in New York to "send . . . a few currant slips in newspaper," and hoped that she could "find a division of a pie plant root not weighing over two to four ounces" and enclose it in a letter, "perhaps with a little moss around it." Writing to her son at Harvard in 1854 (during the height of the Anthony Burns trial), Mary Jones of Georgia apologized for having "no better seeds to send you; five years' absence has made sad havoc with the flowers." California gold-seekers were particularly active in the transcontinental exchange of seeds. "I have nothing to present you with but a few flower seeds," Franklin Buck informed his sister in Vermont in 1853. Benjamin Wingate in San Francisco and his wife Mary in Connecticut regularly posted and discussed seeds in their correspondence.[49] European immigrants did the same in their correspondence with the Old Country. At the close of a letter to his family in Prussia in 1840, Wilhelm Stille of rural Pennsylvania made a two-part final request: "I ask all of you together to take as good care of our dear old mother as you can and be so kind as to send me a few seeds from the big curly cabbage and a few sweet pea seeds."[50]

Mailed seeds were not, in most cases, simply horticultural expedients or experiments. They were celebrations of the miracle of the mail that affirmed the proximity of ostensibly distant correspondents. Transplanted vegetation could transport a displaced correspondent back to a place of origin, as the Harvard law student from Georgia affirmed in response to his mother's gift. "The musk-cluster roses and sprigs of verbena did indeed remind me of many past pleasures at home," Charles Jones wrote, "while their sweet perfume was but an index, a representative, of that atmosphere fragrant with love and tender remembrance ever cherished there."[51] More generally, the arrival of a seed in the mail underscored the same wondrous feature of postal transmission that so struck Henry David Thoreau upon receiving an international letter from Ralph Waldo Emerson. "It is hard to believe that England is so near as from your letters it appears," Thoreau wrote to his friend, "and that this identical piece of paper has lately come all the way from there hither, begrimed with the English dust . . . from England, which is only historical fairyland to me, to America, which I have put my spade into, and about which there is no doubt."[52] Posted letters did not only bear intimate thoughts, timely news, or tokens of personal identity—they could also transport the terrain.

Few American postal users needed a shipment of seeds to remind them that physical objects could be transported and transplanted across the country—or the ocean. The piles of banknotes passing daily through the U.S. mails made a similar point. But cash, which remained in circulation, emphasized the perpetual movement of posted materials, while seeds, which could be planted, promised an enduring relationship between sender and addressee. How seriously or profoundly this poetic suggestion resonated among the large number of ordinary postal users who sent seeds is an open question, but these practices registered, at the very least, a broad awareness of the kind of material exchange that the post made possible and, by 1845, affordable.

Every mailable object introduced into the daily experience of ordinary Americans by mid-century shaped the meaning of the newly inclusive post. Among the more surprising and evocative of such objects was the vaccine. The mail figured recurrently in epidemiological anxieties in antebellum America, even before miasma theories began to recede as authoritative explanations for the spread of disease.[53] After mid-century, such concerns grew. Albert Janin, describing his joy at receiving a letter from his girlfriend in 1871, confessed to having kissed it "over and over again," in willful disregard of "the small-pox epidemic at New York."[54] But of course if some worried that mail might spread illness, the capacity of the post to transport medical remedies was even clearer. During the Civil War, Confederate Congressman Warren Akin enclosed an ounce of calomel and "some vaccine virus" in a letter to his wife, and instructed her to inoculate his "whole family, black and white." Lucy Breckinridge of Virginia also received vaccine in the mail during the war, which she promptly used.[55] In 1864, Norwegian immigrant Gro Svendson wrote to her parents in Scandinavia about her concern to vaccinate her son, a practice she feared was uncommon in her new country. "You can't come here to help us, and I can't send my boy over to you. Is it impossible to send the vaccine in a letter?" Several months later, Svendson was thanking her father for sending her three bottles of vaccine, one of which survived the journey intact. With the help of the post, a viral sample from Norway could now immunize an immigrant child in Minnesota against local pathogens.[56]

As with seeds, banknotes, and daguerreotypes, the transmission of viruses through the mail concretized the connections that the postal system enabled once it moved beyond its initial function as a site for broadcasting news. By the middle of the century, mail consisted not simply of the circulated information necessary for the conduct of public affairs but of every conceivable form of human contact, commerce, desire, and interdependence.

THREE

PLAYING POST OFFICE
MAIL IN URBAN SPACE

Peering across the Atlantic in 1867, the editors of Edinburgh's *Black-wood's Magazine* sounded the alarm. Relations between the sexes and between the generations were in disarray once again in the young republic—but this time the culprit was the post office. Of course, from the perspective of contemporary British observers, almost any social institution in the United States during the nineteenth century could serve as a dangerous source, a telling index, or an apt symbol of democratic and egalitarian excess. But in many respects the particular target was surprising. The post was not exactly an American innovation, and the British, on average, posted mail far more frequently during this time period than the Americans. To *Blackwood's*, though, whose views were reprinted with qualified approval in an American journal, it was not so much the post itself that underwrote the unique freedom enjoyed by young women in the United States. It was, more specifically, what the author called the "post-office system."

Postal service, as *Blackwood's* understood, involved more than just mail routes and transmission schedules. The impact and significance of the post depended on the forms of access the new users had to their mail. And on that score, the American system stood out. "The unmarried girl of nineteen or twenty," the article noted, "has the privilege, if she chooses to exercise it, of her own private box or pigeon-hole at the post-office of the town where she resides, where she can have her letters addressed." While her European counterpart depended on the "confidence of a third party" (perhaps the neighborhood pastry chef or stationer, the author supposed) to transmit secret letters, "the post-office system offers a facility for clandestine correspondence which no respectable father or mother on the European side of the Atlantic would think of without a shudder."[1]

Concern over unsupervised female correspondence had become commonplace by the middle of the nineteenth century, inspiring reams of conduct manuals, epistolary guides, and sentimental literature on both sides of the ocean. But here was a novel (and in some respects counter-intuitive) suggestion. What gave the post subversive force in the United States at this moment in history, *Blackwood's* argued, had to do less with the ostensible privacy of the sealed letter and more with the potential secrecy of the anonymous post office. Though this anxiety (or fantasy) about clandestine pigeon holes provides a partial and misleading image of the relationship that ordinary American women had to the mail, *Blackwood's* was astute in highlighting the role of the physical space of the post office in America's growing communications network. Along-side the named postal user, the other basic unit of exchange in this network was the post office, which was of course a building as well as a bureaucratic entity. By mid-century there were close to twenty thousand post offices in tiny towns and large cities, and all mail exchanges passed through these buildings.[2] Popular understanding of the post was in many respects inseparable from popular understanding of the remarkable places where letters, correspondents, and expectant users of the network all came into contact.

Post offices were, above all, paradigmatic sites of public life. This was true not only in small towns, where the post might be the only point of regular contact with the outside world and the only visible embodiment of government authority, but also in the nation's growing cities. Prior to mid-century, however, post offices were not conspicu-ous, purpose-built structures. In smaller communities, postmasters dis-charged their responsibilities in general stores or private residences. The history of the post in antebellum Brimfield, Massachusetts, for example, tracks the movement of the office from the home or business of one postmaster to that of another. In Guilford, Connecticut, around mid-century, postmaster Elisha Hutchinson made a small addition to the north side of his home to accommodate the town's mail. In rural com-munities in the antebellum South, one chronicler later recalled, neigh-borhood life was oriented around "a store where everything of a miscel-laneous character was kept, and at the same place was the post office." In what would later become the most famous post office in small-town America during the antebellum period, residents of New Salem, Illinois, collected their mail at the grocery store, where a young postmaster named Abe Lincoln (not the store's proprietor) kept receipts in an old blue sock and carried letters in his hat. An 1846 story published in Hudson, New York, began with the observation that "amusing incidents often occur by persons mistaking" local stores and businesses for the post office.[3] Even in metropolitan centers, postal spaces were distinguished less by their stately architecture than by their function and location. Post offices in cities were typically housed in converted buildings of varying types, ordinarily on principal business streets, often abutting, adjoining, or inhabiting a merchants' exchange. The office in New York, to take the most populous example, occupied a two-story wooden house in Lower Manhattan in 1825 that was known as the Academy Building. Two years later, the post office moved to the merchants' exchange, then to the rotunda near City Hall, and from there in 1845 to a Dutch Reformed Church, where it remained until after the Civil War. Baltimore's post office occupied rooms in a hotel in 1830, and as late as the mid-1850s the government was renting space for the post from the Exchange Company. During the 1830s and '40s, the city post office in Washington, D.C., resided in a Masonic hall, a former bank, and a saloon. Urban post offices moved frequently in the antebellum era; the Detroit office, for instance, switched locations half a dozen times between 1831 and 1849 and did not occupy a building specifically designed or constructed for its use until 1860.[4] But unlike their equally itinerant small-town counterparts, city post office spaces, however temporary, were centers of urban sociability, in large part because they were frequently the sole location for collecting or depositing mail in a densely populated metropolitan area. They were central post offices in an important sense, and their use, if not their architecture, reflected this fact. The Salt Lake City office, for example, housed city council meetings and served as that community's unofficial lost and found. Advertisements for missing objects, ranging from white handkerchiefs to red steers, would direct readers back to the civic space of the post. According to one observer in 1853, the post office in that city was "the most important place in the Mormon territory, not excepting the Tabernacle."[5]

Throughout the nineteenth century, the public nature of the post office rested on more than the presence of the federal government. During the first half of the century, urban post offices were privileged locations within a mercantile public sphere organized around the newspaper. Serving primarily as central depots for the arrival of the news and secondarily as a service center for the commercial users whose high postage fees subsidized newspaper transmission, the public spaces of the post bore the distinctive cultural imprint of the mercantile and partisan journals that filled the mails. For this reason, the contiguities and affinities between post offices and merchant exchanges were quite natural. The *Mobile Register* complained in 1841 about the "want of a place of general resort and *re-union* for gentlemen engaged in commercial and professional business." In the absence of a building specially designed for such people and purposes, "the post office corner, or the bar-rooms of the hotels" offered "the only places approaching to the character of a business 'Exchange.'"[6] After the great fire of 1835 destroyed the Merchants' Exchange, which had housed the post office in New York, the business community fought hard to prevent the office from remaining uptown in City Hall Park, even though the population center (though not the commercial center) had already drifted north by that point. Merchants were sufficiently anxious to preserve the proximity between downtown and the post that they donated $50,000 to enable the government to acquire the church building on Nassau Street. Before the 1840s, post office buildings had not yet acquired their status as sites of popular gathering and use. Instead, they joined merchants' exchanges, reading rooms, hotels, and coffee houses as centers of a particular kind of bourgeois society.[7]

By the middle decades of the century, the public character of the post office had begun to shift. Already in the 1830s, the link between newspapers and the post was attenuated by the arrival of cheap dailies in large cities that circumvented the mail altogether. Then the 1845 postage reform radically diminished the proportion of newspapers in the mail and helped to transform the post from a broadcast medium to an interactive communications network. This of course had a dramatic impact on the character of postal spaces. Post offices became places where ordinary people congregated in order to participate in the increasingly inclusive practice of circulating mail. This was especially true before the Civil War, when the post office did not offer free home delivery and (with limited exceptions late in the antebellum period) did not collect letters from alternate deposit locations. In mid-century New York, to take the most dramatic illustration, a single post office building (not counting a branch office that charged additional fees) served 750,000 city residents and countless more visitors, who together posted close to 62,000 letters every day. (By 1878 the New York post office would be processing 679,094 letters daily.) The sheer popularity of the postal network, as well as its implicitly inclusive claims on the attention of most Americans, made urban post offices unusually crowded and newly public arenas.[8]

As cities grew in the antebellum period, their post offices came to resemble congested and heterogeneous streets rather than gentlemanly merchant exchanges. At post offices, both strangers and acquaintances were more likely than elsewhere to encounter one another as they went about their daily business; they were places of high visibility and broad access within an increasingly diffuse urban environment. They were also noisy and bustling. In essence, the post office provided an extreme instance of the crowded thoroughfare, with all of the dangers associated with the dense concentration of bodies. Pickpockets, for example, haunt antebellum descriptions of the city, and the post office appears as a particular point of vulnerability in cautionary tales about urban life. Already in the early 1840s, the *New Orleans Picayune* published numerous such accounts, warning readers on one occasion that "several pockets were picked yesterday at the post office and other places," symptomatic of what the newspaper characterized as a vast and organized threat against the city's population.[9] Not coincidentally, perhaps, this particular warning appeared the day after the publication of a dead letter list, when higher volumes of customers might be expected to collect mail—perhaps many of them unaccustomed to life in the big post office. At a time when money was routinely transmitted by letter, a crowded post office could pose a major temptation to an urban thief. Mail robbery looms large in our image of the nineteenth century, but we often overlook the susceptibility of individual postal patrons (as well as bags, stagecoaches, and train cars) to such depredations. Bigger cities and broader participation in the postal network meant that post offices became worlds of strangers, intense microcosms of the urban settings in which they were prominently situated.

This crucial shift in the character of urban post offices in the United States coincided with the most important development in post office architecture during the nineteenth century. Before the 1850s, the federal government had constructed few buildings outside of the nation's capital (and not many more in Washington, for that matter), and the design features of local post offices had not been a matter of bureaucratic policy. Consequently, there was no such thing as a characteristic (let alone standard) post office space, architecturally speaking, in the United States during the inaugural years of cheap postage. But in the early 1850s, the new construction branch of the Treasury Department initiated a systematic redesign of the nation's custom houses, and in the process revolutionized the design and construction of urban post offices as well. Overseen by Alexander Bowman and implemented by Ammi Burnham Young, an architect who had joined the department in 1850, the new system of architectural supervision would produce forty-six new custom houses between 1853 and 1856, tripling the number of buildings under the control of the Treasury. And in a single fiscal year ending in September of 1858, twenty-one new buildings were opened.[10] Although initially identified with the Treasury Department's responsibility to administer and collect tariffs, most of the custom houses created by Young during this period were also designed to serve as post offices, and their postal function was typically foregrounded. The edifice constructed by the Treasury in Milwaukee during the 1850s, for example, was officially designated as a custom house, but the façade bore the prominent inscription POST OFFICE above the entrance.[11] From the perspective of local residents and visitors, the primary purpose and identity of the new buildings was clear enough. Within a few years, the postal system suddenly had its first set of spaces specifically designed for the collection and distribution of mail.

Perhaps more important to postal users, these new post offices were designed to resemble one another. The custom house/post office projects of the 1850s employed standard building types and were tightly controlled, down to the smallest detail, by a central bureaucracy. In several cases identical blueprints for different sites were produced from the same lithographic image. The Young post offices appearing just after mid-century in large and small cities all across the country, from Portland, Maine, to Galveston, Texas, and from Richmond to Cleveland, were all remarkably similar in appearance, which was not true for any other period of post office design in the nineteenth century. Some of the plans, such as the ones for Chicago, New Haven, Buffalo, Milwaukee, and others, are essentially indistinguishable.[12] All of these post office buildings were built in the Italianate palazzo style (see fig. 1), which marked a clear departure from the neoclassical designs that had dominated both federal architecture (such as existed) and other prominent civic structures in the first half of the century. Typically, the city's central post office occupied the main entrance floor of these two- or three-story buildings. After the Civil War, the Office of the Supervising Architect of the U.S. Treasury shifted course, abandoning the Italian style that Young had favored (Supervising Architect Alfred B. Mullett, who took over in 1866, preferred more elaborate buildings in the French Second Empire fashion) and, more significantly, rejected the policies of centralized control and standardized design that Bowman and Young had pioneered. There was no retreat, however, from the practice of designing large and conspicuous buildings for the purpose of housing a post office, and, as the century wore on, post offices disentangled themselves from the other spaces of federal activity (courthouses and custom houses) with which they typically shared a roof in the mid-century plans. Post offices built in the late 1860s and the 1870s tended to be more striking in appearance and more spacious inside. New York's new post office on Broadway at Park Row (occupied in 1875), perhaps the most famous post office from the Alfred Mullett era, was a stately and imposing structure that briefly dominated the Manhattan skyline during the 1870s (see fig. 2).[13] Despite the changes that took place after 1865, however, the legacy of the Ammi Young period was profound and enduring. During the ten years before the Civil War, a generation of similar urban post offices appeared throughout the United States at the same time as the

— FIGURE I —

U.S. CUSTOM HOUSE BUILDING, WHEELING, WEST VIRGINIA; 1860 PHOTOGRAPH.

post was becoming an inclusive and interactive network. Going to the post office, especially in America's growing and proliferating cities, was becoming a recognizable mass activity with a distinctive character.

But how did Americans relate to their evolving postal spaces? Most commonly, antebellum observers were fond of emphasizing the density and heterogeneity of life at the post. Post offices appear in sources from the 1840s as among the public spaces where miscellaneous men ("groups of idlers" in the phraseology of one short story) might congregate. Reverend William Taylor noted that the post office in Gold Rush San Francisco was "the greatest local attraction of the heterogeneous masses," and postal clerk James Rees wrote in the 1860s of the "motley crew" that gathered at the windows of the Philadelphia office.[14] Paintings of urban post offices from the 1850s and '60s also emphasize the disorderly character of these spaces. In contrast to the celebrated images of John Lewis Krimmel (1814) and Richard Caton Woodville (1848), which portray quiet scenes of absorbed citizens gathering political news from afar, artistic renderings of the post office from the third quarter of the century often focus on cities and feature crowds, bustle, and a multiplicity of social purposes and pursuits.[15] David Blythe's amusing *Post Office* (see

— FIGURE 2 —

VIEW OF MANHATTAN IN 1876, PHOTOGRAPHED BY JOSHUA BEAL DURING THE
CONSTRUCTION OF THE BROOKLYN BRIDGE. ALFRED B. MULLETT'S POST OFFICE IS
THE LARGE BUILDING ON THE LEFT.

fig. 3), which he produced during the Civil War, presents the newly
opened Pittsburgh office as a congested site of urban dangers and bawdy
pleasures. While a mixed-sex group of six or seven patrons cram com-
petitively into the small opening at the general delivery window, a young
pickpocket plies his trade in the foreground. The dominant character,
centered in the canvas but seen only from the rear, is a woman whose
large, billowing skirt is rendered with shades of rose that stand out
against the rest of the painting. Blythe's other post office painting, from
the same period, presents a calmer view of the office interior, but here too
a crowd of mutually indifferent patrons are gathered in the vicinity of a
collection window, and the floor is strewn with envelopes—the ephemeral detritus of a busy exchange. Perhaps the most carnivalesque image
of the urban post office, Thomas Prichard Rossiter's *Post-Office: In the
City*, was one of three post office scenes produced in 1857 (during a crucial
period of growth and transition in postal history) by the famous Hudson
River School artist. Even his rendering of a *Rural Post Office* emphasized
a striking degree of congestion and variegated postal activity.[16]

More popular representations of post offices reinforced many of these
same themes. The drawing of the post office lobby shown in Figure 4,
which ran across the width of a page in the popular weekly, *Frank
Leslie's Illustrated Newspaper*, in 1857, is relatively reverent, but shows the

— FIGURE 3 —
DAVID GILMOUR BLYTHE PAINTING, *POST OFFICE*, CA. 1859–63. (COURTESY OF THE
CARNEGIE MUSEUM OF ART, PITTSBURGH.)

New York post office as a place of diverse and promiscuous interaction.
Exterior views of urban post offices in pictorial magazines routinely foregrounded the crowds and activity in front of the buildings.[17] Lithographs
on letter sheets from Gold Rush San Francisco picture long lines of expectant postal users spilling out into the streets while jubilant forty-niners
read their mail in public view.[18]

In many published expressions, fascination with the way that mail
jumbled together America's disparate elements focuses on the correspondence itself. In an 1857 novel set in Philadelphia, a visit to the post office

LOBBY OF THE POST-OFFICE, FACING ON PINE STREET.

— FIGURE 4 —

VIEW OF THE NEW YORK POST OFFICE. FROM *FRANK LESLIE'S ILLUSTRATED
NEWSPAPER*, 1857. (COURTESY OF AMERICAN ANTIQUARIAN SOCIETY.)

occasions a lengthy, melancholy reflection on the diverse mass of letters
that entered the deposit box every day. Both the commercial and the personal, the narrator observes, love letters and bills, congratulations as well
as condolences, all entered the same space, "jostl[ing] each other as they
slid down the brass throat" of the post.[19] Postal agent James Holbrook described the letter bag in 1855 as a social microcosm, "an epitome of human
life," a mixed multitude of emotions and peoples, a leveler of human difference "as great as the grave," and a "confusion of tongues . . . worthy of
the last stages of the tower of Babel, or of a Woman's Rights convention."[20] But however struck Holbrook and others may have been by the
poetic capacity of personified pieces of mail to dramatize social contrasts
and juxtapositions, it was potentially far more unsettling to imagine the
congregation of all of the actual people who sent and received that mail.

Holbrook's humorous and trivializing reference to women's rights
betrayed some of the larger stakes of postal intermingling. Like feminist
conventions, mail bags and post offices threatened to collapse, if only
for a fantastic moment, divisions of gender. While many cultural commentators worried about the privacy of the letter as a source of disorder
between the sexes, others worried about the publicity of the post office.
In mid-century America, as *Blackwood's* had observed, the post office
box allowed all women to receive and send mail beyond the regulatory
reaches of friends and family; but to enjoy such privacy, women had
to enter an intensely public space. Not coincidentally, that space was
marked in many respects as a male preserve.

Visiting the post office was, in this period, a normatively masculine activity, its role in the division of sexual labor inculcated from a young age. Child-rearing advice from the 1860s listed going to the post office among the light daily duties to which boys ought to be habituated around age eight or nine, while girls were being introduced to the responsibilities of dressing smaller children or helping their mothers set the table. Anecdotal evidence suggests that trips to the post office would be assigned in many cases to young boys, male servants, and male slaves, but far less commonly to women.[21] Part of what marked the deposit and collection of mail as a male task was that it frequently necessitated a trip to the center of town or a venture down crowded thoroughfares or congested business districts. Unexpected encounters and disturbing scenes took place on the way to and from the post office. On election day in Washington, D.C., in 1857, Benjamin Brown French recorded in his diary the spectacle of "an organized body of scoundrels, calling themselves 'Plug Uglies'... [who] came on from Baltimore to *regulate* our elections." Though the display of force at the polls had apparently begun a bit earlier, French noted that the "first I knew of it was at 11, when I was on my way to the P.O."[22] Both en route and upon arrival, an errand to the post might entail contact with the more rugged and boisterous elements of town and city life. Many observers worried about the effect of this journey on young men as well. Postal reformer Pliny Miles pointed to court records to support his contention in the 1850s "that there are a large number of errand boys, clerks, and servants corrupted and convicted of crime every year through the temptation thrown before them in carrying letters to and from the Post Office," and though his concern may have been more with the temptation of carrying money, the postal errand seemed to pose a special threat of corruption, even for clerks who were generally exposed to large amounts of currency. At any rate, such perils were normatively subsumed under the expanding category of dangers facing young men in the city.[23]

Throughout the period, men dominated the life of the post office. To some extent, this may reflect the preponderance of men as users of the postal network. But it is also true that the physical presence of women in post offices introduced particular problems and triggered particular anxieties. By mid-century, postal spaces were designed to regulate and mitigate the forced heterosocial intermingling that Blythe's images of the post office accentuated. Separate windows and entrances for men and women, which *Blackwood's Magazine* saw as contributing to the dangerous secrecy of the American post office system, were intended primarily to protect women from the inconveniences and discomforts associated with entering a social space that was, in the apt phrase of Richard R. John, "aggressively masculine [in] character."[24]

Perhaps the most striking common feature of the standard post office designs of Ammi Burnham Young was their nearly universal commitment to segregating men and women as they sent and received letters. Some of Young's plans called for gender-specific windows, some created distinct waiting areas or "ladies' vestibules," and several set aside separate entrances. At the Philadelphia office, designed in 1861 and arguably Young's crowning achievement, the ladies' vestibule was divided from the general lobby by a wrought-iron screen. In addition to a ladies' delivery window, a separate counter was established for men collecting letters addressed to women, an innovation that had appeared earlier in San Francisco, in postal spaces not designed by the Treasury Department. Segregated counters, waiting areas, and entrances were institutionalized as standard features of urban post office design as early as there was even such a thing as standard post office design.[25]

In providing special spaces for female postal patrons, federal architects were making a significant and underrecognized contribution to what Mary P. Ryan has characterized as a "major civic project during the latter half of the nineteenth century": the clear and deliberate demarcation of public spaces for women in U.S. cities. There were precedents, to be sure, for the kind of spatial compartmentalization featured in mid-century post offices. Distinct parlors for women had appeared on steamboats as early as the 1820s, and twenty years later women would occupy special sections of railroad cars or, in some cases, cars reserved exclusively for their use. By that time, special parlors and dining areas for women or for families were common in major urban hotels as well. But none of these spaces was created by the government, and none constituted the same sort of fixed, public space as the mid-century urban post office. In some ways the closest analogues to the ladies' areas and facilities at the post may have been separate reading rooms for women in libraries. Before the 1850s, however, urban libraries were typically private, elite institutions, and the provision of women's rooms and counters in public libraries was not common until well after the Civil War.[26] For men and women using the new post office buildings, the more obvious comparison might have been to the federal courtrooms, which frequently occupied the floor immediately (or in some cases two stories) above the post. In Philadelphia, Detroit, Cleveland, Dubuque, Richmond, and several other cities, plans for separate entrances and waiting areas for women using the mail contrasted with plans for gallery seating in the courtrooms without reference to gender. At the post office, urban Americans encountered an early attempt on the part of designers to come to terms with shifting attitudes toward the presence of women in public space and evolving dilemmas about the dangers and pleasures of city life.

Segregated counters and lobbies had the (presumably deliberate) effect of marginalizing women's participation in this arena of postal life and reaffirming the masculinity of the larger space. Separate entrances promised the further benefit of concealing the presence of women in the post altogether. An 1869 article about the Dead Letter Office in Washington, D.C., where numerous women were employed, pointed out that "strangers visiting Washington, and admiring the style and architecture of the General Post Office building, would never know that there are numbers of ladies seated behind the plate-glass of the second-story windows. Indeed, few people residing in the Capital are really aware in what part of the building these women are stowed away."[27]

At the same time, architectural attempts to keep the movements of women out of general view inevitably called attention, at the very least, to the threats of heterosocial contact they sought to minimize. And as much as spatial segregation marginalized the female postal user, ladies' windows became sites of popular interest in the post office.[28] Moreover, it is by no means clear that separate facilities always served to keep the sexes apart. Descriptions of the San Francisco post office cast some doubt on whether segregation at the counters restricted the access that men and women had to one another. At the ladies' window, one witness bragged, men waiting to collect letters for "their wife, or sister, or perhaps sweetheart, or other lady friend," gallantly offer their places to the women behind them. Another account, appearing originally in the daily newspaper in 1855, confirmed this chivalrous practice, expressing satisfaction that the addition of a second clerk to handle "the call of gentlemen for ladies' letters" was now expediting the distribution of mail. Before the change, at least, the ladies' window was clearly not a space of strict segregation, and it presumably facilitated various interactions, chivalrous and otherwise.[29]

Still, the message emanating from all of these attempts at spatial regulation may have confirmed public perceptions that the post office would be used primarily by men. How accessible and congenial these spaces were to various classes and groups of American women is open to question, but it is clear that for many women, both urban and rural, a postal system that required regular trips to a central post office may have reinforced dependence upon husbands, fathers, and male associates, instead of undermining such dependence. As increasing numbers of women relied upon men to pick up and deliver their letters, participation in the postal system occasioned complex domestic negotiations. Fanny Fern, the best-selling novelist, was fond of calling attention to these conjugal conflicts in her popular newspaper sketches. An 1856 tirade against negligent husbands excoriates the man "who carries a letter, intended for his wife, in his pocket for six weeks." Three years later, Fern's advice to engaged women includes the following prenuptial test: "Give him a letter to drop in the post-office, and find out if it ever leaves that grave—his pocket."[30]

"Annie Heaton," a short story published in the *Ladies Repository* in 1851, the year of the second major postal reform, dramatizes the dependence produced by the post office system quite elaborately. The young title character, who lives under the reign of a joyless, workaholic patriarch, falls in love with her father's apprentice. After he leaves her father's employ, Annie hopes desperately for a letter, but must summon up all her courage to ask her father to inquire at the post office on her behalf. When he repeatedly ignores her requests, she and her sister engage in elaborate ruses to induce him to go, eventually emptying the family larder of various household staples to force him into town. Upon his return, the sisters sit in impatient silence while the father indicates nothing about a letter. When one of them asks whether he visited the post office, he replies that he did but says nothing further. They continue to wait, watching with disappointment as he fumbles in the pockets of his coat and removes only the groceries he has purchased. Only at the end of the evening does Annie's sister finally break into the patriarchal coat and, sure enough, find the desired letter.[31] The postal system may, in theory, have allowed women the privilege of their own private box, but for many the mail box was inside the coat pockets of men.

Women's letters were thus contested objects to which men often staked an initial claim. Men would request letters addressed to women, even those to whom they were not related, as the earlier reports of the San Francisco post attest. The creation of a special window for men collecting women's letters acknowledged and encouraged such practices, glossing over any potential conflicts that might arise. One female postal clerk who worked at the ladies' window in New York complained that "men would come to the window and insist on her getting the letters of their lady friends for them." The Chicago post office in 1835 issued a directive requiring that "any person calling for letters for their friends, to prevent mistake, will please bring written orders for them," but such strictures do not appear to have been commonly enforced in mid-century America.[32]

In many instances, especially if she was married, a woman's correspondence was expected to pass through an intermediary who would save her a trip to the post. A poetic address on an 1856 letter from one Indiana woman to another, for example, presumed that the recipient's husband would pick it up.

> To Columbus go,
> In Bartholomew Co.
> To Mary J. Bass,
> I have come at last;
> And without any doubt;
> You may please take me out.
> —Care T. Bass State Indiana

In a more unusual case brought to the attention of the postmaster general in 1859, a man asserted his right to all letters addressed to his estranged wife. The Post Office denied his claim, charging that it violated the proprietary rights of the sender, but the husband's presumption emerged within a postal culture in which husbands frequently handled and monitored their wives' personal correspondence.[33]

In both popular fiction and in the diaries and letters of real women, the post office appears frequently as a place to which women (especially those confined to the home) had only partial and impeded access. In *The Hidden Hand*, the highly successful 1859 novel by E. D. E. N. Southworth, Clara Day desires to communicate with her betrothed and his mother but is discouraged by the realization that "it was perfectly useless to write and send the letter to the post-office by any servant at the Hidden House," since the letter would be diverted into the hands of her enemy. Similar dilemmas confront the heroines of Harriet Wilson's *Our Nig* and Maria Cummins's *The Lamplighter*.[34] The wartime letters of Elizabeth Blair Lee express frequent frustration at her dependence upon men to deliver letters from her husband. Writing in 1861, she complains that seven letters that had been waiting for her in the Atlantic City Post Office were belatedly forwarded to her in Philadelphia. "Mr. Dick went to the Post Office & I daily reminded to enquire for me—& he did for Mr. Phillips Lee—but not for Mrs. S. P. or E. B. Lee." Mary Boykin Chesnut complained in 1863 that her "letters always come from the P.O. *open*." For Emily Hawley, a twenty-two-year-old woman living with her family in rural Iowa, indirect access to the post meant that her parents could monitor her correspondence. After her younger brother brought a "good letter" to her from a young man, Hawley's mother took the opportunity to share her disapproval of "letters from strangers."[35]

Faced with such constraints, many women did of course venture to the post office, where they encountered numerous obstacles and nuisances. Mary Jane Megquier, living in San Francisco without her physician husband in 1856, described to her daughter back in Maine an incident that sheds some light, despite the particularity of her circumstances, on dilemmas that many women faced when seeking to receive mail. Mail steamers from the East Coast arrived only twice a month, so on this particular steamer day, Megquier was eager to inquire for letters as soon as the mails would open at 10:00 p.m., about six hours after the ship docked. She announced to those assembled at her house that she intended to go down to the post office that night, but no one responded to what she had intended as a cue for an offer to accompany her or to run the errand on her behalf. When the hour for the opening of the post office arrived, Megquier was playing euchre with several men. Dropping her cards and gathering her hat and shawl, she "asked if any of the gentlemen were going into town," but they just "looked at each other," so Megquier "turned on [her] heel and was off." In recounting her journey to the post office, she complained of having to travel "such an outlandish street that is not lighted for three quarters of a mile alone, in such a place as this." Once inside, the line at the ladies' counter was sufficiently shorter than the numerous lines of men (divided in San Francisco by section of the alphabet) to allow her to pass quickly in front of "a crowd of hundreds, a privilege a lady has," and return home with her letters in hand, the whole trip having consumed only twenty-five minutes. Still, she was "cross as a bear." Resentful at having to traverse the city in darkness, appreciative of not having to stand in line, and unwilling (even in retrospect, when charged with having left in excessive haste) to wait for her mail, Mary Jane Megquier understood well some of the difficult choices women encountered under the post office system.[36]

What Megquier did not register was an awareness of how her presence in public space appeared to onlookers. Despite attempts to regulate or conceal the intermingling of men and women, post offices remained dangerous and transgressive places in the eyes of many contemporaries at a time when women, especially those in the middle class, were enjoined to avoid public self-presentation. The inevitable interactions among strangers, especially in urban areas, reinforced the aura of anonymity and promiscuity that *Blackwood's* identified as fundamental to the post office system. Women who entered these public spaces came under suspicion of being public women. Virginia Penny's 1863 survey of women's employment opportunities counted as one of the hazards of working in the post office the troubling phenomenon that "the class of women who go to the general post office constantly for letters, are of a kind a respectable woman would not like to come in contact with. The majority receive letters under fictitious names."[37] Penny alluded in part to the well-known fact that prostitutes used post office boxes in order to contact clients, a practice made known to those who had never even been to an urban post office by the late 1840s when the *National Police Gazette* published the correspondence of Helen Jewett, the famous New York prostitute who had been murdered in 1836. Jewett's correspondence, as Patricia Cline Cohen has underscored, highlights the role of drop letters—letters that entered and exited the same post office—in a certain branch of the sex trade.[38]

Post offices figured as well in the sex lives of amateurs. "The stations are the favorites of intriguers of both sexes," observed Junius Browne in his sensational 1869 guide to New York, "and are frequently made rendezvous for interdicted communication and illicit pleasures." Post offices were places where adulterous couples could simply run into each other by concealed prearrangement, or where strangers might initiate and develop relationships. Even if a couple did not meet in the post office, drop letters facilitated the conduct of secret affairs. In the waning days of his relationship with his mistress, Madaline Edwards, in 1847, for example, New Orleans insurance agent Charles Bradbury wrote her a letter in an attempt to arrange a date. After crossing out a suggestion (still legible) that he would "call to morrow night between 7 & 8 o'clock and if the gate is open I will enter and if it is locked I will pass," Bradbury instead offered to visit her at home "any night which you choose to designate, by a note to me through the Post Office."[39] The emerging urban practice of soliciting strangers through personal ads in the daily newspapers typically involved postal addresses as well. "Will the lady in Brooklyn who addressed a note to a gentleman in New York please write again," the classified section of one New York daily advertised, "as her letter was not received until Saturday?" Some notices referred to boxes, others simply invoked standard practices of inquiry, but either way the daily spectacle of miscellaneous individuals connecting, reconnecting, misconnecting, and communicating obliquely reinforced the association between the public space of the post office and the most promiscuous features of modern urban life.[40]

Beyond the popular associations between the post office system and sexual promiscuity, what was transgressive or unsettling about the appearance of women at the urban post office was that central post office buildings were not simply places where people quietly deposited and collected mail. They were special places to see and be seen—sites of self—presentation and confrontation. For most users who did not rent private boxes, a trip to the post office typically entailed a public encounter with a postal clerk that did not always go as planned. For one thing, inquiries for mail were frequently unsuccessful—a New York postal clerk was quoted in 1863 as estimating that "nine out of ten of all callers at the 'general delivery' window fail to receive a letter."[41] But even when letters lay waiting, the process of collection was not always simple or straightforward. Americans with distinctive accents or limited facility in English struggled hard to make themselves understood. Martin Weitz, a German immigrant living in Rockville, Connecticut, in 1856, explained to his family the problems that he experienced at his small-town post office. After three unsuccessful visits to the post, Weitz finally received a letter from home after he saw it listed in the local "*Nusbeber*" (in Weitz's transliteration) as uncollected mail. "I had been there a few times before and asked if there was a letter, he always said no, this is how you ask in English (*Gat ju Lether vor mi dies Män telt mi Nasser*)." Weitz's annoyance at having his letter delayed several weeks may suggest the larger frustrations of non-English speakers at the post office, to the extent that his formulaic inquiry for mail ("got you letter for me, this man tells me nothing") incorporates as a standard expectation some prior failure to communicate with the clerk.[42]

Some patrons blamed the incompetence (or malice) of post office employees for such breakdowns and lapses in the mail system. "Post-office clerks are models of unconcern if not rudeness, all the country over," observed Junius Browne, who found postal workers as a group more difficult than any other class of employee encountered in everyday life. "I have often believed they were born only to have their noses pulled; and it is a great pity they so often miss their destiny. It is wonderful how such dull fellows can be so ingeniously offensive. All the capacity they have is directed to disobligation."[43] Other accounts and anecdotes of postal life emphasize the outrageous demands and unreasonable behavior of postal patrons. Kate Harrington's humorous (and presumably imaginative) description of "A Half-Hour in the Post-Office," which appeared in a Cincinnati literary magazine in 1854, lampoons the diverse collection of needy and unsophisticated customers (most of them, interestingly, female) who approach the postal counter with blundering pronunciations, thick accents, laughable requests for discounts on stamps, or humble entreaties for an amanuensis.[44] Whether seen from the perspective of long-suffering clerks or inconvenienced and mistreated patrons, though, the post office was the site of fraught and potentially adversarial inter-actions.

Especially in larger communities, these ordinary encounters took place in large public gatherings. Naive or inexperienced users might face the derision of more than just an ornery clerk. A "tall Missourian" walked into the San Francisco office in 1853 and inquired among the long line of people waiting for the general delivery to open whether this was "*whar they got letters?*" Striding past the line and rapping on a closed window at the counter, "he poked his head in as far as possible, and inquired if there was a letter '*thar for Eph. Shinner?*'" The bemused clerk answered that there was and then slammed the window shut. "[B]efore Eph. could recover from his astonishment," the newspaper account of this event noted with some satisfaction, "he was rapidly hurried to the door, amid the jests and hoots of the crowd." On the other hand, a successful visit to the post could provide an occasion for a proud public display. Having mailed a letter of his own composition, Horatio Alger's Ragged Dick enjoys the (characteristic) fortune of being seen emerging from the post office by a former colleague in the bootblack trade who did not know that Dick could write.[45]

In multiple ways, the post office was a force for public exposure, trans-forming the ostensibly intimate epistolary contact into a broadly visible event. "Did you ever watch the faces of those whose eyes devour letters just received?" asked Junius Browne. "If you be a skilled physiognomist, you can learn the contents by the reflections above them." The privacy of the sealed letter evaporated under the gaze of the savvy frequenter of the post office. "Glance at the ladies' window," a sensational guide to the Philadelphia post office exhorted readers, so that they might "see that tall female upon whose face you can trace the dark lines of sorrow. . . . " "Watch the politician," the tour of the postal lobby continued, "by his looks you can read the secret of his heart."[46] William Taylor the minis-ter took special care to "mark the countenances and conduct of men as they turned away from the delivery windows" in San Francisco, sharing with his readers such images as that of a forty-niner breaking open a letter, "trembling till black with agonized emotion."[47] Descriptions of public displays of intense emotion recur with such frequency, especially in portraits of the San Francisco Post Office during the Gold Rush, as to form something of a postal trope in antebellum American culture. In one typical example appearing in *Harper's Monthly* in 1857, a postal clerk narrates the story of Mary Martin, a middle-aged woman with an "honest look" whose daily disappointment at not receiving a letter was so clearly imprinted on her face that the clerk took special notice of her and found her missive, misplaced in a pile of dead letters.

> I gave it to her, and she tore it open, read a few lines, screamed, and fell to the floor. I stepped out and aided her to rise, and soon learned the brief, sad story. Her only son had gone West to get work; a letter from him a few weeks ago had told her that he had found a place, and should send her money soon. This letter was in another hand, and to say that her son had sickened and died—in his last hours talking of his mother, and wishing that he might die on her breast. . . . Such scenes as these in the Post-office, in the midst of the business of every-day life and a heartless world, strike on the soul as if there is indeed another world than this of business, and there is but a step out of one into the other; indeed, they often come into contact, as when a mother weeps for a dead son on the floor where cent. per cent. and the price of flour are more thought of than death or love.[48]

The juxtaposition of the mundane and the tragic, filthy lucre and maternal love, on the literal floor of the post office parallels and encodes, of course, the uncomfortable contiguity of men and women.

Popular perceptions and widespread discussions of the urban post office as a site of publicity, promiscuity, and exposure formed part of the crucial cultural context for a remarkable set of changes that took place in America's post office system during the Civil War period. Highlighted by the introduction in 1863 of free home delivery in America's largest cities, these changes amounted to nothing less than a radical reorientation of the place of the urban post office within the growing mail network and a gradual but fundamental transformation of the relationship between postal space and public space.

Already at mid-century, critics of the postal system began to wonder why Americans needed to go to a central post office to send or receive mail. In 1849 Representative John G. Palfrey of Massachusetts questioned the efficiency of such a system, calling his colleagues' attention to the spectacle of so much wasted "time daily spent . . . in going backwards and forwards on errands to the Post Office."[49] For Palfrey and like-minded observers, the call for a broader distribution of mail services was part of the larger project of reforming the post by standardizing its operations, lowering users' costs, and increasing its use. In this particular cause, as in all the other postal reform initiatives of mid-century, the most tireless and visible advocate was Pliny Miles, America's counterpart to the famous British postal reformer Rowland Hill. Throughout the mid-1850s, Miles argued against what he regarded as an antiquated post office system that poorly served the needs of urban users and stunted the growth of the mail network. "Except by the labor of private parties," Miles pointed out in 1857, "we have hardly an improvement or facility for distributing letters in cities to-day that did not exist seventy years ago." In big cities, he maintained, the "legitimate wants of people" require multiple mail deliveries every day and stations for buying stamps or posting letters located "at every one or two hundred yards." Finally, letters ought to arrive at the homes of their intended recipients.[50]

In many respects, Miles's position extended the themes and arguments of the campaign for cheap, uniform postage that he had championed during the previous decade. As he did in the earlier cause, Miles encouraged his countrymen to look to the British example, where intracity mail was delivered frequently, and users did not have to pay extra to avoid traveling to a central post office. The most striking disparity between American and British use of the mails, Miles noted, lay in the volume of local letters posted in cities. Postal participation was disproportionately urban, but in American cities a relatively small portion of the urban mail was local. As late as 1850, the number of letters posted within London amounted to more than half the total correspondence of the entire United States. Even after the explosive increase in mail use in America in the early 1850s, London's annual output of local letters for 1856 was forty times greater than that of New York, and the difference accounted almost single-handedly for the statistic that the British sent more letters per capita than their American cousins.[51] Just as Americans had followed the British lead in establishing low, uniform rates of postage, reformers argued, adopting such British innovations as outdoor mailboxes and home delivery would improve the post and stimulate greater correspondence.

Numerous continuities linked the new push for postal reform with its predecessor. Both positions relied on the economic rationale that the high fixed costs of postal delivery warranted efforts to increase the volume of mail delivered, and both positions assumed that high or complex postage costs were the principal obstacle to greater participation. As with postage reform, the campaign for home delivery affirmed the benefits of both rate uniformity (patrons should not have to pay additional fees for delivery services or for the private boxes that expedited receipt of one's mail) and government monopoly (the post office should not cede business to private carriers or service providers).[52] Finally, this next phase of postal reform proved most popular in the Northeast and was clearly identified with urban, commercial interests.

At the same time, Miles's attack on the central post office system introduced a conceptual innovation in postal reform. In arguing for more frequent delivery within cities, Miles sought to break the familiar identity between a city as a community of postal users and its central post office as a single, irreducible unit of postal exchange. Only user demand and letter volume should determine delivery schedules, he maintained. If mail traveled three times a day between New York and Boston and once a day between New Orleans and Charleston, then within large cities the rate of frequency should be six to twelve times every day. The post should connect users, in Miles's view, not incorporated localities.[53]

The significance of this paradigm shift was not trivial. Whereas the United States postal system had been initially designed to facilitate long-distance news transmission among a dispersed populace—in part to encourage popular involvement with politics while avoiding urbanization—by mid-century reformers were arguing for a postal system in which distance was irrelevant and a dispersed citizenry was not essential for the survival of a republic. Home delivery appealed to Miles for the same reasons he favored frequent intracity mail runs. Post offices should serve as final delivery points only in rural societies; a truly modern post ought to be adaptable to metropolitan conditions. Labeling the British system *free* home delivery was misleading, he insisted, since it was entirely consistent with the principle of uniform postage to deliver letters without additional charges. A single rate should be assessed for transporting mail from its origin to its terminus, and in "cities and towns [this] means to the door of the person addressed."[54] Post offices appear in this model as processing stations rather than as integral sites in a network.

Over a period of several years, the implementation of this alternative vision of the urban post office unfolded somewhat unevenly. During the late 1850s, letter boxes began appearing in city streets in New York, Philadelphia, and Boston, supplementing the smattering of tin containers that were placed in bars, hotels, and public buildings. In 1858, Albert Potts received a patent for a mailbox built into a lamppost (see fig. 5), and within the year more than three hundred boxes were attached to lampposts throughout the city of Philadelphia, a development lauded by *Scientific American* for "bringing the Post-office to everyone's door." Not everyone shared the magazine's enthusiasm for the new boxes. "There is great complaint" about mail security, asserted the *New York Times* in 1860, after that city began adopting the Philadelphia lamppost box. "The lid can be raised, and with pincers letters can be caught and withdrawn," the paper observed, adding that several individuals had been apprehended for just such a crime.[55] Boxes were not immediately and

POTTS' IMPROVED STREET LETTER-BOX.

— FIGURE 5 —

ALBERT POTTS LITHOGRAPH OF THE LAMP-POST MAIL BOX.
SCIENTIFIC AMERICAN, CA. 1859.

universally adopted, and no American city would boast a network of
official mail receptacles in the 1860s comparable to London's pillar-box
system, which had been in place for years and was probably familiar to
many American readers.[56] Still, a new system was spreading: 574 lamppost boxes were in place in New York (all below 55th Street) as of 1860,
and their contents were emptied and delivered (for a fee of one cent)
to the post office or to one of six substations recently established, all
within three miles of the central post office. Back in the city of their
birth, the boxes were growing in popularity. During a particular quarter
in 1864, Philadelphians posted close to three-quarters of a million letters in lampposts. By the 1870s, a guide to life in San Francisco would

declare that "the system of iron postal boxes, placed at convenient intervals throughout the city, is greatly appreciated by the citizens, and is
conducted efficiently."[57]

Outdoor mailboxes on the European model were part of the disman-
tling of the other box system that foreign observers identified with the
American post office: the grids of pigeon holes and locked boxes inside
the post office building, which individual patrons rented for their private
use. Such boxes were most popular in large cities, but even there only a
small percentage of patrons rented them. In the late 1850s approximately
4,200 private boxes were rented at the New York Post Office at a rate
of six dollars per year. An average of three persons were served by every
rented box, which could be shared (and were often leased by private companies who would then deliver the contents to their clients), but in a city
of more than 750,000 inhabitants, this amounted to small though active
minority of those who used the post office. The box system came under
attack during the 1850s for high rents, excessive restrictions, or preferential treatment, but postmasters had come to rely upon the income
they generated and defended private boxes as integral to the post office
system. "[T]he box system . . . has been so long in use that it could not
be discontinued without great discontent," New York postmaster John
Dix insisted somewhat defensively in 1860, "even if its discontinuance
were desirable."[58]

Throughout the antebellum period, the Post Office had also spon-
sored letter-carrier service in large cities, charging two cents in additional
postage (later reduced to one cent) for patrons who wanted their letters
delivered to them.[59] Coexisting uneasily with the box system, the carrier
system never achieved its goal of putting private companies out of the
business of delivering mail within cities (in the 1850s, two private firms
operating in New York delivered nine times as many letters as the city
carriers) and, more importantly, failed to satisfy the complaints of those
who bemoaned popular dependence on the central post office building.
The vast majority of letters sent and received in America's largest city
were still being deposited and collected at the post office at the time of
the Civil War, and a leading congressional critic maintained that the
current state of delivery service "furnishes little accommodation to the
public."[60] Not until 1863 did postal reformers achieve significant progress
in their battle against the post office system. In 1863, the Post Office
extended Cleveland's model of home delivery for all patrons, free of
charge, in close to fifty large American cities, reducing congestion in
the busiest post offices and striking a decisive blow against many of the

private delivery firms that had served businesses and well-to-do patrons for decades.

Congressional sponsors of the new legislative initiative justified the move with many of the same financial and administrative rationales that Pliny Miles had advanced several years earlier, and by 1863 the wartime composition of Congress had muffled the resistance of those who were indifferent to the needs of urbanites and suspicious of the growth of a government bureaucracy. In this sense, free home delivery was in line with other important extensions and standardizations of the role of the federal government that took place during the Civil War, when Democrats from the South were conveniently not serving in Congress. By a vote of 73 to 35 in the House of Representatives, urban Americans were to begin receiving their mail at their homes and offices.[61]

Outdoor mailboxes and free delivery expedited the transmission of mail within cities, though not enough for many critics. Outraged complaints about the relative irregularity of intracity mail persisted through the 1860s. "The City mails are particularly deranged," Junius Browne charged. "You can send a letter to Boston, or Albany, or Chicago, with a tolerable certainty of its reaching its destination some time. But if you mail a missive from your office in Pine or William street to your friend in Grammercy park, or Lexington avenue, or direct a note to your cousin round the corner, the chances of its ever being heard from are slight." The Reverend L. W. Bacon lodged similar charges in 1868, and even conducted an experiment to demonstrate the inefficiency of postal service within New York. The letters Bacon posted from various post offices and mailboxes in Manhattan and Brooklyn to a downtown address fared better than Browne's remark suggested (all arrived at their destinations), but several took more than twenty-four hours, an intolerable lag by the author's standards—and by those of the London post, to which the American system was invariably and invidiously compared.[62] But if the innovations did not instantly meet the demands of commerce, they certainly reoriented urban mail use away from the central post office and from all that the post office represented and evoked.

From its inception, the appeal of home delivery transcended issues of federal power, administrative uniformity, and postal finance. Supporters of the new reform understood that they were addressing problems of gender relations in urban life as well. In his presentation before the House, Representative John Hutchins of Ohio quoted John Palfrey's earlier speech in support of delivery, which had cited the needs of "the female of humble condition, [who] is compelled to go to a public place for the letter she is expecting, and await her turn to inquire for it, amidst the annoyance of a crowd."[63] Such concerns resonated beyond the halls of Congress. For more than a decade, numerous observers had linked the problems of the antebellum post office system to issues of gender. Discussions of post office site selection, for example, frequently reminded readers of the presence of women in public space. A Buffalo site commission argued in 1854 for choosing a location protected from lake winds, out of special concern for "females & children as all must visit the Post office frequently." A magazine review of the proposed Boston post office in 1858 singled out the convenience of its location for "the ladies, whose accommodation ought to be provided for in establishing a post office." Business interests might argue for a site closer to the current location in the Merchants' Exchange, the article conceded, but women "pay a large part of the postal revenue, and have a right to be considered."[64]

From an alternative perspective, of course, female patrons would be better served by not having to visit the central post office at all. When lamppost mailboxes were introduced, admirers pointed to their particular utility for "the gentler sex," and a lithograph promoting the new invention features a well-dressed woman depositing mail (see fig. 5). By 1868, when the site for the new Alfred Mullett post office in New York was being debated, *Putnam's Magazine* pointed out that questions of accessibility were no longer as important. "[S]o long as the Post-Office *is not inaccessible,*" *Putnam's* observed, "it cannot long matter whether it is especially *convenient of access* or not." The magazine approved of what it accurately saw as an attempt by the postal authorities "to bring about, what ought long ago to have been established, such a system of collection and delivery of mail-matter as will make it unnecessary for any body to go to the Post-Office in New York for his letters and newspapers, as it is, to-day, in London or Paris. In fact, he means to break up the system of box-delivery altogether—has already begun to break it up."[65] What was breaking up, or what was being dismantled, was not only a distinctive inconvenience of American postal communication, but also one of the most intensely promiscuous public spaces in nineteenth-century America.

Home delivery helped to allay particular concerns about the kind of public space that men and women entered when they used the mail. Standard recent explanations of the 1863 reform emphasize the centrality of gender troubles at the post office. James Bruns, founding director of the National Postal Museum, argues that private delivery was a "humane reaction" to the "emotional trauma" suffered by women who received news of the death of loved ones during the Civil War. Rather than subject female patrons and male postal clerks to this discomfiting scene, Bruns implies, the department turned to home delivery.[66] Though such an interpretation might seem to reconfigure and displace the problem that many male observers had with the promiscuous space of the post office, the importance attributed to intimate war correspondence, to the display of emotions, and to the exposure of women to male scrutiny reflects larger preoccupations in American postal culture during the 1850s and 60s.

To be sure, by switching the site of mail collection from the crowded post office building to the private residence, home delivery raised other concerns about heteroerotic relations that have become familiar subjects of popular humor over the past century. An early expression of anxiety about the entrance of mailmen into domestic spaces appeared on the minstrel stage in a blackface farce published in the mid-1870s but performed earlier. Charles White's *The United States Mail* features Post Office Sam, a black letter carrier wearing a dandyish outfit including "Jockey cap, Yankee trousers, and fancy coat." The plot revolves around a young white woman named Lucy who is anticipating mail from her beau announcing an intended visit. Lucy is concerned that his letter might have been delayed, "as there is no regularity with the carriers now they are all such a stupid set of black apes," and when Post Office Sam arrives with his mailbag, he confirms her worst suspicions, as he turns out to be an illiterate carrier prone to opening letters and stealing their contents. The beau's letter appears from the mailbag, but when the woman reads the note aloud it is loaded with racist mockery of black speech and Sam vows revenge. First he tries to overcharge her for postage due, but is interrupted by the arrival of the letter's author in the flesh. Panicking, she hides Sam in his own mailbag to avoid discovery. When the beau, who trades suspicious accusations with Lucy about having spotted her with another man about town, turns on some music, Sam begins involuntarily to dance inside the bag. He is discovered, a group dance ensues, and in the mix Sam manages to exact some physical revenge on the pompous beau. While feeding northern white audiences the minstrel stage's familiar menu of racist stereotypes, physical comedy, and bawdy burlesque of social norms and pretensions, *The United States Mail* also served up a cautionary reminder that the delivery system could undermine the intimacy and confidentiality of an epistolary overture by inadvertently sending a sexual rival into the home of the addressee.[67]

Concerns about contact between carriers and patrons do not appear to have tempered the enthusiasm of postal reformers for the changes that were taking place in the urban post office system. Within a year of the 1863 legislation, free home delivery had spread to a total of sixty-six different American cities, and over the next quarter century the total would approach five hundred. By the end of the nineteenth century, free delivery would extend to rural postal users as well, thus completing the slow but steady transformation of the post into a communications network in which the home served as a constitutive address and a primary site of exchange for a majority of users.[68] In the middle decades of the nineteenth century, however, the growing, bustling post office building was a far more comprehensive metonym for the U.S. mail. It also stood as a monument to a modern, centrifugal, and potentially disorderly world.

By the time of its penetration into the daily experience of most men and women living in the United States, the postal network presented two strikingly different images of human connection. On the one hand, mail communication brought together friends, family, and acquaintances who were physically separated. On the other hand, the system also brought people (often strangers) into physical proximity. These contrasting models of postal contact suggested some of the conflicting implications of the mail for social relations, implications that would be worked out in the new postal culture.

Postal Intimacy

∽FOUR∾

EMBRACING
OPPORTUNITIES
THE CONSTRUCTION OF THE
PERSONAL LETTER

Shortly before the 1845 postage reduction took effect, Frederick Clapp of Worcester wrote to his brother in another Massachusetts town; this is the earliest of Frederick's surviving letters to bear a postmark. Whereas their previous correspondence appears to have been occasioned by news of illness, Frederick underscores the decidedly quotidian status of this particular missive: "Dear Brother, / Having an opportunity to write you and hapning to think of the promise we made each other before you left, I have concluded to take my pen in hand and see if I could not manufacture one of those little things which the man at the Post Office sometimes hands out to the man of letters."[1]

Thrusting himself wryly into a world of elite status ("the man of letters"), Clapp also imagines participating in the familiar ritual of post office life. Such gestures registered some of the challenges and ambiguities associated with entering the postal network after 1845. The post had been many things in the memory of mid-century Americans—a news source, a medium for business communication, a resource for making special (typically tragic) announcements—but it had not been a broadly interactive network, and its rites and rhythms had no fixed place in everyday experience. As a newly accessible and increasingly indispensable communication network took root in the 1840s and '50s, American correspondents sought to articulate new models for postal relationships. A great deal of cultural work went into the production of the codes and ideals of intimacy that shaped epistolary communication. What emerged most generally during this period was a set of practices, discourses, and beliefs—a postal culture—that redefined the very status of mail. More specifically, Americans began producing and circulating in massive numbers something that had never before been an instrument of everyday sociability among ordinary people: the personal letter.

To write, receive, post, or expect a letter in the newly inclusive U.S. mail network was to engage a system that had been, for some time, deeply linked to the transmission of news and the spread of the market. New users of the post both adopted and adapted these associations in an effort to make sense of what it might mean to conduct interpersonal relationships through the mail. In an 1854 transcontinental letter, for example, Benjamin Wingate directed his son to think in new ways about the value and purpose of writing letters:

> It is a very good plan for you to correspond with your relatives in Wis[consin]. It will do you, and them, good, in several ways. Do not neglect it. Do not fall into the notion, that you cannot write, unless you have some *news* to tell. Items of news may be gathered from the newspapers; but a friendly correspondence has, or should have, another purpose—to express sympathy and good feeling, and to keep up an acquaintance with and a pleasant remembrance of, each other. Write as you would talk to them.[2]

The distinction between news and "friendly correspondence" was not, of course, an innovation, and the epistolary ideal of writing "as you would talk" enjoyed an established pedigree. At least since the sixteenth century, English-language guides to letter-writing had defined the craft as "Oration written," a trope that had become a well-worn cliché by the time of Wingate's letter.[3] What was new to this period was the notion that a young person of middling income and status no longer needed to model his correspondence on news or justify his use of the post by the announcement of an extraordinary occurrence or the sharing of some recent intelligence. The post could be used to cultivate and sustain "an acquaintance" over long distances. In an 1859 letter to his son in Alabama, Iowa minister and land speculator J. H. Williams opened by acknowledging that he was "sitting down to write to you from habit rather than from any thing important, I have to communicate."[4] For family and friends living at a distance, it was precisely this "habit" that characterized the new postal connection.

While mid-century correspondents negotiated the relationship between letters and news, they also wrestled with a closer model for interpersonal postal exchange—the business letter. Despite a long tradition associating letters with polite society, despite a continual emphasis in etiquette books on letter-writing as an act of personal self-presentation, and despite the construction of letters as windows into the soul in popular epistolary novels, Americans at mid-century understood that the prototypical letter-writer was a businessman. Postal reforms gave ordinary Americans access to a mode of communication that had previously been the province of bankers, merchants, and clerks. In the same 1845 letter in which Frederick Clapp imagined himself as a "man of letters," his wife Sarah mobilized a more current metaphor. "I have been thinking about writing to you, for some little time," she explained, so she and Frederick "entered into partnership, to write you a letter." Sarah had little news to report, she added, as "F. has had a little more than his share." To understand the attitudes that new users had to their postal relationships, one must begin by taking such business metaphors seriously. "The day has gone by when the post-office was thought to be only for the merchant," a Massachusetts magazine announced in 1850, but that day was not so distant, and its imprint remained palpable.[5] Mid-century correspondents were entering a terrain stamped by the culture of the market.

The link between letters and commerce transcended the fact that business correspondence, as contemporary observers acknowledged, accounted for most of the letter volume of the mail even after the postal reductions. Letter-writing was in many ways the paradigmatic activity of the business world. While cargo might ride on railroad cars or steamboats, and while crucial messages might pass along expensive telegraph wires, much of the conduct of long-distance trade took place via the post, and much of the labor associated with the mercantile economy consisted of writing, copying, and filing letters. The antebellum workplace, with its compartmentalized desks and grids of pigeonholes, was organized around postal correspondence.[6] Decades before achieving infamy as a financier, a young Jay Cooke spent his days in the 1840s as a clerk composing such correspondence, "some days fifteen or twenty letters to all parts of the United States."[7] Clerks like Cooke were part of a new breed of white-collar employee, for whom entry-level, salaried positions—dissociated from artisanal traditions or productive skills—served as badges of middle-class status and promised upward mobility. Their jobs were increasingly defined in the public eye as mental rather than manual labor, but the responsibilities of a clerk were in a literal sense intensely manual. Clerks and businessmen handwrote letters for a living.[8]

What this meant is that the skills associated with correspondence were also the qualifications for entering middle-class professional life. Guides to success in business emphasized the importance of composition, orthography, and penmanship, not only because those features of correspondence (especially penmanship) would be taken as reliable signs of character, but also because so much of commercial life revolved around the production of letters. An 1872 manual told the story of a Philadelphia clerk whose road to success was paved with proper attention to business correspondence. The Liverpool branch of his firm "noticed how admirably his letters were written, and had him transferred to that city, where he rapidly rose to a partnership, and retired with a fortune of $800,000."[9] Significantly, the title character in Horatio Alger's *Ragged Dick* (1867) begins his journey up the social ladder by learning how to write a good letter.[10] When Dick ultimately lands a promising position as a clerk, mid-century readers would recognize that his voyage has reached its terminus.

Letters exchanged among friends and family were profoundly (if ambiguously) linked to the world of business. As new users joined the postal network after 1845, they wrestled with the question of how their mail related to the dominant model of correspondence. One especially illuminating illustration of this struggle appears in evolving attitudes toward composing letters on the Sabbath. Sunday Sabbath observance had been at the heart of two major political controversies before the first postal reform, and both controversies focused on mail. In the 1810s, and then again in the late 1820s, powerful Sabbatarian movements had organized in opposition to the transmission of mail on Sundays. As Richard R. John has argued, Sabbatarians targeted the post not simply because it was the most visible embodiment of the federal government, but in large part because the U.S. mail represented the government's role in the market economy and the conduct of commercial and financial transactions.[11] The Sabbatarians failed to close down the postal system on Sundays, but their identification of the post with business was broadly shared (many of their opponents simply felt that the market could not afford to be hamstrung by a day of rest). As letter-writing became more common, correspondents who observed the Sabbath faced a dilemma. Was the medium they were using inherently worklike? Bradford Morse, a young clerk in San Francisco during the 1850s, acknowledged this quandary in a letter to his mother in Massachusetts. "I intended to have replied to your letter last evening," he explained, "but knowing your ideas about using the Sabbath for such purposes I delayed until this morning."[12] Morse invokes his mother's Sabbatarian concerns to excuse a breach of filial piety, but he also distances himself from those concerns, leaving open the possibility that he might have written letters to someone else on Sunday. Morse and his mother may have found themselves on opposite sides of a generational divide. Seven years later, teenaged Lucy Breckinridge of Virginia noted in her diary that although the minister's wife "considers it very wrong to write letters on Sunday, ... I cannot see any harm in writing to people that you love." Much of the conflict hinged on a crucial but slippery distinction between different types of letter-writing. Breckinridge conceded that "it would be sinful to write formal business letters," but cited "love" as a mitigating factor.[13]

For a new generation of Protestant postal users, especially those far from home, letter-writing came to shed its associations with business and to acquire affinities with the proper observance of the Sabbath. William Allen Clark, a soldier in the Union Army in 1862, proudly claimed to his Baptist family in Indiana that he had written them "each Sabbath since I left home except when marching."[14] For soldiers, travelers, and migrants, letters from far away offered the promise of an absorptive reading experience linked both to Bible study and, moreover, to the imaginative recreation of idealized home life in the midst of a transient and frequently acquisitive existence. This was especially true during the Gold Rush, when letters from home were celebrated and even fetishized as symbolic counterpoints to the worldly preoccupations and the money-making ethos that governed everyday life. Recalling the frenzy that greeted the arrival of a mail steamer in the 1850s in California, Hubert Howe Bancroft reminded his readers that letters had provided the sole bridge to a distant world "of civilization, of Sabbath and home influence, of all the sweet memories and amenities that make life endurable."[15] Letters, in this view, were themselves tokens of Sabbath observance. Historian Alexis McCrossen cites several examples of westward migrants who used Sunday as a day for writing, reading, and rereading letters, and she reaffirms their sense of letter-writing as a sacred activity. "Sojourners and settlers treated Sunday differently from the other days of the week," McCrossen notes of the mid-to-late nineteenth century, "whether they engaged in more than usual gambling, drinking, and fighting, or in letter writing, introspection, and devotions."[16]

During the middle decades of the nineteenth century, the tension between the transmission of mail as the classic transgression of the Sabbath and the personal letter as an apt symbol of Sabbath observance reflected deeper uncertainty about the meaning of postal contact. To resolve this tension, cultural commentators and epistolary guides were quick to insist upon the validity of Lucy Breckinridge's distinction between business mail and personal mail. Business letters should be particularly "brief, plain, and straightforward," advised a "practical guide to business," and *Godey's* recommended that "business letters should be as brief as is consistent with perspicuity." Such correspondence was not to be confused with other kinds of letters. An 1856 issue of *Ladies' Repository* offered a taxonomy of the varieties of mail, stigmatizing business letters as if they were a marginal, regrettable category of postal material: "In this world of material interests we must have *business* letters too. There is not an atom of genuine love to be picked out of one in a thousand of these necessary documents. It is a trade to write them. Good penmanship and correct arithmetic qualify the writer." In a similar vein, some postal users emphasized the relative triviality of business letters. Bancroft spoke of savoring a missive "that breathed of tender memories and pure affection" amid a "pile of business correspondence." Others accepted grudgingly the priority that business mail claimed. Forty-niner Henry Dewitt informed his mother that her other son Alfred would have no time to write, "as he can hardly answer his business letters." "He is now writing," Henry reported. "I expect it will be daylight before he gets through."[17] In both formulations, the distinction seemed clear enough. As categories of correspondence, business letters and personal letters took discrete forms and marked separate practices.

In practice, however, the line proved blurry. Drawing upon many of the same skills, competing (as Henry Dewitt acknowledged) for the same time and attention, and arriving in the same mail bags, business letters were not always easy to distinguish from personal letters. Unlike that of later times, mid-century business correspondence was handwritten, authored (if not always written) by a person familiar (at least by name) to the addressee. Letters between friends and family, for their part, often dealt with financial matters and routinely enclosed money. To which camp—business or personal—does one assign a letter from a forty-niner to his wife offering detailed instructions about the collection of a debt or the management of a store? Under which rubric belongs the correspondence between an Alabama slave and her absentee master, providing crop reports and detailing family news?[18]

If the business and personal categories were not as mutually exclusive as critics pretended, letter-writers themselves nonetheless grappled with the division. In his recent study of the literate habits of young clerks in antebellum America, Thomas Augst has observed subtle (and perhaps unconscious) differences in the way young, middle-class men wrote when their audiences or subjects belonged to the emerging world of white-collar work. Augst finds that handwriting, for example, might be more elegant when a clerk wrote about domestic topics or corresponded with female relatives than when he wrote to colleagues about business.[19] Inevitably, however, there was overlap. Jay Cooke apologized to his brother in 1840 for a slippage between what he knew ought to be distinct modes of epistolary address: "I write so many letters that I almost lose the form and spirit of a private one," he observed, speculating that his "business way for expressing things," must frequently intrude upon the intimacy of his brotherly exchange.[20]

Distinctions between what was business and what was personal in the steady stream of mail transmission were part of the complex project of constructing epistolary intimacy. At the broadest level, more widespread and frequent use of the mail required some negotiation of the boundaries between public and private in the new postal culture. The ostensible privacy of the sealed letter was—and remains—the subject of a great deal of earnest discussion and mystification. Antebellum Americans inherited a deep ideological faith in the *privacy* of letters, though a number of different concepts were subsumed under that rubric. The right of confidential correspondence was in fact a centerpiece of English notions of liberty and English suspicions of government tyranny. In 1844, accusations that the government spied on the private correspondence of Joseph Mazzini, a well-connected Italian exile living in England, precipitated a major crisis in British politics.[21] The immunity of the mail to government inspection and interference had been a legal cornerstone of the American postal system since 1792—though an important exception was made in the antebellum South in the case of abolitionist literature. And while Americans did worry on occasion about the vulnerability of letters to unwanted third-party intrusion, their concerns usually focused on postal theft.[22] But the insistence upon the privacy of correspondence in antebellum America was more than a matter of political or economic rights; letters were private because their contents were intimate.

During the eighteenth and nineteenth centuries, an elaborate mythology of epistolary privacy surrounded the exchange of letters. Though they were hardly the first to formulate the connection, epistolary novelists such as Jean-Jacques Rousseau and Samuel Richardson produced popular celebrations of the personal letter as a uniquely authentic and sincere form of expression. Correspondence, according to a false etymology peddled in Richardson's *Clarissa*, was "coeur-respondence," communication from the heart.[23] Characters in epistolary fiction might send letters through messengers, but mail bags were public repositories of private expressions. As a German cabinet official put it in 1814, "What is locked up most carefully in the heart, in one's own living room, is entrusted without hesitation to the postal service by everyone, by hundreds of thousands every day. The postman's satchel thus holds incomparably more secrets, and no less securely under proper administration, than the seal of confession, and the symbol of discretion is none other than that of the postal service."[24]

Americans paid frequent homage to the integrity and reliability of the postal confession booth. The popular mid-century novel *Reveries of a Bachelor* dubbed letters "the only true heart-talkers . . . a true soul-print," unsullied by the distortions of other forms of social interaction. "As in a mirror one shows his face to himself, so in a letter one shows his heart to his friend," journalist Theodore Tilton wrote to his wife in 1866, before the scandal surrounding her relationship with the Reverend Henry Ward Beecher turned the intimacy of their foundering marriage into a public spectacle.[25]

Even as cheap postage democratized correspondence, the personal letter retained its sacred status as a private text in popular literature, the periodical press, and the flurry of epistolary guidebooks that were published during the antebellum period. In innumerable texts and contexts, authors belabored a series of clichés that were central to the ideology of epistolary privacy. Calling letters "the treasured mementoes of the absent, the loved, and lost," an 1868 guide published in San Francisco and "peculiarly adapted to the requirements of California" invoked many of the stock images and terms with which an increasingly ordinary activity was resanctified:

> [H]ow they are read and re-read, wept over and kissed; how they are locked away in secret cabinets, to be taken forth only in solitude, as a miser gloats over his gold; how they are worn almost illegible by the throbbing of soft, white bosoms, and how often they are hidden in the still folds of the winding sheet.... Letters of friendship, love, and affection are sacred things, and should be so imbued with the spirit of the writer as to render them worthy of the devoted attention they call for.[26]

Letters were secret (in several senses), they bore metonymic traces of the (typically female) bodies that composed them, and they dealt in the currency of human intimacy. Items of personal correspondence, in the words of Hubert Howe Bancroft, "breathed of tender memories and pure affection."[27]

Lest new postal users find such an enterprise a bit daunting, commentators and advisers reminded them continually of the old saw that a letter was still nothing more than written conversation. An 1841 composition textbook defined the epistolary genre as "a conversation carried on upon paper between friends at a distance," while one guide after another assured readers that "letter-writing is but 'speaking by the pen.'"[28] When Horatio Alger's Ragged Dick contemplates the task of composing his first letter, he doubts his abilities. "Like a good many other boys," the pedantic narrator of the 1867 novel explains, "he looked upon it as a very serious job, not reflecting that, after all, letter-writing is nothing but talking upon paper...."[29] There was a tension, of course, between the mystifying claim that letters were treasured revelations composed in solitude and the ostensibly demystifying claim that letters were simply ordinary conversation. The analogy between correspondence and speech did, however, have its own mystical resonance, implying that a properly composed text might somehow incarnate an absent friend. At any rate, both descriptions of the personal letter were extremely common in mid-century writing, and both were crucial to the cultural construction of mail as an intimate social exchange that could form the basis for an ongoing relationship between correspondents who did not see each other.

New postal users encountered the ideology of epistolary privacy at every turn during the middle of the nineteenth century, whether or not they purchased letter-writing manuals. Prevailing assumptions about the personal letter surfaced in a number of major news stories, for example, in which correspondence was introduced into public view. One of the most famous concerned the New York prostitute Helen Jewett, whose murder in 1836 was a foundational event in the formation of a popular daily press in urban America. Jewett had used the post office frequently to conduct business and to negotiate personal affairs, and an elaborate correspondence between her and Richard Robinson, later her accused murderer, was seized at the time of the crime. Though they played little part in the trial that exonerated Robinson and figured only marginally in the flood of press coverage surrounding the case, the Jewett-Robinson letters made a public appearance more than a decade later (in the period of postal reform) when the *National Police Gazette* published them in full as part of an elaborate serial story on Jewett. George Wilkes, the editor, drew no sensational conclusions from the letters, but simply offered them to his readers as a point of access to the life of the victim.

Purportedly intimate letters appeared on the public stage two decades later in a bizarre episode involving the disposition of Mary Lincoln's clothes. Beset by staggering debts accumulated while she was in the White House, Lincoln traveled incognito from Chicago to New York in an attempt to raise money by selling off her wardrobe. As part of her fund-raising strategy, the former first lady wrote a series of letters to a jewelry broker describing her poverty, which he then threatened to publish (and ultimately did) in the newspapers. None of this succeeded in selling the goods (or otherwise raising funds), but the circulation of Mary Lincoln's letters was central to the "Old Clothes Scandal" of 1867, paralleling the unseemly exhibition of her personal belongings. In a final twist to the scandal, Lincoln's seamstress and confidante, the former slave Elizabeth Keckley, printed several of Lincoln's letters to her in a memoir. Keckley propounded various defenses for her actions (which earned her widespread condemnation in the press as well as the ire of her friend), claiming among other things that she "excluded everything of a personal character from her letters" and excerpted only those portions that "refer to public men." But Keckley recognized at the same time that the value of the documents as evidence was that they "were not written for publication." Mary Lincoln's letters, Keckley pointed out, were "the frank overflowings of the heart, the outcropping of impulse, the key to genuine motives." Far from being public papers, these letters were distinctively private, and uniquely revealing. They would enable Keckley to defend Mrs. Lincoln in public by "lay[ing] her secret history bare."[30]

Similar confidence in the sincerity and veracity of unguarded intimate correspondence underlay the publication of letters in the Beecher-Tilton scandal that captivated metropolitan readers in the mid-1870s. Theodore and Elizabeth Tilton had conducted and preserved an extraordinarily rich correspondence during the late 1860s, and many of these letters were introduced (by both sides) as evidence in court in 1875 during civil proceedings against Henry Ward Beecher for allegedly seducing Elizabeth and alienating her affections from her husband. During the previous year, however, Theodore Tilton had taken the unusual step of having the journalist George Alfred Townsend, his principal advocate in the press, publish 201 letters between the couple in the columns of the Chicago *Daily Tribune*. The correspondence was intended to vindicate Theodore Tilton's depiction of a happy marriage disrupted by a fiendish intervention and thereby to discredit the story that Elizabeth was then telling of an oppressive and unsatisfying relationship. Elizabeth Tilton's letters in particular provided "testimony," in Townsend's words, of her emotional state "before she had any occasion to submit such testimony to the manipulation of lawyers bent on crushing her husband for the sake of saving Mr. Beecher."[31] Decoupled from the question of Beecher's culpability, the Tilton letters were also a major literary sensation whose merits were debated throughout the nation. In the process, large numbers of readers digested what was essentially a collection of testimonials to the power of romantic correspondence. Letters, this remarkable act of publication seemed to suggest, were repositories of the secrets of the conjugal bedroom and the human heart.[32]

The Jewett, Lincoln, and Tilton episodes confirmed what was popularly understood to be intimate about the mail, even as they raised the specter of the eventual publication of ostensibly private communication. Letters emerged in these news stories as material artifacts of private emotional life that might be used to violate the very privacy they registered. But the power of that violation depended, of course, on widespread belief that letters were sincere and confidential disclosures made in the insulated context of an intense emotional relationship. At a time when the post was becoming a broadly participatory network, the implications of this ideological assumption were considerable. Almost everyone, it might appear, from ministers to prostitutes, from ex-slaves to the wives of presidents, conducted these intense and intimate emotional relationships and left a paper trail of sincere confessions.

In reality, of course, postal relationships conformed rather imperfectly to the model of a sealed intimacy between two correspondents. Whether or not letters were published in the press, postal users encountered daily evidence that the status of personal mail was far more complex. Letters were frequently addressed to more than one person, and even when addressed to a single person, they were commonly shared. This might take the form of showing a letter prior to sealing it. The surviving correspondence of Helen Jewett reveals that she would on occasion mail a letter to a more intimate third party, with the instruction that he read, seal, and repost the letter to its putatively intended recipient.[33] More typically, however, the circulation of personal letters took place after the initial posting and with the presumed consent of all parties. Mary Paul, writing from Vermont to New Hampshire in 1852, explained her enclosure of a letter from one of her brothers in a way that nicely captures the circuits along which family correspondence might travel. "I received a letter from Henry last night inclosing yours from William," she opened, referring to two of her brothers. "He (Henry) said you wished me to send it back to you as you were going to send it to Julius," yet another brother.[34] Letter-writers often explicitly authorized and encouraged this practice in order to save time or postage. Overland migrant Louisa Cook made such a suggestion to her mother and sister in an 1862 letter from somewhere in Nebraska. "I do not have time to write to any one but you & if any of the friends wish to hear from me they can do so through you. If you go over to the Debolt neighborhood give my love to the friends there & if you like you can let them read my letters."[35] In other cases, writers might renounce confidentiality in order to avoid the impression that they had something to hide. "I am perfectly willing for you to show Mother my letters," Franklin Buck wrote from New York to his sister in Vermont. "I don't intend to do anything that I am ashamed to have her know."[36]

Despite the rhetoric surrounding intimate correspondence, letters were often written for larger audiences. If a writer had journeyed to a distant location, his or her mail could serve as a travel guide or as a kind of sensational literature, and many letters from the West reflect this awareness.[37] Letters from European immigrants to their communities of origin were especially likely to be circulated—partly because of high rates of international postage, which persisted well into the second half of the century and made writing separate letters to different friends and family members a costly proposition. Mail from new arrivals during the antebellum period also played a prominent role back home in collective discussions and deliberations about migration, and were often so clearly composed for communal consumption that historians have dubbed them "America Letters" and classified them as a species of public literature.[38]

Even under more ordinary circumstances, letters were typically displays of writing skill and performances of good taste. Frequent comments about spelling mistakes in the epistolary admonitions of parents and siblings, as discussed in chapter 1, reinforced this point. Adults were not exempt from such pedagogical direction, especially women. A San Franciscan writing to his sister in the East expressed, "strictly *entre nous*," a wish that she might develop "a less careless habit of letter writing; for as a young lady, you may presently be called upon to write letters, which you would not like to contain *errors*." While men might send "letters of a very indifferent appearance" (his own compositions, he admitted, were "monsters of deformity"), a young lady could ill afford such carelessness. "So pray read over your letters after they are written, and supply such words as you have left out.[39] In an 1861 letter to his wife Pamelia, James Fergus commended her improvement: "This is the best you ever wrote me and contained the most interesting news," he wrote, though her spelling and writing were found wanting. Dismayed by the errors, James instructed her on the proper way to compose correspondence. "Write your letter first out on your slate," he directed, "rub out alter and correct untill you think the spelling is all right, and [the letter] is as good . . . as you can get it. Then write it on paper with a pencil, correcting any further errors you may have, then copy it in ink, and your letters will certainly look better than they do now." An intimate communication between a husband and a wife was still an occasion for care in one's self-presentation.[40]

For some postal users, the imagined readership for personal letters extended to future generations. Theodore Tilton, after exclaiming to his wife that letters approximate and register a moment of physical contact ("there is something in the exchange of letters that ranks next to the greeting of palm to palm"), confessed a desire to save her letters, put them in an iron safe, and bequeath them to their children, in order to show future grandchildren "how much their grandfather and grandmother loved one another in the olden time." Earlier that month, Elizabeth had praised his letters as "a legacy to my children when I no longer live to preserve them." Though the fate of the Tilton correspondence would take an uncommon twist, preserving letters was a common practice. Louisa Cook asked her correspondents to save her letters, "as I have written a great deal that I have not in my journal & when I come back I should like to have them to refer to." In asking his wife to "preserve all my letters carfull on file," James Fergus cited their value as business records (a useful reminder of the merging of letter types), but he saved all letters from her, whether or not they dealt with business matters.[41] Merchants and clerks routinely kept copies of the letters they sent (late-eighteenth century innovators, including Thomas Jefferson, had even experimented with mechanical devices that created a duplicate copy of a letter), a practice taken up by postal users who were not in the business world. A business guide recommended that "not merely the merchant, but the farmer, mechanic, and even those engaged only in private affairs, should keep a copy of every business letter they write," but some correspondents also copied letters to friends and family, either to send duplicates to others, or for some other purpose.[42] Immigrant correspondence, for example, might be copied for circulation, a practice that compounded the self-consciousness of unpracticed postal users. An 1857 letter from a Norwegian immigrant asked that the recipients take advantage of the copying process to correct his mistakes. Another letter home to Norway assumed that letters were ordinarily copied for precisely such purposes—and perhaps also to censor inappropriate discussions of intimate life. "You do not have to copy this letter and make omissions," he insisted. "[L]et every iota stand and let anyone see it as it is, for it is written by a soldier."[43]

Whether or not correspondents imagined the future utility or interest of their mail, they understood that their letters, once posted, lay beyond their control and often circulated outside the one-to-one relationship that the form of the sealed epistle seemed to imply. Some worried, understandably, about the fate of their letters. Abigail Malick, who moved to the Oregon Territory at mid-century and corresponded regularly with her daughter and son-in-law in Illinois, asked her daughter to avoid discussing a certain man in her letters as he "Alwais wants to see All the Letters that you write to me." In 1859, James Stuart of Mississippi warned his sister to be careful in her letters home, as "Aunt Mary always takes the letters and reads them and at the table makes it a point to comment upon anything she pleases." Edwin Horton, a solider in the Union Army, asked his wife not to show his letters to anyone and admonished her for having done so in the past.

> I am real Sorry I rote such a lot of stuff in that letter since it has cause so much trouble but a better way is Nell not to show any of my letters I dont never show any of yours I always burn them up as soon as I read them I dont burn them because I am ashamed to keep or read them to others but I burn them becaus I dont think it is a good plan to keep a lot of old letters for others to read and chuckle about as soon as a mans back is turned.[44]

Requests to burn or shred letters became common during this period, though they were not always fulfilled. In an 1848 missive, a postal user from Boston instructed his aunt in Vermont to "tear this letter up.... You never tore up my letters last summer when I was up as you promised did you." Junius Newport Bragg, an Arkansas physician in the Confederate Army, refused his wife's request that he destroy her letters, claiming he could never do such a thing to things she had written—"unless they were inevitably to be made public."[45] The threat of inevitable publicity haunted many who wrote personal correspondence. An etiquette guide from 1859 expressed a bizarre anxiety about letter-writing, counseling women against writing to men they did not know well, lest their intimate correspondent "show the superscription or the signature, or both to his idle companions and make insinuations much to her disadvantage, which his comrades will be sure to circulate and exaggerate." The same guide also noted the practice of certain women with insatiable epistolary appetites who "inveigle" gentlemen into correspondence and then profit by "selling the letters for publication."[46]

All of these practices and prescriptions reflected and confirmed a heightened awareness of the limits of epistolary privacy. Still, the seal on a letter or (increasingly after 1860) on the envelopes in which they were sent remained sacrosanct in the eyes of many Americans. The wise adult character in Mrs. John Farrar's didactic *The Youth's Letter-Writer* (1834) refuses to open a letter addressed to his son, reaffirming an older view of the sealed letter as "a sacred thing" and added that he "consider[ed] it very improper for one to break a seal belonging to another, or to read a letter without leave to do so, after the seal is broken."[47] In this strict view, the violation of the privacy of both the author and addressee of posted correspondence was an act of "trespass, ... which no intimacy can justify." In common practice, however, people often invoked intimacy as a defense for breaching the walls of the private letter. Parents frequently regarded their children's letters as properly subject to surveillance. In 1849, newspaper publisher Richard Cary Morse rationalized opening letters addressed to his daughter in the following terms: "I recognize the sacredness of a seal & the seal of [my daughter's] letters no less than others.... But I take it for granted that she has all confidence in me, & that her secrets ... are safe in her father's keeping. Yet children can never know the interest their parents take in them. We regard our children as part of ourselves."[48] This was hardly a unique or original line of defense: in 1798 another parent had explained, under similar circumstances, that "no one has a better right to know my children's secrets nor more ardently wishes their happiness."[49] But it became a bolder claim after 1845, when more young people had frequent and independent access to the post.

Parents were especially vigilant in monitoring the epistolary practices of their daughters. The famous diary of Mary Chesnut records an incident in which the author was shown a letter "from a girl crossed in love" by parents who objected to the match (Chesnut cites orthographic errors in the letter and says that "for such a speller ... a man of any social status would do").[50] Mary Akin informed her husband, a Confederate Congressman, that a young man had written to eighteen-year-old Eliza, his daughter and her stepdaughter, and that Eliza had asked for permission and advice. "[A]s it was John," Mary reported, "I told her to write to him if she chose to do so that it was a correspondence she could drop whenever she thought proper, and she has written to him."[51]

In consulting her stepmother, Eliza was respecting a powerful social norm. An 1837 guide to women's conduct recognized the value of honoring a request to maintain a confidential correspondence, but insisted that a young woman "make an exception in favor of [her] mother ... for young ladies under age should gracefully acknowledge their parents' right of inspection." In 1873, the "Young Woman's Column" in the *North Carolina Presbyterian* took a harder line, decreeing that "a girl under nineteen or twenty should never be allowed" to correspond with a young man, "and certainly never without the inspection of her mother or some very much older friend." The taboo against unsupervised correspondence by young women (a central theme in conduct guides and epistolary novels during the previous century) reinforced the notion that letters constructed intimate (and potentially transgressive) connections insulated from social scrutiny.[52] Armed with such cultural ammunition, husbands would sometimes make claims against the privacy of their wives' mail, a point raised in an earlier chapter. Caroline Loomis Edwards expressed her relief in 1841 that her brother's wife was "not like some ladies of my acquaintance who refuse to let their husbands see their letters and throw an air of mystery over their actions."[53]

Discussions of the possibilities and perils of private correspondence in the new postal culture continually highlighted the distinctive letter-writing habits of women. "Ladies' epistolary" was even the name of a standard mid-century penmanship style. Many critics and commentators saw correspondence as a peculiarly feminine craft. "Letter-writing, particularly the lighter kinds," wrote Lucy Fountain in *Putnam's Magazine* shortly after the Civil War, "needs a delicacy and brilliancy of touch particularly feminine." An 1860 letter-writing guide "for the use of ladies" acknowledged that "our sex have been complimented as the possessors of a natural taste for epistolary composition." Other observers were more contemptuous of female correspondence, mocking their propensity to indulge in lengthy and numerous postscripts or the feminine impulse "to indite beautiful little notes, with long-tailed letters, upon vellum paper with pink margins sealed with sweet mottoes, and dainty devices, the whole deliciously perfumed with musk and attar of roses."[54] Both critics and advocates affirmed a kind of two-sex model of letter writing, distinguishing male and female correspondence in clear terms. Letter-writing manuals often targeted one sex or the other, elaborating different styles and presuming different motivations for writing letters. Even modern historians, most notably Marilyn Ferris Motz, distinguish masculine and feminine epistolary modes during the nineteenth century.[55] The important point, however, is not whether women and men wrote (or received) a fundamentally different kind of mail (an unlikely and oversimplifying hypothesis for which we lack sufficient evidence), but that the association between gender and particular modes of correspondence was quite popular at mid-century. Such gender stereotypes appear frequently in the writings of ordinary postal users, especially in the letters of men. Fred Worth, a nineteen year-old clerk living in San Francisco, apologized to his grandmother for the brevity of his 1859 letter. "If I had the favor of *streching out a letter*, as some ladies have," Worth explained, "I might make this medley of a letter about twenty five pages in length, . . . but not having that faculty I must bring this letter to a abrupt termination, by filling the remainder with *love*."[56] Claims about the epistolary practices of men and women, many of which were fairly old clichés by the time of the postal revolution, served some new and interesting cultural functions at mid-century. A popular discourse about gender and letter writing helped Americans map out boundaries between business and personal correspondence in everyday life and between the public and the private in the world of the post.

The personal letters that passed through the mails in unprecedented numbers during the middle of the nineteenth century were artifacts of a postal culture and not just expressions of individual needs and circumstances. Paradoxically, the collective insistence by published commentators that a letter is (or ought to be) a spontaneous effusion of sincere feeling from one person to another accomplished much of the cultural work that went into producing the modern personal letter. At least as important, however, were the letters themselves, which elaborated, reinforced, and circulated the principal themes of the ideology of epistolary intimacy.

Mid-century correspondents were as relentless as published guides in defining letters as a kind of intimate conversation.[57] Lucy Smith of Michigan asked her mother in 1843 to reciprocate with "a real long letter just exactly as you would talk." At the close of an especially descriptive and rambling 1856 letter, Abigail Malick reflected "Dont I write guest As if you ware here And I was A talking to you." Confederate Congressman Warren Akin offered a related apology for a long letter to a friend in 1864: "Pardon my many *words*. When I commence writing to you I feel like I'm talking to you, and I hurry on without stopping to think much." Others cited the familiar analogy between letters and conversation to excuse informality rather than length. As Lethe Jackson, an enslaved woman living in Virginia, explained in an 1838 letter to her master's daughter, "I hope I have not made too free in any thing I said—I wanted to write as if I was talking to you."[58] More often, letter-writers simply incorporated the analogy in their descriptions of the act of composition. A recent arrival in San Francisco in 1850, John McCrackan introduced a letter to his sister Lotte in these terms: "I am seated . . . at the close of a very busy day, having just finished 'a glorious good dinner' to have a quiet chat, so now give me your hand and we will commence at once." Another forty-niner, Samuel Adams of Maine, explained to his absent wife, "[I] must talk a few minutes with my loving partner before retiring for the night." Mary Wingate wrote to her husband Benjamin that "the family have all retired and now I will finish my letter for I like to be alone when I talk with you." Warren Akin made the point more explicitly and provocatively. "Are you not mistaken when you sometimes say I dont talk to you?" he teasingly asked his wife. "I'm sure I have held sweet converse with you every day this week, to a considerable extent. And, indeed, it is a sweet converse, darling to sit down and thus speak to my dear wife."[59]

By repeating the traditional trope of correspondence as conversation, ordinary letter-writers indulged and encouraged a fantasy about the bodily presence of distant persons. Built into this fantasy, however, was some recognition of the frustrating gap that letters could never quite close. "It is with pleasure that I seat myself to converse with you a few moments today," Sabrina Swain began a letter to her husband in California, only to add "would that it were verbally."[60] As a young law student, Charles Jones acknowledged that although he looked forward to the "regular receipt" of mail from home with "zealous anticipation," letters were still "not equal to positive conversation"—they were inferior to the bodily contact they evoked. "[S]eeing these lines, traced although they be by your hand," he confided to his mother, "is not equivalent to beholding the form that dictated them."[61] Captain Jacob Ritner's letter to his wife Emeline during the Civil War betrays a similar awareness of the way conversational letters stood for both presence and absence:

> Well, dear, it is late Sunday night and if you are not too tired and sleepy and will sit on my knee and listen, I will try to tell you what we have been about since I last wrote. I have a "bushel" of news to tell, but can't tell it all tonight, if I have to write it down. I wish I could sit down and talk to you till midnight, don't you! But I am very thankful that I have the privilege of writing to you—it is more than I expected sometimes through the week.

While the letter opens as an oral exchange embedded in an intimate physical encounter, the medium of writing winds up imposing time limits on what can be said, disrupting the analogy. Franklin Buck acknowledged a similar problem in one of his early letters to his sister after leaving Vermont. "It is hard work for me to write my thoughts," he admitted. "If I was with you I could talk more in five minutes than I can write on two sheets of paper." But in Jacob Ritner's case the fantasy of being able to "sit down and talk to you till midnight" reads less as a wish for more time than as a wish for more bodily contact.[62] If only the image of correspondence as laptalk were real, he seems to suggest.

For Ritner, as for many mid-century correspondents, the conventional description of the personal letter as surrogate speech gave way to a complex fantasy that the mail might simulate bodily presence more generally. Perhaps encouraged both by the increasing speed and frequency of the mails and by the spread of the telegraph, letter-writers frequently imagined being brought into some sort of instantaneous communion with the people they addressed. "I wish you *could* be taken up bodily," journalist Joseph Lyman wrote from New York to his wife in Massachusetts, "and set down here with me a day and a night."[63] Such erotic fantasies were fairly common in nineteenth-century letters, but the thought of being physically transported along with the mail went beyond the familiar expression of sexual desire; it called attention to both the possibilities and limitations of the personal letter as a bearer of physical presence. On a steamer bound for California in 1849, John Ingalls articulated a standard version of this observation to his foster brother. "I wish I had the power to bring you on board the ship Pacific by an effort of the will," he wrote in his letter. Warren Akin offered a slight variation in a letter to his wife. "If I could move with 'the speed of thought' I would now be sitting by the fire with you and my dear children this cold night." Mollie Dorsey, who moved west with her family at the age of eighteen from Indianapolis in 1857, described in her diary three years later how one day, disconsolate at not receiving letters from home, she stared out eastward across the Colorado plains. "I wished myself a fairy or spirit," she recorded, "that I might fly away to the old home and see them all once more, and soon I transferred my longing to paper."[64] Fantasies of simultaneity and instant travel reflected and reinforced heightened expectations of contact in a society transformed by increased use of the post. But they were also gestures by which ordinary postal users ratified the claim of the mailed letter to be an intimate act of interpersonal communication.

Everyday acts of correspondence were crucial to the cultural construction of the personal letter, and not simply because letters frequently affirmed the ideology of epistolary intimacy. Ordinary letters shaped popular understanding of interpersonal correspondence even when they did not articulate explicit views on the value of letter-writing. Every use of the post, of course, informed both the sender's and the recipient's sense of what it meant to correspond by mail, and the range of circumstances, exigencies, desires, anxieties, obligations, and pieties reflected or expressed in the daily mail was, as commentators were fond of emphasizing, unimaginably diverse. Yet much of what appeared in personal letters during the mid-nineteenth century (and no doubt subsequently) was highly formulaic. This was, in fact, one of the most important senses in which ostensibly private correspondence was conspicuously public. Broadly shared conventions of salutation, address, and expression forged a powerful link between the individual letter and a larger epistolary discourse. Letter-writing formulas and clichés were largely matters of propriety and habit. They provided reassurances that an author was qualified and experienced in the practice of correspondence, and thus they could be useful in enabling, excusing, or even disclaiming whatever intimacy might follow. Formulas, in other words, explicitly framed the intimacy of a personal letter as a particular instance of a popular practice subject to norms and conventions.

It would be an enormous task to catalogue the innumerable formulaic expressions that recur throughout the archive of mid-century correspondence, but many of them rehearse a few basic themes. As literary historian William Merrill Decker has demonstrated, popular letters in nineteenth-century America repeated a series of tropes about separation, absence, and death with which correspondents had been preoccupied for centuries. Standard assurances that the author is still "in the land of the living" or stock expressions of pious confidence that the parties might be reunited in some better future were not simply clichés, as Decker observes. Such formulas affirm, albeit in unoriginal and unself-conscious ways, the "transcendental principle of enduring presence" that underwrites epistolary intimacy, enabling correspondents to make sense of long-distance relationships.[65] Another cluster of formulas relate to reciprocity, including typical opening lines that mark and date the arrival of an incoming letter ("Yours of the 9 inst came to hand last evening"; "I received your welcome letter yesterday evening"; "Your very affectionate letter of the 24th came to hand today"; "Your very kind and interesting favor of the 30th ult. was this moment received")[66] or bemoan the addressee's failure to write ("To-day's mail in and no letter for me. I can't tell you how much I am disappointed"; "I am satisfied now that I shall get no letters from you by this mail").[67]

Perhaps the most common opening in mid-century correspondence spun some variation on the following formula, adopted in this example by the Midwesterner Samuel Tripp. "Dear father and mother," he began an 1849 letter. "I now take my pen to write you a few lines to inform you that I am well at present sincerely hoping that these few lines will find you all enjoying the same blessing." Tripp started other letters to other correspondents almost identically ("Dear sir. I again take my pen to write you a few lines to let you know that I am well at present and enjoying good health and I sincerely hope [illegible smudge] enjoying the same good blessing") and read similar openings in the mail he received ("Dear sir I now take my pin in hand to lit you no that I am well and I hope that these few lines may find you the same").[68] This formula obviously reflected an anxiety about health, but to read the astonishing recurrence of this greeting simply as a reflection of the fragility of life in nineteenth-century America would be to miss a major point. Ordinary correspondents resorted to formulaic expressions precisely because of their status as gestures whose semantic content was dulled by familiarity.

Personal letters began with references to taking "pen in hand," inscribing "these few lines," or having "an opportunity," not because such locutions necessarily captured the goals and values of correspondence, but because they marked a piece of writing as properly epistolary—in defiance of the edict that letters mimic ordinary conversation. The ubiquitous invocation of the "opportunity" to write, which was typically "embraced" or, slightly less frequently, "improved" (both expressions mean to capitalize upon), was a relic of an earlier era when letter-writing occasions were typically created by the fortuitous availability of a personal courier.[69] It may not be coincidental that the words *embrace* and *improve*, which emphasized two different sets of values central to correspondence (interpersonal intimacy and literate upward mobility), loomed so large in the formulaic opening (on occasion the recipient might replace the opportunity as the direct object of the intended embrace),[70] but surely for most users those terms had lost much of their edge.

The sheer volume of personal letter-writing during the early years of cheap postage makes generalizations hazardous, but formulaic expressions at the start of personal letters appear to have been particularly common among postal users for whom written correspondence was most unfamiliar. Enslaved African-Americans, recent immigrants from Europe, female mill workers just off the farm, Civil War soldiers from small towns, and rural migrants heading westward relied most frequently upon standard announcements about taking pens in hand, embracing opportunities, writing a few lines, and hoping the reader is enjoying the same blessing of good health.[71]

The division between correspondents who resorted to these formulas and those who did not was not always predictable, however. Even within the same family, approaches to the epistolary formula could vary. David Lee Campbell and his brother James were born in 1824 and 1826 in Kentucky and moved to Adams County, Illinois, with their parents in 1831. They attended the same district public school in Brown County, both married (within three weeks of each other) in 1849, emigrated in tandem to California in 1850, and returned from there together two years later. Yet despite their shared background and experiences, the brothers' letters home to Illinois (first from the overland trail and then from California) reveal a striking difference. James, the younger brother, begins a typical letter to his wife with the conventional explanation that he has "taken another opportunity to inform you that I am well and in good spirits and hoping that you and John Sidney are enjoying the same blessing."[72] Four months later, this time from California, James's letter to his wife's parents strikes the same pose: "I take this opportunity to inform you that I am well and hope these lines will find you all enjoying the same blessing." Almost a year later he addressed his father in terms almost identical (save for the spelling): "I take this opportunity to wright a few lines to let you know that David and myself are well and hope you are all enjoying the same blessing."[73]

But while older brother David may have been enjoying that same blessing, he did not typically adopt the same formulas to say as much. "Dear Father, James & myself are in good health," he begins abruptly in a letter to his father from Scott's Bluffs. Other letters open similarly, announcing simply "We are well," or "Brother James and & [sic] myself have finally arrived in California." Once in California his letters occasionally refer to "tak[ing] an opportunity to inform you that I am well," and one surviving letter to his father even indulges in James's formulaic expression of hope about the shared blessing of good health, but this is a notable deviation from his ordinary pattern. In almost all cases David's correspondence begins with either a direct report of his condition or the confirmation of receipt of mail.[74]

James Campbell's consistent and energetic preference for conventional openings may have reflected any of a number of influences and considerations, but as personal correspondence proliferated during the middle decades of the century, his practice ran the risk of being read as a sign of epistolary inexperience. The *New Orleans Picayune* mocked the inappropriate use of standard formulas by unsophisticated letter writers in an 1841 item purporting to be an actual "Western Love Letter" penned by one "Kathrun An Tilden." Replete with misspellings and encumbered by several postscripts (a habit associated derisively with women's correspondence) and bits of doggerel, the letter opens as follows: "My Deer Henry—I embrace this opporchunity to let you knough as I am had a spell of the aigur. And I hope theas few lines may find you enjoying the same God's Blessin!" Frank J. Webb's novel *The Garies and Their Friends* (1857) uses the same joke to mark the dividing line of literary sophistication separating different strata of African American society in antebellum Philadelphia. Webb juxtaposes two letters addressed to young Charlie Ellis informing him that his home has been destroyed and his father injured by mob violence. Along with a proper, forthright epistle from his sister Esther, Charlie encounters the awkward, rambling, and orthographically irregular composition of his friend Kinch Sanders de Younge. Kinch, the son of an illiterate clothing dealer and a poor student, had been struggling for some time to produce the letter. "DEER SIR AND HONNORED FRIEND," it began. "I take This chance To Write To you To tell You that I am Well, And that we are all well Except Your father, who Is sick; and I hope you are Enjoying the same Blessin."[75]

Even less comically inappropriate applications of the formulaic expression came in for criticism. An 1863 piece of serialized fiction in the *Southern Illustrated News* disparaged the embraced opportunity as a "trite and apologetic expression." Earlier in the period, Mrs. John Farrar had advanced a far broader indictment. In Farrar's popular epistolary guide for young readers, Anna, the most authoritative and accomplished of the book's adolescent characters, makes the point that good letter-writers have no need for "any set phrase for a beginning." Later in the story, a younger farmhand seeks Anna's advice as he struggles to compose a letter, which he has begun with the familiar "This comes to inform you that I am well, and hope you are the same." Anna explains that such an opening is unnecessary. "'Every letter,' she said, 'comes to inform one of something; and therefore it is unnecessary to say that it does; and unless you have been ill, and there is great anxiety about your health, there is too much egotism in making that your first topic."[76] An 1852 article similarly criticized the appearance of stock phrases in business letters:

> It is to be presumed that you do not write without a quill pen, or a metallic substitute, and there is therefore no particular necessity for informing your correspondent that "you take your pen in hand." Nobody, except the remarkable personage without arms who was exhibited a few years since, takes the pen between the toes. Neither need you tell your friend that your letter "comes hoping," It may leave *you* 'hoping;' but that any emotion of hope or despair can be predicated of a sheet of paper is hardly to be asserted.

By the time of the Civil War, formulaic openings may also have begun to seem old-fashioned, as teenager Mary Trussell implied in an 1860 letter to her foster sister, Delia Page. Trussell mocked the salutatory "I now take my pen in hand to let you know I am well, and hope you are the same," as the standard fare of "old times," though she conceded that "a good many" letters still adopted the deplorable practice.[77] Formulaic expressions were recognizable icons of personal correspondence, but many letter writers took pride in avoiding them.

How James and David Lee Campbell, or anyone else for that matter, acquired the literary habits that framed their personal letters is of course difficult to surmise. Published letter-writing guides were enormously popular throughout the nineteenth century, but they probably played no major role in training readers in the use of formulaic salutations or openings. Though one 1839 guide published in New York offers two examples of letters that begin by marking "the opportunity of writing these few lines to you," and expressing hope "that you are in as good health as I am at present" (significantly, one of the letters is attributed to an apprentice),[78] the overwhelming majority of model letters in epistolary manuals avoid such formulas.

More important, it is unlikely that many correspondents relied upon letter-writing guides for basic instruction.[79] The appeal of these texts probably owed more to their status as conduct guides or as a kind of epistolary fiction. A remarkable number of the featured letters in antebellum epistolary manuals affirm norms of behavior among young men and women and describe the same sorts of familial conflicts and heterosocial dangers that dominate the popular epistolary novels influenced by Samuel Richardson. Richardson's own venture into the genre of letter-writing guide, *Familiar Letters on Important Occasions* (1741), left a heavy stamp on American manuals more than a century after its initial publication. An 1853 *Complete Letter Writer* published in San Francisco, for example, recycled many of Richardson's letters without citation, entertaining readers with virtually identical versions of the master's "From an Uncle to his Nephew, an apprentice, on his keeping bad company, bad Hours, &c" or "From a Daughter to her Father, pleading for her Sister, who had married without her consent"—along with the father's reply.[80] There is little reason to assume that readers of *The Fashionable American Letter Writer* or *The Ladies' and Gentlemens' Letter-writer* were any more eager for (or susceptible to) practical letter-writing advice than were the consumers of *Pamela* or *Clarissa*.

Composition books used in schools were probably more influential than letter-writing guides in shaping the epistolary practices of ordinary people, and some of them may have contributed to the popularization of stock expressions and formulaic gestures. As Lucille M. Schultz has observed, composition textbooks taught by formal precept rather than by anecdotal model, and were probably more widely read (though fewer different titles have survived).[81] And unlike epistolary manuals, composition books prescribed compulsory, mimetic exercises. At least one antebellum composition text instructed students in the use of formulaic openings to personal correspondence. The first skeletal model for a letter in Charles Morley's 1839 *A Practical Guide to Composition* prefaced a letter to a sister with the familiar "I take this opportunity to write you a few lines." Subsequent sentences were governed by guidelines rather than prescribed text. The first substantive line ought to "mention the state of your health, and that of your friends," while the next should speak of progress in school. Additional letter models, one to a friend in Europe and another to a brother, open similarly with formulaic introductions before launching into news.[82]

Undoubtedly, the most powerful influences on ordinary letter-writing habits came in the form of personal correspondence itself. As performances of proper penmanship and respectable character, personal letters were central exhibits in the larger didactic projects to which epistolary guides and composition textbooks contributed. Letters, as several scholars have demonstrated, were important sites for the elaboration and circulation of antebellum cultural norms, especially those of gender and class. But correspondents also exchanged something more specific about the construction of letters themselves. The personal, handwritten missive was not simply an instrument of cultural pedagogy; it was also, in some interesting ways, a pedagogical goal in and of itself. In admonishing their correspondents to write more frequently, more neatly, or more expressively, parents, siblings, and friends were not only encouraging the cultivation and display of skills and qualities that could be usefully deployed elsewhere. They were teaching and modeling the art of the personal letter at a time when postal correspondence was becoming both financially affordable and socially indispensable.

Americans during the middle decades of the century taught one another how to compose letters and how to recognize letters as gestures of self-expression. That they emphasized themes and images that had been, in many cases, familiar *topoi* of epistolary discourse in previous centuries camouflages the novelty of this development. Codes of intimacy, reciprocity, and self-presentation that organized (and in some respects standardized) mid-century correspondence may have rehearsed older ideas about presence and absence, speech and writing, or words and flesh. But once those codes entered the everyday experience of large numbers of Americans who expected to maintain some of their most important relationships through the post, the stakes were much higher. The structural conditions of epistolary practice were now the structuring facts of everyday sociability.

The novelty of the personal letter as a model of intimacy in the antebellum period is easy to overlook. Though posted letters had in ancient and medieval times been paradigmatically public artifacts, in the early modern period new and ideologically charged associations emerged between the handwritten letter and privacy in its two fundamental senses: solitude and intimacy. Furthermore, letter-writing became central to the project of self-fashioning and self-improvement in the United States well before the arrival of cheap postage, but especially in the early national era, as aspirations and access to gentility spread among middling Americans.[83] But as this process spilled beyond the borders of self-conscious pedagogical interventions and extended to a broader range of the population, something different was emerging. Instead of simply teaching epistolary self-presentation as a mark of refinement or a badge of respectability, Americans valued and practiced epistolary intimacy as a basic mode of social and familial interaction. By the 1870s most Americans recognized the personal letter as a vehicle for everyday expressions of intimacy and everyday performances of the individual self.

FIVE

PRECIOUS AS GOLD
MOBILITY AND FAMILY IN THE GOLD
RUSH AND CIVIL WAR

When Charles Stanton left Chicago in 1846, his brother Philip in Brooklyn received the news enthusiastically. After ten years in the fledgling Illinois city, the trip westward marked, at least from the perspective of an older sibling, a reawakening of Charles's dormant ambitions. Recalling the events two years later under the pall of his brother's tragic odyssey, Philip noted that he had learned of Charles's plans only upon receiving a letter posted from St. Louis, followed "almost on [its] heels" by one from Independence, Missouri—a jumping-off point for the Overland Trail. From his home in Brooklyn, Philip proceeded to track his brother's progress across the plains. "From the time my brother left Independence," Philip remembered, "I had a map lying before me on my table, and whenever I received a letter from him, I would trace out his course on the map, and his letters being in full detail, I was enabled to travel along with him." Separated by most of a continent from a brother traveling through unfamiliar territory, Philip followed along, reassured by the way the postmarks and datelines of arriving letters conformed predictably to the map of the aggressively expanding United States. Even as he crossed the Rocky Mountains (through territory not yet taken during the war that had officially begun a few months earlier), Charles corresponded frequently, incorporating his brother vicariously into the trek. "So much attention did I pay to this," Philip wrote, "that the whole route became perfectly familiar to me." Only when the letters stopped did Philip begin to lose his confident grip on Charles's progress. Though he took some comfort from a warning in Charles's last letter that a projected trip through the Bear River Valley might cause an interruption in communication, Philip grew "extremely anxious" for a report. Most of a year passed before a news item in the *New York Tribune* informed him of the grisly fate of Charles Stanton and the other members of the infamous Donner Party.[1]

As letter-writing became more common, and mail service more regular and extensive, the post allowed people to track mobile friends and relatives and imagine their activities within a shared temporal framework. Along with railroad routes, maps, and telegraphic service, the rhythms of mail helped plot and place the movement of goods, information, and—above all—people across the country.[2] When Theodore Tilton embarked on a midwestern lecturing tour in 1869, his wife Elizabeth in Brooklyn depended on the patterns of his correspondence to follow along. "Your change of route upsets my reckoning," she complained on one occasion, "and I am not able to place you tonight, which I regret because, as I told you before, I have known not only what place you are each night, but also which letter of mine you will find there."[3] Until this unexpected shift in itinerary, Tilton had remained within the familiar and reassuring parameters established by postal habits and expectations. By 1870, in other words, the post had become a crucial component of American geographical movement, shaping the experiences of both everyday individual migrations and momentous mass mobilizations.

Throughout the middle decades of the century, the meaning of the post in American life was shaped in part by a popular celebration of its ability to anchor disrupted relations among dispersed friends, lovers, and families. Although much of what passed in the mail conformed to very different models of postal use—business correspondence, anonymous solicitations, print publications, fan mail to celebrities—letters between friends and (especially) relatives who had once resided in the same place and were now (perhaps only temporarily) separated by long distances figured prominently in the popular imagination. The importance of correspondence among mobile and displaced kin was not simply the logical consequence of a confluence of economic changes, transportation innovations, and the spread of the post (though that confluence was significant and certainly necessary). Americans, both in their letters and in a growing public discourse of the post, acknowledged the value of mail as a conduit for familial affections and long-distance social interaction. By elaborating codes of postal reciprocity and narrating dramas of personal relationships conducted through the mail, Americans constructed during the 1840s, '50s, and '60s an understanding of the post that shaped the meaning of family and community. In an era of widespread transition and dislocation, the posted letter became for many Americans a powerful symbol of personal continuity and a badge of membership in some distant network of personal relations. More specifically, mail became the privileged mode of performing familial affiliations, especially for a growing middle class.

The claims of correspondence to such values and functions surfaced in and around countless acts of composing, sending, and expecting mail, in innumerable real and imagined postal exchanges among ordinary people uprooted from their homes. These claims had the broadest cultural impact, not surprisingly, in moments when migrants were the focus of public discussion. During the California Gold Rush and the Civil War, to take the two most striking examples, the possibilities of using a postal network to connect temporarily separated family members were demonstrated before a national audience. Throughout the period, though, the spectacle and the phenomenon of Americans on the move formed a defining context for the newly accessible postal system.

Whether they were rich or poor, male or female, free or enslaved, most Americans who moved during the middle third of the nineteenth century did so with the novel expectation that they might maintain a connection to the people they left behind. These expectations were, of course, unevenly fulfilled, and the diaries of men and women recently displaced from home are replete with expressions of disappointment and incredulity when letters failed to appear.[4] Still, by mid-century it was common for new transplants to devote considerable time to maintaining postal relationships. Several years after leaving Philadelphia with her husband for South Carolina, Anne Sinkler Whaley LeClerq remained in close contact with the city of her birth. She noted in 1848 that letters sent on Monday from her plantation via ferry to the Charleston Post Office would reach Philadelphia by Friday. On one occasion, this predictable postal link had brought LeClerq a bounty of twenty-two letters in a single mail delivery, shortly after the first postage reduction.[5]

Postal relationships became increasingly indispensable to maintaining kin networks. Roxana Brown Walbridge Watts of Vermont confided to her granddaughter in 1853 that her "children all left home and some gone so far that I do not ever expect to see them again." Her son Dustan described to his sister Sarah a decade later a common plight among New England families: "[W]e are scattered all over the world and writing is the only means by which we can communicate with each other." As matriarch of this scattered clan, Roxana posted scores of letters to her relatives— close to two hundred written in the decade or so after postal reform have survived. These letters may not have diminished the sorrow of seeing her family disperse, but surely whatever continuous claim the idea of family had upon the descendants of Roxana Watts was anchored to the post.[6]

By mid-century, postal users turned to the mail to preserve relationships during physical separation, even when they, like Donner Party victim Stanton, embarked along unfamiliar paths toward uncertain destinations. Westward migrants on the overland trail from the late 1840s onward did their best to maintain postal contacts as they traversed territories over which the U.S. Post Office had few if any established routes. Charles Hinman, en route from Tazewell County, Illinois, to California in 1849, was surprised not to find any letters from friends and family waiting for him at the post office in St. Joseph's. Anticipating several months of being able to compose but not receive mail, he testily wrote to his wife that "I cannot but co[n]clude where there is so much indifference about writing there must be as much about hearing from me."[7]

After crossing the Missouri River, travelers faced the problem of locating post offices. James Fergus of Minnesota, bound for the West Coast in 1860, wrote to his wife from Nebraska, warning her not to expect another communication until he got to Denver, which was the site of the next office on his route. More than any other landmark, the appearance of a post office reassured westward migrants that they inhabited the same world as friends and family. When the traveling party of Julia Ann Archibald passed the "last frontier Post Office" at Council Grove, along the Santa Fe Road, in 1858, they shared a sad recognition that there would be no mail for a while. For six months, it turned out, "we were to be imprisoned from the world and our friends."[8]

Having ventured off the main map of the postal network, many migrants crossing Kansas, Nebraska, Colorado, Wyoming, and Utah relied upon chance encounters with eastbound travelers of varying reliability to carry letters to post offices within the States or (by the 1850s) to federal forts in the Territories. Somewhere halfway between Fort Childs and Fort Laramie, Charles Inman's wagon train encountered "a Mail carrier from the Salt lake" who offered to wait thirty minutes while letters were composed. Six members of the westward travel party contributed toward the dollar and fifty cents necessary to detain the envoy. "He will take this as far as St. Josephs Mo.," Inman explained to his wife. Ten days later Inman found an "opertunity of sending you a letter by paying 25^{cts} if the fellow dont lie."[9] Inman was not alone in his suspicions of unauthorized letter-carriers. Lucia Lorraine Williams wrote to her mother upon reaching Oregon in 1851 that she had sent her a letter through Fort Laramie via "a mountaineer calling himself the mail carrier but have since learned he was an imposter and that the others were in pursuit of him, so you may not have received that." A decade later Louisa Cook informed her mother that she had "sent a letter some 2 or 3 days ago to you but I am much afraid you will never get [it] as I sent it to an office by an emigrant a perfect stranger & on the plains one does not know who they can trust." Scams of this sort were not uncommon. Overland traveler Alonzo

Delano described a roadside sign promising to bring letters back to "the States" for half a dollar. "Many a half dollar was left," Delano recalled a few years after his 1849 journey, "but those letters which our company left for the friends never reached them, and it was only a pleasant ruse to gull travelers, and 'raise the wind.'" Even honest couriers might fail to deliver the mail, as several migrants acknowledged. In an 1846 letter to his father from Fort Hall, Charles Putnam allowed that some of his earlier missives may have perished en route, "for the persons who return to the States have no convenient way of carrying them, being on horseback." He had on several occasions during his travels witnessed the disheartening sight of "letters on the road broken open which were directed to the States." Undaunted, westward travelers turned optimistically to the kindness of unidentified strangers. In an unmanned post office informally established in 1846 on the North Fork of the Platte River, migrants deposited letters in a recess in the wall, hoping that other travelers would carry them back across the Missouri.[10]

Throughout the 1850s, post offices of all kinds sprouted up in the Plains Territories, and by the 1860s, as new states entered the Union, makeshift mailboxes began appearing on upright posts along the most-traveled roads so that letter carriers could deposit mail addressed to postal users living within a ten-mile radius.[11] For much of the antebellum era, however, postal access to the States was irregular, and patrons often had to engage expensive express services. Having moved in her late teens from Indianapolis to Nebraska and then to Colorado, Mollie Dorsey noted in her diary that in 1860 a letter between Indiana and Denver (in either direction) cost twenty-five cents at her end, and that consequently "we won't write every day."[12] Before 1851, postage to and from California was comparably prohibitive, and those without easy access to the post would often pay additional charges to private parties. A few months after reaching California, Charles Inman paid a man bound for Naperville, Illinois, fifty cents per letter to carry mail to that state. Inman and several others also paid five dollars each for someone to inquire for letters on their behalf in Sacramento and San Francisco. Stephen Chapin Davis, an enterprising teenager from Massachusetts who emigrated in 1850, conducted a brisk express business delivering letters to the mines, charging $1.50 for 40-cent letters mailed to San Francisco via steamer.[13]

In many respects, travelers to California from the eastern half of the continent during the decade following 1849 constituted a unique class of new postal users in American history. Gold-seekers, especially those from New England, the Mid-Atlantic, and the Midwest, journeyed to the San Francisco Bay and the foothills of the Sierras, and usually expected to return soon to their home communities with increased wealth and enhanced status. Unlike westward migrants who sold farms and uprooted families in search of cheap land (and more than forty-niners from China, Chile, France, or Australia), California-bound voyagers from the East were apt not to anticipate major disruptions in their social relationships. Moreover, the discovery of gold in California took place precisely at the historic moment when postal reductions and reforms were redefining the mail as a mass activity suitable means for maintaining long-distance relationships. And though in the initial years of the Gold Rush it was unclear how smoothly and effectively California would be incorporated into the expanded postal network, new American postal users at mid-century were well situated to imagine the possibility of maintaining their places at home even while living at a great distance.

Postal service between California and the eastern states was slow and relatively infrequent throughout the 1850s, especially in the period 1849–1851. For those in the diggings, a letter had to make it through a series of intermediate stages on its circuitous route over Panama, not least of which was the express company that brought letters from San Francisco to the mines. But even in cities on the bay, correspondents depended upon the schedule of Pacific Ocean steamers, which came either once or twice a month for much of the Gold Rush era. Deterred by high costs and concerned about the dependability of the mail, new arrivals in California sometimes sought ways around the post, but soon most accepted the place of the postal network in their lives. Forty-niners began advising their eastern correspondents to have faith in the system. "Never send by private hand—not if your own husband was the person," Franklin Buck instructed his sister in 1850, shortly after his arrival in Sacramento. Experience had already dissuaded Buck from pursuing that strategy. "The person always dies on the way, goes to the mines or to the devil." A few months later, David Dustin took a similar line with his brother. "I wish you to send all your letters by mail & not trust to *friends*, as it is very difficult to find acquaintances here, besides the liability of being detained on the way."[14] Neither of these admonitions amounted to a ringing endorsement of the post, and precautions were often in order. Frustrated by the failure of his wife's letters to reach him in San Francisco, Benjamin Wingate urged her to send letters to New York well in advance of the steamer's scheduled departure and even encouraged her to send two copies of her letters via rival express companies.[15]

Newly arrived Californians continually assured friends and family back home that any lapse in communication was the "fault of the mails" and generously invoked the same explanation to excuse their correspondents' apparent failures to write more frequently.[16]

Despite the lapses, lags, and surcharges that made postal communication to and from California more difficult than many American migrants had recently come to expect, the post was a central feature of the Gold Rush experience. Surviving samples of Gold Rush correspondence, which form an extraordinarily voluminous epistolary archive, bear witness to the tenacity with which fortune seekers maintained contact with absent friends and, especially, family. Letters sent eastward did not simply express love and longing; they performed a range of practical functions that bound Americans in California to the places they called home. First and foremost, posted letters bore money, in the form of banknotes, drafts, and specks of gold. Money was, of course, a staple of postal exchange in mid-century America, but in the case of the Gold Rush the transmission of money played a particularly meaningful role in maintaining the unity and identity of the family. Men who left their families with the promise to return could reaffirm their status as temporary travelers acting on behalf of an economic unit back in Vermont, New York, or Illinois.[17] One might even compare the posting of money during the Gold Rush to the wages sent home by mill girls at Lowell to their families on New England farms. The crucial difference, of course, was that gold-seekers were typically adult males who sent back money sporadically and often unexpectedly to families over which they exerted economic control. Still, sometimes, the flow of money could go in the other direction. More typically, discussions of money in Gold Rush correspondence were framed by the prospect that the California party might at any moment send a large sum. "I have no money in hand to day," Benjamin Wingate informed his wife in January, 1854, "but expect to receive $250 next week & will send it to you by the mail of Feb. 1 so that you will have it about the 1st March."[18]

Promises of sending money were, to be sure, embedded in larger emotional negotiations through which separated family members adjusted to the unusual circumstances of the Gold Rush. But they were also crucial to the process by which the mail allowed displaced heads of household to participate in the conduct of affairs back home. Letters between husbands and wives, parents and children, and brothers and sisters routinely took up the details of daily economic life. Thomas Megquier, a New England doctor who traveled back and forth with his wife between

Maine and California, would send explicit directions to his son-in-law on how to manage the family farm:

> [L]et Deacon Cole take the cow, if he will, or some other one, & hire the colt wintered & pay the money & let the hay in the barn remain & if it is thought best in the Spring to sell, do so & not have it taken out by small parcels & by different persons. If you have not found a tenant before this, you had better write Milton, (If it is not already done) to have the barn fastened up securely & windows boarded.... I wrote John Morrill to be sure to leave the fences secure, but I think he must have left before receiving the letter.[19]

Benjamin and Mary Wingate engaged in detailed discussions of whether she should pay a postage bill to a local storeowner in Connecticut.[20] Forty-niners were equally insistent on maintaining their other roles, admonishing children to be good, to practice their writing, or to observe the Sabbath.[21] Benjamin Wingate even saw fit to remind his wife about her oral hygiene. Do not, "on any account, neglect your *teeth*," he implored. "You know they have a strong tendency to early decay; and if you do not clean them regularly and carefully, and have the cavities filled as soon as they occur, you will loose [*sic*] them."[22]

Displaced Californians used the mail to bridge the geographical gap in other ways as well, insinuating themselves into the worlds of their correspondents. Franklin Buck's letters to his sister in Bucksport, Maine strike a defiant note of continued engagement, even as his stay in California stretched beyond what he might have initially imagined. "Talk to me about a man's forgetting old times and losing his interest in his home and friends—it is all humbug," he assured her toward the end of 1849. "The farther I am removed from you and the longer I stay, mine increases." Supplied by her letters with a steady stream of local information, Buck took some satisfaction in being "posted up on events from down East, to the latest dates," and offered her his thoughts on the most recent town gossip. Two years later, working in the mines, he continued to request that she describe "all the affairs in and about Bucksport as anything will be interesting." In 1853 he was playfully asking her to submit specific propositions to the Bucksport Lyceum for discussion. His fellow miners had debated (inconclusively) the night before such questions as whether a bat is a bird or "Does not whisky preserve some men while it kills off others?" and they decided to refer them to the folks back home. "Please answer by next mail," he added.[23]

Beyond soliciting and exchanging the sorts of local details that might make them feel closer to home, forty-niners and their families turned to the mail for visual access to one another. Most commonly, new arrivals in California posed for daguerreotype portraits and posted them to loved ones. Daguerreotyping, introduced in the United States in the decade prior to the Gold Rush, flourished as a trade in California, particularly in San Francisco, where portrait studios lined the central streets near Portsmouth Square.[24] Correspondents on both sides of the Sierras waxed poetic about the significance of these miniature photographs— "likenesses," as they most frequently called them—and elaborated fantasies around the specter of presence that daguerreotypes evoked. "I am only sorry that it is not the original that is to go and the likeness to remain," one miner wrote to his fiancée. She received the portrait with "unexpected joy," observing that her absent beloved "could have sent nothing but yourself, that would have been half so acceptable." Another forty-niner informed his wife that he stared at her likeness "generally when I go to bed and when I rise. . . . I enjoy looking at you much."[25]

Gold Rush correspondents were not simply interested in iconic keepsakes or erotic visual aids. They also wished to track changes and developments in the physical appearance of loved ones whom they could not otherwise see. This was especially important in the case of very young children. Mary Wingate mailed a daguerreotype of their daughter to Benjamin, but cautioned him that the camera could not capture the "roguish twinkle in her eye" when she played. Such disclaimers appeared frequently in the letters that included portraits. The sender often apologized for the sobriety of the image or insisted that it failed to do the sitter justice. Responding to critical comments by his sister, Franklin Buck defended his portrait, but saw fit to add that "my friends say it looks rather older than the original. Sarah says more care worn." Another brother's letter relayed his friends' positive assessment of the portrait he enclosed, but assured his sister that he was capable of better: "I have been very much disposed to send one taken in my hat, which is white and really makes a beautiful contrast in the picture. Still I shall reserve this and you may see it one of these days." Yet another new arrival in San Francisco deferred the portrait altogether. "I would send you my Daguerretype by this letter if I was in good trim," he explained to his sister, "but I am very poor in flesh." He assured her that he was rapidly gaining weight, though, and that "as soon as I look decent I will send it and when I do I want you to send me yours."[26] Daguerreotypes facilitated a certain kind of discourse about the vicissitudes of weight and hairstyle (one correspondent predicted that his likeness would prompt tonsorial criticism from his mother—"Mother dear it is expensive here to visit the barber," he remonstrated preemptively).[27] But even when daguerreotypes were not enclosed, forty-niners used the post to keep their correspondents up-to-date on changes in appearance. Young Henry Perry, writing to his parents in Connecticut from a mid-journey stop in Rio de Janeiro in 1849, assured his mother that he now weighed 140 and 1/2 pounds, "10 lbs more than I weighed the day before I left new York."[28]

Images and descriptions of California bodies were matched by visual representations of the physical surroundings in which new arrivals found themselves. Some forty-niners drew pictures of their homes (real and imagined) and even their neighbors.[29] Those not inclined to produce original artwork could still provide visual access to curious family and friends back home. Many of the personal letters posted from San Francisco and the mines appeared on illuminated stationery. Sold in enormous quantities throughout the 1850s, pictorial letter sheets and illustrated envelopes provided the principal visual access to life in and around the Gold Rush for correspondents from all over the world (and they remain, in the words of their leading curator, "the major surviving visual account of California in that era").[30] Ranging in price from ten to fifty cents, letter sheets were especially popular in the first half of the decade, when postage to California was still assessed on the basis of sheets rather than weight and a single piece of foldable and addressable stationery had additional advantages. Many of these sheets were almost entirely covered (at least on one side) with archetypical images of miners, picturesque views of California flora and fauna, and vignettes of California life, including numerous takes on the spectacle of mail steamers arriving in the harbor or forty-niners gathering at the post office (see fig. 6), leaving little room for long letters. One miner writing from Murphy's in 1854 admitted that pictorial stationery was popular with forty-niners inasmuch "as it helps to fill out the sheet & thereby save the trouble of writing long letters which by many is considered a great task."[31] Though the full extent of their popularity is hard to reconstruct, the volume of illustrated stationery purchased during the early years of the Gold Rush was clearly considerable. The publisher of "The Miner's Ten Commandments," one of the most famous of the few hundred different pieces that have survived (see fig. 7) later claimed to have sold ninety-seven thousand copies of that image alone during a period of roughly one year in 1853–54. A Sacramento bookseller boasted in 1858 of a collection of ten thousand "assorted California letter sheets." The significant business done by publishers and stationers confirms the popularity of postal correspondence in and around mid-century San Francisco. More specifically, cheap lithographic pictures designed for postal exchange catered to the desire of new (and putatively temporary) Californians to

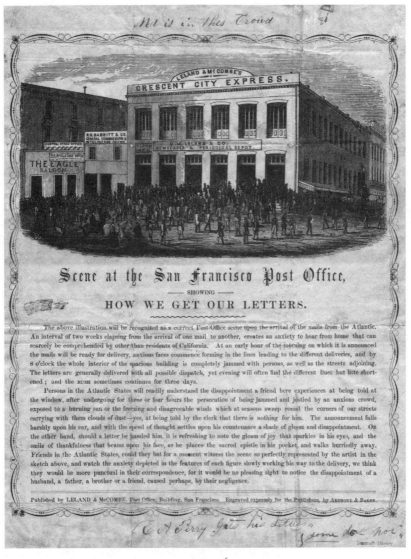

— FIGURE 6 —

LETTER SHEET FROM 1854 DEPICTING SCENE AT THE SAN FRANCISCO POST
OFFICE, WITH NOTATION BY ITS USER. (COURTESY OF THE BANCROFT LIBRARY,
UNIVERSITY OF CALIFORNIA, BERKELEY, BANC PIC 1963.002:0137 (VARIANT)-A.)

maintain the sort of immediate visual contact that the post seemed to
offer.[32]

The letter sheets and illustrated envelopes published, purchased, and
posted in San Francisco were early model postcards—not by philatelic
criteria, of course, but insofar as they introduced and popularized the

— FIGURE 7 —
"THE MINER'S TEN COMMANDMENTS," 1853 LETTER SHEET.

link between mail and preprinted visual representation. Like the picture postcard (which first became popular in the United States at the end of the century) the letter sheet bore the traveler's implicit claim to have encountered scenes of interest to friends and family back home. Soon after arriving in California, Mary Jane Megquier wrote to her friend

Milton Benjamin in Maine, somewhat at a loss for how to gratify the curiosity of those at home about life on the West Coast. "I know not what to say now that will be interesting after so much has been written about Cal. but we send you a very fine view of the bay." Megquier's stationery anticipated—and served—one of the principal purposes of correspondence during the Gold Rush.

Like daguerreotype portraits, images of California shaped the meaning of postal exchange by enabling correspondents back home to imagine themselves close to their displaced loved ones. Mary Wingate expressed to her husband "a great desire to know in what part of the city your residence is so that we can find it on [the] picture you sent me." One sentence later she pushed the fantasy to its predictable next step. "How I wish I could be in your room to night when you come home if it was only for a few minutes." On other occasions Wingate asked her husband for maps and pictures of San Francisco and California so that she could see "the place where you spend most of your time."[33] Upon receiving a letter from her forty-niner husband, Chastina Rix took some solace in learning of his work, "for now I can know something what his daily business will be." Though she longed to be "*there*" (emphasis in original), of course, she could not. Still Rix saw fit to conclude her description of the letter by mentioning that Alfred sent "five dollars and some engravings of San Francisco."[34] Portable (and mailable) paper images were central to the value of the post as a medium connecting parties who did not expect physical separation to disrupt social ties.

Given the circumstances and timing of the Gold Rush migration, it is not surprising that so many of the new arrivals spoke explicitly and plaintively about their desire for correspondence. Nor is it surprising that this extraordinary dependence on the post for contact with distant homes focused a great deal of attention on the times and places at which mail arrived from the eastern states. In the days following the arrival of mail steamers, post offices in San Francisco and Sacramento were sites of spectacular congestion. Contemporary published accounts of the Gold Rush painted scenes of long lines snaking around the block, crowds surrounding the building, and even broken windows. Bayard Taylor's *Eldorado*, one of the early classics of this genre, offered readers a detailed view of the San Francisco post office in 1849, documenting the handling of a summer's worth of mail that arrived on board the *Panama* that October. "The excitement and anxiety of the public can scarcely be told in words," Taylor explained. "Where the source that governs business, satisfies affection, and supplies intelligence had been shut off from a whole community for three months, the rush from all sides to supply the void was irresistible." Taylor's unrelated namesake, the Reverend William Taylor, called the San Francisco post office "the greatest local attraction of the heterogeneous masses." Hubert Howe Bancroft, who came to San Francisco in 1852, characterized the "feverish, fidgety days" when mail steamers came and went as "the great tickings in social and commercial time," and waxed poetic about the "nervous pulsations" that gripped the entire population in anticipation of a citywide mail call. "The ordinary routine of business was suspended," recalled a local guide in the 1870s, "and the city was in a commotion."[35]

With some sixty thousand letters arriving on each steamer in the early years of the Gold Rush (and almost as many departing), the post office bore powerful witness to the role of mail in mid-century San Francisco. Perhaps no image was so central to contemporary fascination with this subject as the long lines outside the post office. In 1849 these lines could extend for blocks—"all the way down the hill into Portsmouth Square, and on the south side across Sacramento Street to the tents among the chaparral"—and the wait could last six hours. Three years later, Bancroft reported, lines still "led into and far up and down the street" and formed as much as twenty hours before the office opened. "So anxious were many to receive their epistles," observed another contemporary publication, "that they posted themselves in the evening of one day to be early at the window on the morning of the next, standing all night in the mud, with a heavy rain pouring down upon their heads."[36]

More compelling, even, than the length or duration of these lines was the eagerness attributed to those expecting mail. Tales of men offering money for a better position in line became standard anecdotes in Gold Rush journalism and memoirs. Bayard Taylor wrote of "impatient" postal users paying bounties of "ten and even twenty-five dollars" to those at the front, and other reports cite similar figures. The 1855 *Annals of San Francisco* claimed that "many clever persons made large sums regularly by" selling their places in line. Methodist minister John Steele's description of the crowding outside the Sacramento post office includes the same claim, but tells of being offered as much as fifty dollars for his spot and reports that "even a hundred dollars had been paid for a place near the delivery" in that city.[37] More often than not, descriptions of post office lines during the Gold Rush insisted that these astounding sums were refused. Looking back from the end of the 1860s, a nostalgic report from San Francisco recalled the days when "five, ten, fifteen dollars would often be offered to men who were ragged, hungry, and dirty, but it rarely tempted them."[38] Forty-niners were especially insistent upon this point in their letters home. Robert Smith Lammot wrote to his father about a failed transaction he had witnessed. A man at the end of a long postal line had tried to purchase a better position for fifteen dollars, but was told it could only be had for twenty-five. John McCrackan proudly told his family that he had responded to a bid of sixteen dollars by declaring "that as many hundred could not keep me from my letters ten minutes." John D. Mitchell offered similar testimony. "A man did offer me $10 for my place after I got within 12 of the delivery box," he informed his family, "but I told him I would not sell out for 50, and if any one had offered me $1000 for my letters before I opened them, I mean I would not have taken it."[39]

Such stories might have been read back home as signs of Gold Rush inflation or as further evidence of the money-making opportunities in California, but witnesses told and retold these post office tales to emphasize how desperate transplanted Americans were for contact by mail. Testimony about outlandish offers of money rejected by expectant recipients was part of a larger thematic insistence by gold-seekers that mail from friends and (especially) family were priceless. "How insignificant seems the postage," John McCrackan wrote to his sister, "if it were ten dollars an ounce for every letter, how readily would I pay it to hear from the dear ones in my distant home." J. M. Alexander assured his wife that he "would give anything I have to get a letter" from her. Thomas Megquier told his cousin that letters from her were "better than gold to us." Charles Mulford implored family members to write often, "as we trust each steamer will bring from each of you packages more precious than Gold dust."[40] In the face of imminent epistolary connection with loved ones, these writers implied, gold seemed to diminish in value.

Comparisons between mail and gold were fraught, however, and assertions that no amount of money could outweigh the pleasures of postal contact risked appearing disingenuous to readers at home. After all, the young men who left families in New Hampshire, Missouri, or New York for mining expeditions or related entrepreneurial opportunities had made precisely the calculation they were now calling into question. What did it mean for men who had left the company of parents, wives, siblings, and children in search of riches to insist that letters from home were as precious as gold? The cavalier attitudes of middle-class American forty-niners toward pecuniary considerations when it came to keeping in touch with home may well have reflected a certain degree of guilt or discomfort about choosing to go to California in the first place. Their frequent allusions, however romantic or mystifying, to the relationship between letters and money may also have marked an uneasy awareness of the way in which wealth could become the unarticulated (or underarticulated) subject or object of Gold Rush correspondence. An 1853 article in the *San Francisco Daily Evening News* captured this phenomenon neatly, reprinting a story from a Columbia paper in which a forty-niner whose letters home had gone unanswered for months devised a plan to drum up mail:

> He accordingly sat down and wrote some half-dozen letters to different persons at home, inquiring the price of land, and stock, what he could buy a handsome farm of 200 or 300 acres for, &c; intimating that he had large sums to invest, and was very rich, generally. By return mail he received no less than *seven* letters, all anxiously inquiring after his health, when he was coming home, &c.; and has received three or four every mail since; including some very *warm* ones from an *old* and very *cold sweet-heart*.[41]

Letters, as both sides of the exchange understood, could maintain financial ties through major shifts in fortune and could serve as investments in the quest for gold.

Though individual correspondents may have had various motives for calculating the exchange rate between gold and mail, the trope of the otherwise acquisitive forty-niner undone by his desire for letters was part of the larger cultural construction of epistolary intimacy. The mining communities and instant cities of mid-century California were famously characterized by lopsided sex ratios, and in the mythology of the Gold Rush, personal letters, especially those written by women, became cultural emissaries to a rugged masculine world. Bancroft was particularly unabashed in celebrating the Gold Rush mail call in these terms. Letters from home were "like angels' visits . . . sweet silent messages, whose witching presence can so wean our sordid vision from the seducing mirage of glittering dust!"[42] Other commentators joined the chorus, remarking upon the positive moral influence wrought by these epistolary interventions from a purer realm of middle-class domesticity. Letters from home (and of course letters were crucial to defining what and where home was) did not simply distract the forty-niner from his pursuit of wealth, according to the authors of *The Annals of San Francisco*; they effected a personal transformation eerily resembling a conversion experience. Every word of the letter "awakens in his mind some tender reminiscence. He is now communing with dearest idols of his heart." To the observer at the post office, the source of this inspiration is uncertain, but the gender can be presumed, and the effect is palpable: "The lines upon which his eyes are riveted, were written perhaps by an absent wife, and they have made him already a better man than he was an hour before."[43]

Testimonials to the salutary moral influence of correspondence typically stressed the capacity of letters from wives, mothers, and sisters to curb the nasty habits to which white, middle-class men in California were reputedly prone. Both Bancroft and the *Annals* make much of the example of a respectable middle-aged church member from back East who had drifted away, in Bancroft's telling, from "high religious sentiments and moral purity" and become a gambler, an atheist, and a customer of prostitutes. But when a letter arrives from his wife, "telling him of her deep abiding love, of her patient waitings and watchings, of her deeds by day and her dreams by night, of the hopes and plans that await his dear return; telling of his children one by one, how they have grown in goodness and loveliness, how the little one, whom he has never seen, has learned to lisp its father's name in its evening prayer," he loses his composure and vows to mend his ways. "That night does not find him in the gambling-house, nor elsewhere in search of amusement." That the man later backslides (at least in one version of the story) only reinforces the suggestion that the letter was immediate and almost mystical in its impact—rather than a timely reminder of his enduring value system. In a sense the moral power of the letter was intrinsic to it. Even after a first reading, Bancroft wrote, the letters he received from home "lay filling the room as with a spiritual attendance, throwing their magical influence into every fibre of my being."[44] For a geographically displaced and morally vulnerable male population, writers like Bancroft believed, personal letters were both monitory and regenerative.

Conversely, the failure of a letter to arrive could have disastrous moral consequences. Enos Christman wrote of a young man whose distress in not receiving mail induced him to "raise his voice in blasphemy and swear his friends had forgotten him and cared nothing about him." The next step followed the cultural logic of nineteenth-century ideologies of domesticity: "He called his companions to the bar and they all enjoyed a drunken revel." Christman's fiancée Ellen Apple wrote to him in 1851 that she had heard about men in California turning to "intoxicating drink to enable them to bear the disappointments" of not receiving mail from home.[45] Charles Thompson described an analogous experience in a letter to his uncle. Having gone to the post office and found no letters from his family, he "went straight to the gambling table, and an exciting line I had of it I can assure you." After losing all of his money, Thompson then had to bear the added insult of returning to the office a couple of days later to receive letters from home, including one "giving me good advice, & speaking of the temptations to gamble in this country."[46]

Such explanations of the importance of correspondence have a conventional ring to them, but the widespread celebration of letters in Gold Rush mythology was more ambitious and profound than might at first appear. As icons and instruments of domesticity, letters from home did not simply wield a restraining influence on the vices of new Californians by reminding them of their cultural origins. Mail was invested with powers of physical transformation. At California post offices, observers repeatedly stressed, the contents of sealed, private, epistles became legible in the countenances of their recipients. One telling of the story of the lapsed Easterner receiving a letter from home describes the "unusual twitching of the muscles of the mouth, a growing dimness of the eyes, and tears . . . rapidly tracing down the furrows of his sunburnt cheeks," while the other notes the "twitching of the muscles in his face, the tears trickling down his cheeks, and the bosom swelling with emotion."[47] Enos Christman wrote of "a huge fellow" on the letter line who exhibited "the appearance of a ruffian without a tender spot in his composition." But after paying for his letter and reading it, the man completely metamorphosed. "In a few minutes I looked around again and saw this same burly, stern-looking man, who looked as hard as adamant, *in tears.*"[48] Tears were, of course, the ultimate sign that a letter from home had found its target. John Steele observed weeping miners at the post office on Coloma in 1853, while Stephen Chapin Davis spotted tears not on the cheeks of those who got mail in San Francisco but among those disappointed mail seekers who had to watch their fellows "reading epistles of friendship and constancy penned in the fine hand of a female."[49] The arrival of letters in California became the occasion for a middle-class narrative about gender in which problematically masculine men become domesticated, reformed, even feminized—almost against their will—by the virtual presence of women, represented metonymically by their handwriting.

All of these depictions and experiences of Gold Rush correspondence signaled and reinforced a deep belief in the capacity of personal letters to transmit the emotional content of domestic relations over distance. While the codes and ideals of epistolary intimacy discussed in the previous chapter emphasized self-possession, self-presentation, and romantic connection, celebrations of the personal letter in and around the Gold Rush ultimately pointed to the nineteenth-century ideal of the family—a compact, bounded unit of blood and marital relatives connected through links of affection and influence—as the crucial and sacred site for intimate correspondence. The sanctification of letter-writing during the middle of the century and its legitimization as an appropriate Sabbath activity depended on the attitudes toward mail and family that surfaced conspicuously in mid-century California. "As the work of cleansing my-self of a weeks dirt kept me till I was too late to go to church this fore-noon," a gold miner wrote to his wife, "I have set myself to the next most sacred duty I could think of—that of writing to my family." Franklin Buck also thought Sunday an especially apt time to perform family obli-gations, instructing his sister soon after his arrival in California to des-ignate that day for regular correspondence with him.[50]

The California Gold Rush was, of course, an extraordinary event, and the effusions and pieties that surrounded the mail were responses to an unusual set of circumstances. Still, as an object of national fascination, the Gold Rush was a major event in the development of popular un-derstanding of the possibilities and purposes of the newly inclusive post. While the proportion of Americans who seriously considered moving to California may have been negligible, the spectacle of the San Francisco post office and the mythology of the personal letter were hardly confined to the forty-niners and their correspondents. The rough coincidence of postal reform and the Gold Rush presented a nationwide audience, most of whom had no stake in the price of postage from California or the steamer schedule to the West Coast, with a dramatic demonstration of how the mail could be used to maintain relationships over remarkable distances. That demonstration included a great deal of cultural prescrip-tion about the content, emotional impact, and moral significance that letters could have, particularly in the context of a dispersed family unit.

The one major event during this period that had a greater impact on popular understandings of the post was the American Civil War. Both sides in the conflict fielded armies that were literate without prece-dent in prior military history. Moreover, the men who fought in the Civil War had grown up during the revolutionary changes in postage and had gone to war with expectations that traveling to the front would not mean severing communication with friends and family. Like the men who left home during the Gold Rush, Civil War soldiers hoped (des-perately) to return to their homes and therefore saw their displacement from friends and family as temporary. Far more than the forty-niners, Union and Confederate personnel came from all sections, sectors, and walks of American life, and they mobilized in numbers that dwarfed the California-bound migrations of 1849–1856. Accordingly, the volume of mail generated by the war exceeded anything produced during the Gold Rush or by any other mass mobilization in the nineteenth century. By one estimate, a hundred and eighty thousand letters a day were sent or received by soldiers in the Civil War.[51]

One result of this phenomenal postal outpouring is the survival of an unparalleled epistolary record of the conflict. The published letters alone could fill several cases of stack space. Historians of the Civil War have mined these letters and countless others preserved in manuscript collections, local historical societies, and private holdings for bits of evidence about the nature of the soldiering experience, the course of the campaigns, the motivations of individual participants, and even the causes of the war. What has gone unnoticed in this high tide of archival documentation is the simple phenomenon of mass military correspondence. More than in any previous war, using the postal network was a major part of the Civil War experience, both for those who fought and for those who followed the conflict through correspondence with men (and, to a much lesser extent, women) at the front.

For soldiers and other military personnel, the existence of a widespread, affordable, and broadly inclusive postal network allowed regular contact with their home communities. "If you went into any camp at any time," observed Mary Livermore, a Union Army nurse who worked in the Sanitary Commission, "you would see dozens, and sometimes hundreds, of soldiers writing letters. Some would be stretched at full length on the ground, with a book or a knapsack for a table—some sitting upright against the trunks of trees, with the paper resting on their drawn-up knees—others would stand and write."[52] In addition to providing solace and distraction, the post allowed soldiers to present themselves before an eager audience back home. As Union surgeon Daniel Holt explained to his wife at the beginning of an unusually brief letter from Virginia in 1863, he was corresponding "for two purposes—one to keep *your* spirits up and another to keep *mine* up."[53] Back home, families and friends waited for mail with "anxious expectation," since letters from the front were not only means of continuous connection but signs of life. And the high volumes of mail posted by soldiers further raised such anxious expectations when no letters appeared. "We were quite disappointed at the nonarrival of your letter this morning," Adelaide Fowler of Massachusetts remarked to her brother on the front, "because we have been accustomed to receive them so regularly."[54] While the Mexican War had been the first U.S. military conflict whose progress could be followed in the newspapers (aided by telegraph lines, which by the end of the war connected cities up and down the eastern seaboard), ordinary Americans had a new kind of access to the Civil War via the postal correspondence of individual soldiers.

Civil War letters did not only connect immediate family members. George Drake of Illinois, a teenager during the fighting, described to his parents a "lottery" of sorts held among his fellow soldiers. Eager for "something to do," every man submitted the name and address of a woman ("nothing but virtuous women," he assured them), and the men wrote letters to whomever they drew. A couple of months later Drake also began writing to a woman with whom he had never corresponded before but who had been a correspondent of a friend in his company.[55] William Allen Clark, another young Union Army recruit from the Midwest, complained to his parents in 1863 that he had less reading material at hand ever since he "Curtailed some of [his] Correspondence." Having found that he was receiving letters from people who wished only to "have something to Story about," Clark pursued a new policy of protecting his reputation "by writing only to those that I know to be my friends."[56] Soldiers found themselves in postal proximity to any civilian with a known name and hometown, and to any civilian who knew their name and military unit.

All of this correspondence created an enormous demand for letter-writing materials among soldiers. One index of this demand was the high volume of postal materials produced and consumed during the war, especially on the Union side. Illustrated envelopes celebrating the Northern cause bore mottos, pictures of Union commanders, and various patriotic images. Unlike the pictorial letter sheets of the Gold Rush years, the function of this stationery was not to help soldiers provide their correspondents with visual access to the battlefront. As a three-volume history of the conflict issued shortly after the Confederate surrender pointed out, the use of war-related envelopes amounted to a mass patriotic expression that began soon after Lincoln's war proclamation. Using these envelopes, more than four thousand different types of which appeared within a matter of weeks, "became a passion . . . a phenomenon of the times," and soon after the war they became artifacts of an earlier moment.[57] Their use was clearly not limited to correspondence with the front, though many soldiers enclosed their letters in patriotic paraphernalia. More broadly, ordinary patrons in the North used them to register their support of the war effort in everyday correspondence.

Other materials were more essential to the letter-writing habits of soldiers. Paper and writing implements were always necessary, but during the Civil War soldiers had to carry them (one war novel noted that "soldiers always carry writing materials on a march") and noted often the struggle to keep them at hand. "Wife when you write to me always put in one extra sheet of paper for me to write Back to you on," wrote Confederate infantryman Richard Henry Brooks, "for it Looks Like I cant get any to write on here nor from home either." Requests for pens, pencils, and paper were standard in letters home, and the care packages or "comfort bags" sent to wounded servicemen seldom omitted these crucial items. Postage stamps were equally pressing necessities, since, unlike the westward migrants of the Gold Rush period, prepayment was mandatory for the men who mobilized during the war. Massachusetts artilleryman John Billings recollected that Union soldiers had typically left for the war with "large quantities" of stamps, which were circulating as scrip in many places in the North, but often had trouble maintaining them in usable condition. "Many an old soldier can recall his disgust on finding what a mess his stamps were in either from rain, perspiration, or compression, as he attempted, after a hot march, to get one for a letter. If he could split off one from a welded mass of perhaps a hundred or more, he counted himself fortunate." Soldiers could replenish their supply of stamps only if they had access to post offices or to the right vendors. According to one report, $700 worth of stamps were sold in one day at the Pittsburgh post office prior to the battle of Shiloh.[58] As Union soldiers got further from U.S. post offices, things could get trickier. One Confederate source reported that in the South a single U.S. postage stamp would sell for a dollar and fifty cents in Confederate currency—an exchange rate that may have reflected more than just the depreciation of Southern money.[59]

Union officers could have their letters franked, and other soldiers could use their franks to transfer postage costs to the addressee. Eunice Snow of Connecticut advised her son Henry that he need not stamp his letters to her "when you are short," since "they will let soldiers send them without it," but this practice, which was sanctioned by the postmaster general, does not appear to have been widely adopted except as a last resort.[60] Letters from the front begged for stamps and routinely cited their scarcity as an excuse for not writing. Army surgeon William Watson of Pennsylvania complained of rampant theft among the troops and confessed to having "not one cent of money—nor one postage stamp. The latter cannot be gotten for either love or money," he explained. "I will try to borrow one—and if I fail I will have to get this letter franked. Don't like to do it—'But necessity knows no law.'"[61]

Soldiers did their best to make do with limited postal supplies and constrained opportunities for correspondence. Indiana infantryman William Allen Clark occasionally made ink out of gunpowder and blackberry juice. Confederate surgeon Junius Bragg apologized repeatedly to his fiancée for not having the right paper and complained on one occasion of having to write his letter "on the lid of the Medicine chest." William Walker, an enlisted man from Northampton, shared Bragg's discomfort with having to use official government paper for his personal letters, and Union soldier Charles Boyle also wrote of having to compose in an uncomfortable position ("lying on my back under a shelter constructed of logs & rails"). Confederate infantryman Peter Dekle explained to his wife that he was "writing now on my Knee and it are raining hard as it do for Common and ever thing are wet and the paper are wet . . . and it are past midKnight but it are my chance to wright to you." Soldiers described these inconveniences not only to excuse less frequent correspondence but also to add value to the many letters they did send. Leaning on a log four miles south of the Maryland-Pennsylvania border, Dr. Daniel Holt made this reckoning explicit in a letter to his wife: "If the satisfaction of receiving a letter is commensurate with the trouble, oftentimes, of writing it, they will always be welcome visitors, for, unlike home, where every convenience is at hand for writing, we are compelled to resort to all kinds of expedients to indict a few lines to anxious ones at home."[62]

Despite physical inconveniences and material impediments, in many respects Civil War soldiers enjoyed broad and unconstrained access to the post. Unlike those sent during many later wars, soldiers' letters were not screened through an established censorship apparatus. To be sure, soldiers did worry about exposing military secrets, especially given the possibility that their letters could wind up in enemy hands. Describing the movements of his company in a letter to his father, William Allen Clark reminded himself to "be careful about writing anything Contraband." Sam Evans, a white soldier from Ohio who served as an officer in a colored regiment, also omitted details of troop movements in his letters home, noting that "it would be contraband news and the authorities are very strict just now on that subject."[63] Because letters would sometimes circulate within a company, they were subject to a fair amount of unofficial scrutiny. William Vermilion, an officer in the Iowa infantry, wrote to his wife about a fellow officer who "was in the habit of writing letters home for the boys, which he always filled with *treason*." Not surprisingly, military prisons did censor mail prior to exchanging letters with the other side under a flag of truce, and captured soldiers typically faced additional constraints in their correspondence. Imprisoned Union soldier James Higginson observed that "under such a censorship as our letters are subject to, nothing specially interesting can be told," and in one Confederate prison Union captives were reputedly restricted to letters of six lines. For the most part, however, soldiers' letters bear little visible trace of the mediation or interposition of military administration.[64]

In general, the surviving correspondence of Civil War personnel suggests a relationship to writing, receiving, and expecting mail that was heightened, but not fundamentally transformed, by the extraordinary circumstances of mobilization and war. As in the case of the Gold Rush migration, war correspondence showed a fascinated impatience with the speed at which letters traveled and a gnawing anxiety that letters were miscarrying or disappearing. Soldiers were even more likely than forty-niners (or than their contemporaries) to begin letters with a dated acknowledgment of the receipt of mail from the addressee,[65] but such notices of success could never fully quiet concerns about postal failure, especially since the specter of death and disappearance haunted every letter and every postal silence. Ordinary worries about the mail grew easily under such conditions. "I sent you one letter yesterday," military nurse Cornelia Hancock wrote to her sister, but "perhaps it fell into that place from whence letters are never issued, so I write this to you to tell my whereabouts."[66] If epistolary communication chronically evoked fears of dead letters and dead correspondents, the massive mobilization of Americans during the war fleshed out these fears.[67]

At the same time, Civil War correspondence underscores how the post could provide access to distant friends and family in mid-nineteenth-century America. All of the uses to which displaced Californians had put the mail a decade earlier figured in the everyday postal habits of soldiers and their correspondents: they transferred money, exchanged photographic portraits, sent agricultural samples, and drew hospital layouts. Less concretely, men away from home relied upon letters to exercise paternal authority or otherwise manage family relations, much as their counterparts had during the Gold Rush. "Sell that heifer if you can," an officer stationed in Arkansas advised his wife in Iowa. A Georgian officer in Tennessee confirmed that his wife's "purchase of the hides was very judicious." Much in the same spirit, a Confederate soldier in Virginia preached obedience to his children in Georgia: "You must attend to everything but especially your Mother, as I should be deeply mortified for her to write me [to the contrary]."[68] And with at least as much pathos as lonesome California adventurers, Civil War soldiers described scenes of anticipation and disappointment as they turned "with a wishful eye and palpitating heart for the mail."[69]

Perhaps the most striking similarity between the Gold Rush and the Civil War as episodes in the cultural history of the U.S. mail lay in the wartime rehearsal of the trope of personal letters as vehicles of regenerative (and typically feminine) moral influence. "You can have no idea what a blessing letters from home are to the men in camp," wrote one soldier. "They make us better men, better soldiers." No matter how bad the food or how fatiguing the duty, when the "mail boy brings a letter—a good long one from you, or from mother, or from some of the dear girls on the West Side," happiness prevails. Moreover, the effect is predictably transformative:

> One of our men was drunk, and fought and swore so shockingly, day before yesterday, that we had to send him to the guard-house. To-night he is taking a good repenting cry between the blankets. Do you know why? He got a letter this afternoon from his mother, and I have no doubt that she spoke of the Sabbath-school, the church, and the prayer she used to say when a little fellow at home, when his mother tucked him in bed.[70]

Other military personnel gave similar accounts of the salutary effects of personal mail. Daniel Holt suspected that "old-fashioned and inspiring letters from home," which he mystified as "breathings from the spirit land," made men better fighters and discouraged desertion. Such letters, observed one soldier, spoke "in louder tones than those of the press or pulpit and bid him resist these evil influences and keep himself pure."[71]

More commonly, the effect of letters from friends and family was thought to be monitory and domesticating. In some fairly practical ways, letters to and from the front could subject soldiers' lives to the scrutiny of those back home. Soldiers who sought to escape the expectations of parents or commitments to wives and lovers might be forced to defend themselves against incriminating information (or misinformation) sent home in the correspondence of their fellows and relayed to them through the mail. Sam Evans learned from his cousin Jane that rumors were circulating back home in Ohio about his sex life in the army. "I heared that you had an old darky woman to cook for you and wash for you, and slept with her," she wrote to him in 1862. "I do not believe any such tales, but I thought I would tell you about it. There has bin some mighty bad Tales or anecdotes told on some of you boys here lately." As historian Reid Mitchell has observed, military life "provided little escape from the prying eyes of small-town America."[72] The moral influence of the mail call extended far beyond such practical forms of surveillance, however. In terms reminiscent of the Gold Rush era, soldiers described themselves and their comrades as softened and feminized by the arrival of mail. "I have not shad tears but twice since I left Home," wrote one man to his wife, "& that was when I received your letters." When soldiers were away from camp and out of postal contact, another soldier observed, "they become profane and boisterous, some of them obscene and quarrelsome." But when they return to find a big mail, providing the whole company with "letters and papers from mothers, wives, sisters, and friends," the immediate impact could be quite remarkable: "A great quietness falls on the men; they become subdued and gentle in manner; there is a cessation of vulgarity and profanity, and an indescribable softening and tenderness is *felt*, rather than perceived, among them. Those who were ready to shoot one another a few hours before are seen talking . . . and walking together, sometimes with their arms around one another."[73] Even the pressures of battle and the coarsening effects of military life would give way, soldiers insisted, to the moral force of the letter from home.

Subdued, tender men wrapped in each other's arms served as an extraordinarily vivid demonstration of the transformative power of a certain kind of mail, and it is tempting to read in such images a sort of fantasy particular to the experience war or at least to the masculine environments epitomized by military mobilization. But as in the case of the Gold Rush, wartime affirmations of the domestic influence of personal letters were well-publicized testimonials in a broader national discussion about the performance of family. That letters could convey parental guidance, sisterly affection, or conjugal intimacy with such force and to such discernible effect spoke volumes about the cultural uses of the post.

Away from the fighting, Americans of all descriptions—old and young, white and black, native and immigrant—attended to this discourse about family intimacy as it emerged in the correspondence of soldiers and their loved ones. Beyond the vast numbers of men, women, and children to whom mail from the front was directly addressed, war letters frequently found even broader audiences. Soldiers' relatives recirculated them, not only to share the information among a network of kin or a local community, but also as a way of coming to terms with the war. The bereaved mother of a Michigan man described the impact and fate of the letter he had dictated from a hospital bed in Memphis. She and her daughter-in-law "were both comforted by it," she reported many years later to the woman who had transcribed the deathbed letter, "and read and re-read it," even after they had memorized its contents. Subsequently, whenever "[we] heard of other women similarly bereaved, we loaned them the letter until it was worn in pieces." Sewn back together, copied, and posted to friends, the letter remained "in circulation until after the war ended."[74] Letters of slain soldiers to female relatives and lovers touched the sensibilities of strangers who came across them and became highly celebrated objects of public sympathy and voyeuristic interest that crossed the battle lines. Mary Chesnut describes her reaction to being presented with a "Yankee soldier's portfolio from the battlefield." Observing in her diary that "women—wives and mothers—are the same everywhere," Chesnut conceded that the enemy's letters might induce "a few tears." (She took some political comfort, however, in the "comically bad" spelling.) Meanwhile, in the North, Oliver Wendell Holmes's description in an 1862 issue of the *Atlantic Monthly* of searching for his wounded son in Antietam excerpted a letter he found on the body of fallen enemy soldier, "directed to Richmond, Virginia, its seal unbroken." After quoting a postscript instructing the letter's intended recipient to "tell John that Nancy's folks are all well and has a verry good Little Crop of corn a growing," Holmes imagined that "by one of those strange chances of which I have seen so many, this number or leaf of the 'Atlantic' will...sooner or later find its way to Cleveland County, North Carolina, and E. Wright, widow of James Wright, and Nancy's folks get from these sentences the last glimpse of husband and friend as he threw up his arms and fell in the bloody cornfield of Antietam."[75]

Even letters that were neither momentous nor heart-rending stood a decent chance of finding an extended readership. Soldiers often instructed their correspondents to preserve mail for future perusal or for posterity, an injunction that was reinforced by much public discussion of war letters. "Keep the Soldier's Letters," proclaimed one Union man's contribution to a compendium of war incidents published in Ohio in 1863, which assured readers that "each word will be historic, each line invaluable." Part of the argument for saving mail from the front emphasized its place in the unfolding drama of American nationhood. "When peace has restored the ravages of war, and our nation's grandeur has made this struggle...memorable,...these pen-pictures of the humblest events, the merest routine details of the life led in winning national unity and freedom, will be priceless." But the postal "bundle" held profound personal value as well. Should the writer perish in battle, his letters, "full of love for you, will be [his] only legacy besides that of having died a noble cause." And should he survive, "those letters will be dear mementoes to [him] of dangers past, of trials borne, of privations suffered, of comrades beloved."[76] Confederate officer Charles Minor Blackford excused the length of his letters to his wife by invoking this expectation of future value. "They may some day be interesting as the story of my experiences during the war," Blackford suggested, and might provide the material from which he would later construct a diary—at least a manuscript version for the enjoyment of his family. Half a century later, Susan Leigh Blackford would privately publish the letters themselves.[77]

None of this intense and enduring interest in soldiers' letters is remarkable, and it is hardly surprising that Americans on both sides of the conflict preserved, circulated, and published Civil War correspondence—and have continued to do so ever since. What is worth noting, however, is how a national investment in these letters as historically significant and personally poignant served, in the 1860s, the secondary cultural function of dramatizing the role of mail in everyday life. By 1865, the war experience had given most Americans additional reasons to think of the post as the repository and conduit for the sort of epistolary self-presentation that united families across great distances and preserved family identity over time.

Popular celebrations of epistolary intimacy underscored the distinctive capacity of personal letters to express the private self and foster sincere and affectionate one-on-one relationships. But such affirmations typically emphasized the family (rather than friendship or romantic relations) as the paradigmatic context for personal correspondence. Mid-century American families, especially those of the emergent middle class, were undergoing a major shift during this period. Far more than their predecessors, family units of middling income defined themselves not in relation to a common plot of land but in less tangible patterns of social and emotional connection. Middle-class families, as several historians have argued, oriented themselves toward new expectations that family life should provide a private, insulated environment within which to nurture the skills, values, and appearances (typically subsumed under the notion of character) that served the needs of a new, white-collar economy and met the challenges of a mobile, urbanizing society.[78]

Within the compact, nuclear units of blood relatives that became at this time the hallmark of the modern family, but also within broader kin networks, the regular exchange of letters became essential to the performance of family identity. As historian Marilyn Ferris Motz observed in her study of women's relations in nineteenth-century Michigan, "the fact that two persons were related to one another was considered justification for correspondence," even if they had never met. As one Michigan woman agreed with her cousin in the 1870s, "correspondence should be kept up with or between all known relatives of the Ela family."[79] With postage reduced and simplified and postal habits broadly inculcated, relatives could maintain contact with one another simply by knowing names and places of residence.

But as the Gold Rush and the Civil War dramatized, members of the same nuclear unit might also register their familial standing and commitment on paper. Countless parents, children, siblings, and spouses affirmed the special role of mail in the performance of family duty and the expression of family affection. "I have always fully appreciated the affectionate tone of your letters, my child," Georgia infantry officer Edgeworth Bird wrote to his fourteen-year-old daughter during the Civil War, explicitly linking her evident "improvement in penmanship and style" with his larger appreciation of "the good God who gave me so capable a daughter, and her so efficient and admirable a mother."[80] Even under less momentous historical circumstances, separated relatives waxed poetic about the mundane matter of family correspondence. A nineteen-year-old living in Tuscaloosa described to his family in Tuskegee the joy he felt after a visit to the post office. Letters from his father and sister were to the young Charles Hentz "as refreshing to my soul as 'the dew of Hermon,—the dew that descended upon the mountains of Zion.'" Scriptural quotations and invocations appealed with similar force to Theodore Tilton, traveling in Iowa, who canonized his wife's letters as "a well of living water." Collected, Elizabeth's missives comprised "a little book of sacred writings, . . . a Newer Testament than the New."[81]

The sanctification of familial correspondence drew upon—and contributed to—a much larger cultural project during the middle of the nineteenth century, when family life acquired its status as a sacred counterpoint to the acquisitive, competitive, and corrupt worlds of the market and politics. But if paeans to domesticity typically emphasized the physical home as the site of familial affection and intimacy, the celebration of letters passed between spouses, among siblings, from parent to child, or along more distant lines of kinship stressed the point that families in antebellum America were intensely dispersed and mobile units. With the onset of cheap postage, the personal letter offered most Americans both a vehicle and a model for a kind of ongoing intimacy that did not depend on physical presence (even as personal letters repeatedly and formulaically invoked that presence as an ideal). So long as one stayed in postal contact, one could claim to be participating in the life of the family. Thus, while the idealized family home represented the possibility of stability amid social and economic dislocation, the idealized family letter represented the portability of all the affection, influence, and shared purpose that secured such stability. Events such as the Gold Rush and the Civil War were watersheds in American postal history, broadly visible exhibitions of a new definition of family intimacy in a mobile society.

SIX

MASS MAILINGS

VALENTINES, JUNK MAIL, AND DEAD LETTERS

On a cloudy and rainy Baltimore day in February, 1851, a young medical student confided in his diary a certain detachment from his surroundings. "It is St Valentines day," he explained, "and almost every one seems to be interested either in sending or receiving." Lacking talent as a poet and "too proud . . . to send borrowed verses," William Quesenbury Claytor watched the sending and receiving frenzy from the sidelines, noting simply how the ritual provided "a source of considerable revenue to the Post Office Department." Five days later, however, Claytor was singing a different tune. The weather was lovely for his twenty-fourth birthday, and he received his "valentine for this year, and truly a good one." Invoking the highest standard praise for personal letters, Claytor observed that "it breathes the purity of heart of one of the purest characters which are scattered here and there as bright spots upon the face of the earth. I can seldom think of her without feeling upon my spirits a wholesome calm and due reverance such as we should feel in the presence of the pure and good." But not all valentines earned the same rave review. The very next day's mail brought a greeting from Annapolis, "quite a simple one, speaking relatively. It certainly was not worth the postage."[1] Some letters incarnated absent correspondents and embodied spiritual values; others, even on Valentine's Day, could be measured against the dramatically diminished costs of transmission—and be found wanting.

Valentine's Day offered people like William Claytor a special occasion for assessing the value of mail that was new to the middle decades of the nineteenth century. Before 1840, February 14 was not widely marked on the American calendar, having failed (like many saints' days) to survive the transatlantic passage. An 1832 guide to holidays declared the observance of February 14th "almost unknown" in the United States, and as late as "a few years ago," the *Philadelphia Ledger* remarked in 1845, "we did not observe it here."[2] But beginning in 1840, the country's leading cities were swept up in the annual ritual of exchanging love tokens. That year, eleven hundred Valentine's Day greetings were reportedly posted in New York City alone. Seven years later, the volume had risen to an estimated thirty thousand, and by the end of the 1850s, *Harper's Weekly* was claiming that three million printed valentines were being sold in the United States.[3] In the span of two decades an obscure saint's day had become a major event organized around the mass consumption and exchange of printed commodities.

Arising around the same time as the modern Christmas, with a shared emphasis on the purchase of objects designed to be given away, Valentine's Day was, as its leading historian has argued, a central component in the consumer culture that emerged during the antebellum period. But there was something particular about the celebration of February 14th that distinguished it from Christmas and from the other commercial festivals that flowered during the nineteenth century. Valentine's Day was a postal holiday, a compelling symbol of the forms of social interaction made possible by an affordable mail system.

Though it may be easy in retrospect to overlook the connection, Americans commemorated the occasion of Valentine's Day primarily by sending paper greetings through the mail. Moreover, popular discussion of the annual frenzy of epistolary romance focused on the post office and on the private express firms that delivered the valentines. The *Philadelphia Ledger* described in 1848 the spectacle of "a postman staggering under a huge market basket filled with the dainty epistles" and claimed that one express company "sent them out by the wheelbarrow load." A decade later a San Francisco newspaper announced that "the postoffices are lumbered with wagon loads of valentines." *Godey's Lady's Book* deprecated the "*printed* doggerel, bought in market and distributed through the penny-post," while a Post Office guide from 1851 pointed out that the holiday had become a "prolific source of dead letters." An 1853 magazine article warned that visiting the New York post office on February 14 required a high degree of patience, as "crowds of valentines throng the way" to the delivery windows. When *Harper's* tried to defend the "Valentine mania" against cynicism in 1859, it featured a drawing of the "arrival of the country postman on St. Valentine's Morning." "The rap of the postman, on the morning of the 14th of February," one observer declared in 1855, "causes many a maiden's bosom to throb with love and curiosity."[4]

All of these representations of the new holiday emphasized the sheer volume of postal business that it generated. It became common for newspapers and magazines to mark the passing of the holiday by detailing the number of valentines that had "passed through the post office."[5]

On a single winter day, post office boxes, mail coaches, and expressman's satchels filled with mail from ordinary people, many of whom turned their eyes to the post with greater anticipation and interest than at any other moment. Valentine's Day celebrated, among other things, America's growing dependence upon the post.

As a festival of the mail system, Valentine's Day projected a set of images of postal life that differed strikingly from those in articles about lonely forty-niners or young men at war. Such images resonated, nonetheless, for they indicated uses and aspects of the post that were not about conventional epistolary intimacy. On Valentine's Day, in fact, the post was not in the business of uniting far-flung family members, facilitating long-distance commerce, or otherwise annihilating time and space. The senders and recipients of valentines were typically inhabitants of the same city or town, often members of the same community. In the 1850 story, "Kate's Valentine," they are even members of the same household.[6] What the post contributed on February 14 was not so much a network of routes and conveyances as an impersonal system of anonymous collection and distribution. Valentine's Day depended upon (and underscored) the anonymity of mail, turning the everyday fact that senders could disguise or conceal their identities into a source of excitement and romantic mystery. "How many innocent maidens are now . . . wondering about who could have sent them those beautiful verses!" an 1840 news report imagined.[7]

Anonymity figured not only in the romantic avowals that the holiday enabled and emboldened (scripted by a nascent greeting-card industry), but also in the "mock valentines" that formed an integral part of the holiday by mid-century. Comical or mean-spirited greetings to "a hen hussy," "a dandy," or a childless couple ("Don't look at each other so cross and so cold/You can't have a baby, you're getting too old/So it's no use of fretting each other insane/You're rocking that old empty cradle in vain," read one 1848 sample), mock valentines operated on the same license of anonymity that underwrote the dominant romantic genre.[8] Significantly, Valentine's Day parodies and pranks sometimes drew specifically on the perils particular to the postal system, especially before the era of mandated prepayment. One popular humorist claimed to have received seventeen postage-due valentines, including several of the nasty kind. An 1858 article claimed that before 1851 rival males would "victimize each other with bulky parcels" addressed in "mock feminine hand." New postal arrangements had dulled the blade of that specific deception, the article noted, but the thematic preoccupation with anonymity persisted. "With us, and at the present time," the author noted, "St. Valentine's

Day is held sacred to anonymous practical jokes."⁹ If posted daguerreo-types intensified the identification of a letter with its author, valentines depended for their effect on the provisional suspension or occlusion of that identification.

Valentine's Day foregrounded the anonymity of postal exchange and also presented a rather promiscuous social picture. February 14 was not a matchmaking holiday; it was an occasion for sending greetings to several objects of admiration (or scorn) and for boasting of the number of valentines one received. Valentine's Day celebrated just how prolific the post could be. Newspaper descriptions of the holiday emphasized the spectacle of postal excess (wagon loads, lumber, staggering postmen with huge baskets), and while images of excess could be incorporated into narratives of romantic destiny, as in a Harper's cartoon from 1868 (see fig. 8), more often the valentine itself appeared in the popular press not as a single missive but as part of a mixed multitude. As a temporal analogue to the Post Office's dead letter repository, Valentine's Day mailbags were sites of extreme juxtaposition and intermingling. "What a quantity of flaming hearts, and bleeding hearts stuck through with arrows," a New Orleans newspaper report mused in 1840, imagining "a rhyming and chiming and tingling and jingling, of . . . long and short lines hobbling to the measure like ill-drilled militia stepping out of time!" The collision and confusion of sentimental and comic valentines intensified the image of unseemliness. At the Dead Letter Office, *The United States Post-Office Guide* informed its readers, the results of this confusion are manifest. "Here you see the delicate tribute of love to beauty, and the coarse caricature of the fool and the villain mingled together!"¹⁰ Such images were familiar fare to consumers of the sensationalist literature of the dead letter and the post office, but on Valentine's Day patrons were especially well positioned to appreciate the promiscuous character of a mailed letter.

As with the introduction of photographic portraits, the introduction of the printed valentine greetings in the 1840s was part of the cultural con-text of the postal revolution. The new holiday encouraged, publicized, and celebrated popular interest in the post, habituating new users to the workings of the mail system and demonstrating the breadth of demand for cheap postage. Within a few years of the invention of this festival, middle-class critics were bemoaning the degradation of the sentiments and the art of a supposedly older custom, deploring the "stereotyped, miserable things" that passed through the mail. Such views, apart from being historically false and in many cases self-serving (*Godey's* suggested, not surprisingly, that a more tasteful alternative to a purchased valentine

— FIGURE 8 —
VALENTINE'S DAY CARTOON. *HARPER'S WEEKLY*, 1868.

would be a subscription to the *Lady's Book*), missed the point that the mass rituals of the post were central to the nature and appeal of Valentine's Day.[11]

America's first postal holiday called public attention to a dimension of the new mail culture that was sometimes overlooked in celebrations of the personal letter. Even though Valentine's Day greetings could be intensely intimate gestures between two individuals, their typically anonymous and potentially promiscuous character provided a different model for how interpersonal connections might be fostered through the mail. Not all users and not all uses of the mail in the age of cheap postage adopted the same approach to the promise of the post to permit intimacy across distances. In fact, many of the purposes to which the post was put in the early decades of cheap postage had little to do with the desire of separated friends and family to communicate. In the case of valentines, the intended recipients were often local, and the personal relationship between the sender and the recipient was strategically bracketed or obscured. More commonly, mail might pass between senders and recipients who did not know each other at all. Though they lacked the pageantry that attended the carnivalesque rituals of Valentine's Day, the enormous number of circulars, solicitations, anonymous inquiries, and junk mail that passed through the post after 1845 shaped (and reflected) popular consciousness about the meaning of postal contact. Alongside the practices and norms through which postal patrons sought to construct selves or honor family allegiances by means of the traditional letter, there emerged a newer category of postal exchange that did not depend upon any prior relationship between the sender and the recipient. The traditional promise of an epistle to incarnate an absent correspondent who had been present in the flesh did not apply to many forms of correspondence that flourished during the middle decades of the century. While Americans invested their newly inclusive postal system with the capacity to preserve bonds of affection, they took interest during the same period in the ability to forge new and different connections among strangers through the mail. From the earliest days of cheap postage, users exploited and emphasized the centrifugal, promiscuous, and anonymous features of a network that could bring any two people into direct contact.

As is the case today, much nineteenth-century mail, perhaps even a majority of what passed through the post office in certain times and places during the middle decades, consisted of unsolicited postings to strangers. This category included newspapers and tracts sent as part of direct-mail campaigns, such as the abolitionist mailings of the 1830s that stirred major controversy in the South.[12] But it also included less famous examples and types of postal communication. There were letters of an "anonymous and abusive character," such as the one a postmaster in Lynn felt entitled to open and inspect in 1840, or the mock valentines that sold over a million copies a year by the time of the Civil War.[13] People even

sent letters to strangers seen entering or exiting their homes, such as the
one addressed as follows:

> To the Lady that wears a white cloak Straw
> Bonnet trimmed with Blue & wears a blue
> veil, brown or striped dress
> No——Bleeker street
> New York.[14]

An 1856 inventory of types of mail included an entry for "begging letters,"
which the author thought "ought never to be answered, if the writer be
unknown, or the handwriting suspicious."[15] The same article suggested
enigmatically that "*anonymous* letters may be very good in some times
and places," but warned that "999,999 of the million are almost sure
to be beneath attention. . . . [I]f they are bad or insignificant, burn the
thing; never speak of it, never think of it again."[16] As generally accessible
participants in the network, postal patrons were targets for all kinds of
inquiries and intrusions from outside their circles of acquaintance.

By far the most common of these came in the form of what were called
circulars, a word that denoted printed letters or advertisements posted or
distributed to numerous recipients. Circulars promoted political causes,
announced social events, solicited donations, and advertised goods and
services. Thousands of them entered the mail each day, especially after
1852, when the postage for any unsealed circular weighing three ounces
or less and traveling anywhere in the country was set at one cent. Though
circulars were in some cases timely and interesting to their recipients,
more often they were regarded as a paradigmatic form of junk mail. By
1855, the postmaster general was estimating that advertising circulars for
lotteries and patent medicines alone were filling up thirty to forty bags a
day at some post offices.[17] Even when they were posted less indiscrimi-
nately, circulars could be burdensome. Unitarian minister Henry Bellows
recalled receiving "heavy circulars from a committee of clergymen, who
had charge of a fund of ten thousand dollars, asking us to compete for a
funeral monument." Annoyed that the package arrived postage due, Bellows ignored the appeal, only to receive a second installment, "postage
still unpaid, but inflicting large manuscript letters upon us in respect to
the way in which the designs were to be managed." Most circulars were
lighter (and paid for), but they were not necessarily any more welcome.[18]
Circulars formed a ubiquitous model of impersonal mail against which
more intimate correspondence could be measured. When her sister accused her in 1847 of writing stereotypical and thin letters, Emily Sinkler
went on the defensive. Demanding "to know what you mean by calling

my letters circulars," the exiled cosmopolite countered: "If you only knew how little I have to write about you would think it wonderful that I get through a letter at all. You who live in a city could have no trouble in writing . . . why you ought to write pages."[19] The accusation clearly stung. Already by mid-century, many Americans (principally those in cities) inhabited a world full of paper detritus. Posted circulars may have been addressed to individuals (unlike the posters and broadsides that littered city streets), but they still epitomized the impersonal communication associated with modern print culture.[20]

Circulars usually involved the increasingly ordinary businesses of advertising, fund-raising, and propaganda. Sometimes, however, they were used to perpetrate frauds, swindles, and schemes that took advantage of both the anonymity of the mail and the size of the postal network to reap considerable profits. Postal ruses took several forms, some quite ingenious. Around mid-century, for example, an enterprising teenaged boy sent multiple handwritten copies of a letter stating that he had "received a package of papers for you with six shillings charges thereon—on receipt of which amount the parcel will be sent to you by such conveyance as you may direct." Signing the letter with a false name, the young man netted a significant number of responses from curious lawyers wondering what business they might have in Great Britain, before he was caught by a special agent of the Post Office hired to investigate frauds.[21] Another elaborate stratagem featured personal letters to country clergymen. "Being at leisure this afternoon," the letter began, "I have concluded to sit down and write you, utterly unacquainted save in that sympathy which persons of like temperament involuntarily feel toward one another." As the pastor would read on, he would learn of the author's dissatisfaction with the "coldness and formality of our metropolitan sermons," and his fond recollections of having once heard the addressee speak while passing through his small town. Such recollections were reawakened, it turned out, by a reference to the distinguished country cleric in a "new publication of travels through the States," in which some distinguished foreign author had given him a glowing mention. The letter closed with an invitation to consider a move to the author's wealthy urban parish. Only in a postscript did the true object of the scam surface. "P.S.—If you have not seen the notice of you, (in the book I alluded to,) I will get it for you. I believe it sells at a dollar and a half, or thereabouts."[22]

Frauds of this character drew upon the imagined credulity and naïveté of small-town folk, and the published accounts exposing such swindles resemble other mid-century urban texts in which an accomplished connoisseur decodes the perils of big-city life.[23] Postal frauds differed from the confidence games that filled the pages of sensationalist urban guides, since they extended the threat of metropolitan insincerity beyond the city limits. At core, however, the countless "circular swindles" that were run out of New York shared with the classic confidence man (the city slicker who pretends to know the country newcomer and manages to borrow his watch) a common foundation of anonymity underlying a veneer of personal recognition or common purpose.

Circular swindles were much bigger business, though, and many of them had no need for the complex set-ups of the schemes discussed earlier. A guide to New York published shortly after the Civil War estimated that more than two thousand "swindling establishments" operated out of the city, each one taking in between a hundred thousand and five hundred thousand dollars during its brief business season before closing up shop and reappearing under a new name and address. The schemes could be quite simple. The addressee might be promised some gift in return for subscribing to a newspaper or a benevolent society, or perhaps a special recipe for producing a patent medicine would be offered free of charge (except of course for a postage stamp). Often, the offer would involve something illegal, such as a lottery (prohibited by law in the state of New York) or the distribution of counterfeit bank notes. The addressee would be enlisted, with a great display of confidence, as the agent for an illegal operation, and when he eventually discovered the fraud, he would be in no position to file a complaint with the police. "No fraud is more transparent [or] successful," observed an 1871 magazine article, than these circular swindles. "There is scarcely a city or town in the Union to which circulars are not sent," another sensationalist text maintained, "and from which victims are not secured."[24]

While amusing as illustrations of the limitless avarice and guile of human beings, the circular swindles depended for their success on several interesting features of the emerging postal network. Many of the perpetrators used city directories, professional publications, commercial lists, newspaper advertisements, and other print artifacts which, taken together, formed a growing registry of postal addresses accessible on a national level. The abolitionists had used similar sources in mounting their direct mail campaigns during the 1830s, but by the 1860s many more names were available through such searches. The teenaged criminal mentioned earlier located his victims through the Law Register. The man who sought to flatter and fleece country clergymen presumably had access to national lists of ministers. Operations that did not discriminate on the basis of profession could gather the names of "hundreds of thousands of persons . . . from all over the country" by consulting a range of texts, including, of course the lists of uncollected letters at the post office, published biweekly in the local newspapers. Vice crusader Anthony Comstock discovered that obscenity dealers would locate potential customers by obtaining school rosters or would, like lottery managers or peddlers of postal fraud, purchase old letters and envelopes from specialized brokers "who make a business of collecting names."[25]

While names (and therefore addresses) were publicly accessible for these early purveyors of spam, victims of circular swindles received letters that often appeared quite private, addressed to them as individuals and pitched discreetly under the protective seal of wafer, gum, or envelope. One example of a scheme to "secure the services of a smart and intelligent Agent" for facsimiles of U.S. greenbacks appeared in the form of lithographs so "well executed" that an inexperienced addressee might easily imagine, according to one observer, that he was reading "a written letter prepared for him exclusively." Another outfit employed a scriptorium of eight employees who were so effectively trained "that there was no perceptible difference in the chirography" of the thousands of circulars they produced and disseminated.[26] Not that it would even make a difference, though. Few recipients of a letter promising exclusive ground-floor access to a counterfeiting ring would show it to their neighbors. Finally, these operations exploited and underscored the massive scale of the postal network, which allowed swindlers to cast an exceptionally wide net, sending out of tens of thousands of solicitations without much risk and at minimal expense. Even a small percentage of replies from eager victims remitting a dollar or just a postage stamp could translate into a major windfall.

The stakes of all of these scams were high, because the post was used for the (by and large) irretrievable transmission of objects. Circulars were cheap and interchangeable pieces of junk mail that reflected the light and fleeting nature of postal contact, but the objects they solicited in return emphasized another side of the story. Postal access enabled interactions that made a difference in the lives of the participants. The concept of the postal swindle took advantage of the anonymity and promiscuity of the mail, which permitted one party to extract money from the other. In one fascinating case described in a magazine in 1872, an "ingenious Yankee" from Massachusetts "got up a circular in imitation of those used by the rascals who sell improper books." This circular promised, upon remission of 80 cents, "a handsomely-bound book, with a rich and peculiarly interesting picture for frontispiece," a book that every bachelor ought to have. Those who sent in their money were outraged to receive in return a copy of the New Testament, and complained to the police.

> The sender of the circulars stoutly maintained that he was doing nothing but propagating the Gospel among a class who greatly needed its wholesome instruction, and that he was using the devices of the wicked for good purposes. But as his pious fraud was very profitable—as the Testaments were only worth fifteen cents each—the authorities finally decided that the transaction was a swindle, and compelled the inventor to abandon his little game.[27]

By the beginning of the 1870s, the postal network had become a familiar avenue through which a range of transactions could take place, attended by certain expectations and fraught with certain risks. Postal users greeted the arrival of a circular with eyes both widened and chastened by new experiences of the mail as a source of so many diverse objects. The post might carry the cold type of printed newspapers or the unmistakable traces of an absent body—a lock of hair, a daguerreotype image, or a signature. Letters might include money, fabric samples, or seeds. They might come in the prefabricated format of the printed valentine or a lithographed advertisement. As all of these objects passed through the post, Americans came to take for granted a certain access to the people they did not see, but who were, in one way or another, part of the same network.

Popular interest in what was collective, connective, and *mass* about the mail system may have been the most recognizably modern feature of the new postal culture. Whether they were signed or anonymous, grounded in personal acquaintance or relying on its absence, letters circulated in a network of countless users who were at the same time unprecedentedly accessible and potentially out of reach. Perhaps the principal focus for this interest at mid-century—and a crucial context within which it was cultivated and elaborated—was the phenomenon of dead letters. Dead letters were pieces of mail that had not reached their destinations, either because they were inadequately addressed or, more frequently, because they had lain uncollected in post offices beyond a prescribed period of three months. Beginning in 1825 the Post Office published lists of the addressees of such letters at regular intervals (typically every two weeks) for three months in local newspapers, after which the letters would be sent to the Dead Letter Office in Washington, D.C. This office was designed primarily to recover lost money, vast sums of which were sent through the mail each year, but much of what wound up in Washington was simply unclaimed correspondence. A million letters were declared dead in 1837, neither retrieved nor paid for by their intended recipients. Three decades later the annual figure generally exceeded four million, though as a percentage of letters mailed this was actually a decrease. In the peak year of 1866, almost 5.2 million letters were received at the Dead Letter Office, containing almost a quarter of a million dollars. Throughout the middle decades of the century an astonishing number of letters were waylaid en route to their addressees.[28]

In the 1820s and '30s, before most Americans formed regular habits of postal inquiry, the lists of letters held at the post office functioned as announcements of the arrival of mail. Newspapers were central circuits through which information about the existence of a letter might pass to an otherwise unsuspecting recipient. By the 1840s, however, the lists began to acquire additional meaning. In the age of mass participation in the postal network, letters identified on such lists were often letters whose addressees had moved on. By 1855, prepaid postage requirements reinforced the impression that letters advertised in the newspapers were not going to be retrieved (since they had already been paid for, the addressees had less reason to delay picking them up, and the post office had less of an incentive to hold onto them). These formidable columns of hundreds and even thousands of addressees were a prominent and ongoing feature of the American press throughout the antebellum era (often occupying more space in a given newspaper issue than any other single article, story, or category of advertising), and formed a central part of the experience and spectacle of the post at mid-century.

The letters identified on these lists were not quite dead, but they were certainly in critical condition. Appearance on a list of undelivered mail raised the specter of ultimate disappearance. As names were dropped from these ubiquitous lists, a reader's imagination might drift toward the next destination of unclaimed letters, which was frequently terminal. Apart from the minority of items that contained money, most dead letters were, in the dramatic language of one report, "transported for the last time to a place without the city, and there solemnly burned, no human being but their writers knowing how much of labor and of pain, has been expended upon them, thus to perish by fire and be exhaled in smoke."[29] The link between death and miscarried mail was hardly an inert metaphor. Even the sober, statistic-laden 1855 tract of postal reformer Pliny Miles milked the connection. In discussing the problem of dead letters, Miles cited a recent tragedy to illustrate the life-and-death stakes of postal efficiency. "Who has not seen the account, lately published," he asked, "of the poor man that went to Texas, and, staying longer than he anticipated, sent 150 dollars in a letter, back to his wife in St. Louis?" As the money was lost, or more likely stolen, en route, the wife and their five little children found themselves "destitute, in a land of strangers." The rest of the story brought out an uncharacteristic flourish in the great advocate of cheap postage. "Driven to want and madness, the unfortunate woman threw herself and her infant child into the Mississippi, there to remain till the sea and the rivers shall give up their dead." That this story did not, as Miles was quick to concede, involve a dead letter was beside the point. Delivering the mail was an urgent business, and every letter waylaid in transit raised the possibility of human death. Two years earlier Herman Melville had made the same point in his now-famous invocation of the Dead Letter Office at the end of "Bartleby, the Scrivener" (1853) Ruminating on the tragic demise of his enigmatic copyist, the lawyer-narrator of Melville's classic story, ruminates on the rumor that Bartleby had worked as a dead letter clerk. Each piece of undelivered mail handled by the clerk, observes the narrator, represents "hope for those who died unhoping," and every errant letter evokes a deceased addressee. "Dead Letters! does it not sound like dead men?"[30]

Tragically undelivered letters haunted published accounts of the mail and animated numerous articles in the popular press on the workings of this branch of the system. The Dead Letter Office, according to one author in the 1870s, still "embodies more personal interest than any other in the Post-Office Department." The appeal of this institution rested not so much on the widespread anxiety that mail might fail to reach its target but on the more basic fact that the collection and inspection of undelivered letters allowed users to visualize the post. Accumulated in unsurpassed volumes and systematically pried open, dead letters were concrete and visible representations of the postal practices that masses of Americans were adopting. Nowhere else, not even at the post office, could Americans visualize tens of thousands of letters at a time—millions over the course of year, with origins from all over the world and purposes that spanned the range of imaginable human interaction—accumulating and coming to rest. Moreover, nowhere else could Americans imagine quite the same access to the sealed contents of all of those letters. At the post office one might scrutinize someone's face for visible reactions to a letter—and such betrayals of emotion were standard features of a certain type of post office story. In the pages of a novel or an epistolary guide, one might be allowed voyeuristic entry into a fictional correspondence. But the Dead Letter Office examined actual mail and offered Americans a glimpse of actual postal habits.

Tourists flocked to the Dead Letter Office on F St. and some even sent hopeful inquiries to the Post Office Department about wayward letters or found money.[31] For more Americans, however, access to dead letters came through articles that appeared in the press, where the content and circumstances of ostensibly private correspondence came into public view. Already in 1831, just six years after the establishment of the dead letter policy, an article in the *New-England Magazine* fancifully proposed editing and publishing them under such possible headings as "Periodical and Documentary Record of Mankind's and Womankind's Doings and Undoings," "A Peep behind the Curtain at Humankind," or "Index to the Human Soul."[32] By mid-century, accounts of the dead letter operation had begun to comprise a genre of sensationalist literature, laying bare dark and concealed worlds along the lines pursued profitably by the popular urban guides and city-mysteries fiction of the era. Much as sensationalist journalism led its readers on tours of the urban demimonde, accounts of the dead letter office exposed the mysterious workings of the major bureaucracy of the nineteenth century, while at the same time uncovering the idiosyncratic practices and human dramas that lay buried under reams of traceless and errant pieces of paper.[33] An 1852 article appearing originally in an Albany newspaper enticed the reader with all of the familiar conventions and tropes of mid-century sensationalism:

> Piled in the halls, outside the doors of these melancholy vaults, are great sacks, locked and sealed and labelled "DEAD LETTERS," and ever and anon, appears a grim, sexton-like old negro who, seizing a bag, disappears with it into one or other of the tombs. You may enter with me if you will, and treading carefully over the ashes that lie scattered everywhere beneath your feet, watch the process by weich [*sic*] living thoughts and high aspirations, and love's word-tokens, and the burning phrases of ambition, and hope, and joy, and the fitful dreamings of the poet, the cool calculations of the money getter, the prophetic outgivings of the politicians— all the thousand varied emotions, sympathies and expressions that go to make up "correspondence" are here converted into lifeless, meaningful trash.[34]

Set in tombs stalked by an old, presumably inscrutable Negro, the life-crushing operations of the Dead Letter Office assume the frightful features of a George Lippard novel, at least until the reader is brought safely inside.

Other articles placed similar emphasis on the morbidity of the institution. *Appleton's Journal* in 1873 carried the following: "At another window table, we find half a dozen clerks busily engaged in assorting the letters which are coming in every moment in bags. . . . These are the hearses which convey the dead letters to this great mausoleum, to be given in charge of the force of . . . undertakers." Even once the mortuary metaphors recede, everything about the office is shrouded, even its employees. "Strangers visiting Washington," an *Overland Monthly* report began in 1869, "would never know that there are" women working on the second floor. "Indeed," the article continued, "few people residing in the Capital are really aware in what part of the building these women are stowed away. . . ."[35] Dead letter literature emphasized the gap between what is ordinarily exposed to general view and what lurks beneath the surface.

Several features of the institutional bureaucracy interested the authors of these journalistic exposés. Along with the women sequestered on an upper story and admitted into the building through a separate entrance labored a number of clergymen, "broken in health or fortune," who, like the women, were presumed to be above temptation to steal the contents of unclaimed mail. Employees of the Dead Letter Office appear in the popular accounts as experts who "learn to decipher what to ordinary mortals would be hieroglyphic, or simply a blank." Like the heroes of early detective fiction (and like urban connoisseurs in popular journalism), these postal employees are decoders; they translate illegible addresses on undelivered letters, identifying the word "Squill" as Schuylkill, Pennsylvania and "Kivvist" as Key West, Florida.[36] The department also hired employees who could go through foreign-language mail, including two clerks assigned specifically to German-language correspondence. Most of all, though, reports emphasized the sheer volume of the dead letter business. The 1874 account pointed out that "the Return Branch, which is composed entirely of ladies, sends average dead-letters back to their writers at the rate of seven thousand a day," while the *Appleton's* story a year earlier celebrated the success of the office in returning "nearly all" of $92,867.82 in lost money.[37]

By far the greatest preoccupation of the dead letter stories was with the window this institution opened onto the world of everyday correspondence. A peek into the Dead Letter Office shed light on the postal habits of ordinary Americans—their carelessness in addressing letters, their mobility, their use of poetry to close their letters, the failure of women to sign their full names, or even "the deplorable fashion of a certain class of writers to address their letters from some country-seat or other, with a fancy or aristocratic name, without giving the post-office address." *Overland Monthly* concluded that "the greater number of letters passing through this office are badly written and uninteresting," itself an interesting point of information for the magazine's readers.[38]

Still the most striking and revealing discoveries about the postal network appeared in the mail inventories that were routinely featured in dead letter stories. Even if letters lacked style, wit, and cash enclosures, Americans were clearly using the post in some interesting ways and for some interesting purposes. The "mailable matter" exhumed from dead letters, *Overland Monthly* informed its readers, included "one half-worm gaiter-boot, two hair-nets, a rag doll-baby minus the head and one foot, a set of cheap jewelry, a small-sized frying pan, two ambrotypes, one pair of white kid-gloves, a nursing bottle, a tooth-brush, a boot-jack, three yards of lace, a box of Ayer's pills, a bunch of keys, six nutmegs, a toddy-stick, and no end of dress samples." *Appleton's* found "rings, watches, brooches, ear-rings, chains, eyeglasses, lace collars, cigar-holders, embroideries, fancy slippers, neckties, gloves (by the gross), babies' dresses, bonnets, homemade socks, pocket-handkerchiefs, fans, . . . even sewing-machines, razors, models, mantel-clocks, and books by the hundred." Perhaps the most impressive and artful list appeared in an 1852 *Albany Register* piece:

> Money, bills of exchange, notes of hand, receipts, emigrant passage tickets, lottery tickets, an old wallet, health, fire, and life insurance policies, a bunch of keys, a specimen of wheat, bottles, sugar samples, hanks of yarn, a bed quilt, a rattlesnake skin, two diamond ornaments, an old hat, a draft for ten thousand dollars, a paving stone, a suit of boy's clothing, a box of tea nuts from that indefatigable gentleman, Jno. Junius Smith, addressed to some delinquent correspondent who has omitted to claim them, a pot of ointment, a bundle of watchmaker's tools, maple sugar, a bullocks horn, a galvanic battery, garden seeds, lawyer's papers without end, officer's commissions and discharges, jewelry of all sorts and values, "forget me not" worked in worsted on a perforated card, a screwdriver, patterns of silk, good for city cousins to match for country friends, etc., etc.[39]

These inventories, like the lists of addressees in the press, emphasized the volume of postal business, but with a twist. By enumerating such an array of items, authors turned a mausoleum of forgotten and worthless paper into a cabinet of curiosities. The last catalogue emphasized difference and incommensurability, in stark contrast both to the sea of miniscule, homogeneous type that comprised the letter lists and to the grim statistics that flattened out hopes and expectations into cold aggregates.

Lengthy catalogues of posted objects highlighted not only the variety of mailable matter that washed up in the Dead Letter Office, but also the bizarre juxtapositions that resulted from collecting all of this material in one place. Most of the articles discussed here presented the Dead Letter Office as a site of incongruous intermingling. Bags of dead letters lumped together "missives of all shapes, sizes, and conditions," from the commercial to the personal, from the masculine to the feminine, "from the lace edged, perfumed *billet*, to the heavy, yellow enveloped official dispatch; from the square folded, greasy epistle of the serving girl, to the prim, red-waxed document of a foreign embassy." Collisions of class and gender proved especially compelling. *Appleton's* tried to use this juxtaposition to provide an orderly, hierarchical taxonomy for the varieties of envelopes passing through the mail in 1869:

> There is the large official letter, in its foolscap envelope; the heavy, fat banker's letter, inclosing bonds of other papers of value; the ordinary, oblong, "5-size," buff business letter, with a card printed in the corner of the envelope; the modern, "cold-pressed," rough, and square envelope, with an intricate monogram, in colors on the flap; the dainty little lilac- or rose-tinged *couvert*, directed in a timid lady's hand; . . . and last, but not least, letters without numbers from the kitchen-regions, in thin, greasy envelopes of uncertain colors, with the direction written, in yellow ink, diagonally from the upper left corner to the lower right one, and with blotches and corrections innumerable.

In most of these accounts, variety tended to erode hierarchy, or at least obscure it. Dead letter collections, like the postal system they encapsulated and represented, dramatized the bigness of an emergent mass society.[40]

Public discussions of dead letters gave focus to popular interest both in the massive inclusiveness of the postal network and in its strange aura of anonymity. One of the most remarkable achievements of the post was the assignment of an identifiable address to every person with access to a post office. Once postage was lowered and regular habits of inquiry were institutionalized, one simply needed to know the name of a person and the name of a post office location (this was what facilitated the acquisition of postal addresses for circulars and advertisements described earlier in this chapter). By definition, everyone had an address (this would of course become more complicated as the Post Office turned to free home delivery in urban communities after 1863). And once the use of prepaid stamps became the norm in the 1850s, every addressee was, effortlessly and automatically, a participant in a complete postal transaction. Men, women, and children of various classes, ethnicities, and legal statuses were all part of the network—eligible for the increasingly ubiquitous mail call. But the dead letter phenomenon pointed to a wrinkle in the system. Letters missed their mark when persons or towns were misidentified and when recipients moved, neglected to inquire at the post, or otherwise fell through the cracks of a system that claimed to include every potential user of the mail. Articles about the dead letter office often implied that greater care in the addressing of letters would solve most of the problems, but clearly this was not the whole story. Dead letters floated in the intermediate space between names and people, and between the personal recognition marked by an individually addressed letter and the impersonality of a large, mobile, and uprooted society.[41]

The bags of errant mail that collected in Washington offered evidence of the inadequacy of personal names as the foundation for the postal address system. In addition to the fact that names were misspelled or attached to places that were themselves misidentified, the dead letter collections thrust letters into a world where addressees were unknown, and thus essentially anonymous. At the post office, especially in smaller communities, names in postal addresses might have meaning within a context of local networks of acquaintanceship. In Cleveland in the mid-1850s, for example, a letter reportedly arrived with the following address: "To the big-faced Butcher, with a big wart on his nose—Cleveland, Ohio." According to the account in *Harper's*, the postal clerks "all knew the man, but they were afraid to deliver the letter!" A letter sent to a postal patron in Dedham, Massachusetts around the same time was addressed in care of John Lee, whose common name apparently necessitated the specification "the man that speaks through his nose or with the crucket foot." A subscriber to *Scientific American* from Knoxville complained in 1859 that the magazine was not delivered to a newcomer in that city because his name was not "familiar to those who assist the postmaster in his duties."[42] For more socially prominent postal users, the network of personal acquaintanceship and recognition could extend beyond the local post office. In 1846, at the dawn of cheap postage, a letter arrived at the South Carolina home of Emily Wharton Sinkler, addressed rather vaguely to her friend "Miss Catherine O'Rourke, care of Mr. Sinkler, P.O. South Carolina." The letter reached its intended destination, Emily Sinkler observed, only because Charleston Postmaster Alfred Huger (who achieved some national fame of his own a decade earlier in the abolitionist mail controversy) was personally acquainted with Charles Sinkler. O'Rourke's correspondent might have been observing older protocols of respect in addressing letters. As late as 1854, a republished edition of an older epistolary guide and etiquette book was still advising readers that "in directing your letter to persons who are well known, it is best not to be too particular; because it lessens the person to whom you write, to suppose him obscure, and not easily found." Such advice was quaint and outdated by mid-century (if not earlier), and certainly at odds with most writing on the subject, and indeed Sinkler was right to think the incident odd and remarkable.[43] Despite noteworthy exceptions, whatever minimal name recognition might be invoked at the local post office lay beyond the parameters of the national network on display in and around the Dead Letter Office. Not only were names severed from faces and networks of personal acquaintanceship, they were also especially liable to be shared among several people. In the dead letter lists and the reports from the postal morgue, it was clear that names were not, in fact, unique addresses.

Even at the local level, postal practices ran into the problem of name duplication, something that the letter lists in the newspaper increasingly reflected and emphasized. Lists of letters being held at the post office were, even more than city directories, the nineteenth-century precursor to the phone book, at least to the extent that they provided the most broadly visible evidence of the commonness of particular surnames. As early as 1840, the *New Orleans Picayune* cited as "incredible" the fact that in the most recent list "there were only sixteen for the Smith family, and not one addressed to John." New postal users, especially those living in large or unfamiliar communities, had to adjust to this new condition of alienation from their own names. Writing from San Francisco in 1854, Charles Allen warned his brother in a postscript to "please put my middle Letter in for there is so may [*sic*] by my name here that they take all my letters and papers." Though some of his namesakes returned Allen's mail to the post office, he noted, "some . . . keep them." James Harris Ham suffered from similar confusion during the Gold Rush, and complained that one of his love letters had wound up in the hands of another J. H. Ham. A published anecdote of postal life in Philadelphia told of a man who had received money intended for a namesake and innocently spent it before a discovery was made. A more tragic fate almost befell the letter of the recovered fugitive Anthony Burns, whose letter to lawyer Richard Dana from a Virginia jail cell, described at the beginning of this study, was delayed by its delivery to another man named Dana. The possibility of namesake misdelivery entered into the list of possible explanations and excuses for the failure of letters to arrive. Mary Wingate, responding to her husband's complaints of not receiving mail in 1851, wondered whether it was "possible there may be another of your name that gets your letters?"[44] By mid-century, post office publications were urging those sending mail to "populous cities" to include in the address "the trade or profession of the party, if known, as well as the number of the street," but such advice appears to have gone unheeded.[45] The system required only a name, and names proved to be slippery anchors of user identity.

In the expanded world of the post, patrons needed to be careful when they used names to create personal contact within a large and public network. An 1865 children's magazine warned its readers, for example, about the perils of using putative knowledge of someone's name as the basis for a postal address. In a piece entitled "A Business Letter," coeditor Gail Hamilton (Mary Abigail Dodge) of *Our Young Folks* insisted upon the importance of using correct and standard procedures in corresponding with print publications and their authors. The article describes a scenario in which a reader, upon hearing that J. T. Trowbridge (editor of the magazine) is really a man named Mr. Franklin Smith of Mattapoiset, sends a manuscript to that address. Imagining the destiny of such a manuscript, Hamilton notes that the voting rolls for Mattapoiset list no one named Franklin Smith, though there is a Francis Smith and a Frank Smith, among many other Smiths. The subscriber's letter, submitting an "enigma" (a type of riddle that was a standard feature of that publication) "is taken from the post-office by Mr. Frank Smith, who is an excellent man, but not given to literature, and who never heard of an enigma. He opens the letter with considerable curiosity." Hamilton imagines the wrong Mr. Smith showing the riddle to his puzzled wife, and then leaving the letter in the family Bible, where it lies "forgotten . . . to this day." Another letter for Franklin Smith is mistaken at the post office by a "gay young clerk" of approximately that name for a love note. Upon discovering his error, "Francis Smith" simply burns the letter. Another letter has the good fortune of arriving in the hands of a Smith whose children happen to be subscribers to *Our Young Folks*. Recognizing and solving the enigma, this Smith brings the riddle with him on a trip to Boston and submits it personally, but without the accompanying note, "so that nobody knows whose story it is, and it goes down into a nameless grave." The nameless grave, Hamilton's didactic article implies, is an ironic but just fate for a letter that sought to penetrate the pseudonymous façade of a public print culture with a direct appeal to a named postal patron.[46]

Didactic warnings were necessary, of course, because the temptation to equate a name with a serviceable postal address was great—and often justified. Americans routinely addressed mail to authors, politicians, and other famous people. Enslaved North Carolina barber James Starkey posted a letter to Swedish opera singer Jenny Lind during the height of her 1850 American tour, appealing to her much-celebrated munificence to liberate him from slavery. In the decade after the Civil War, Harriet Lane Levy, a young daughter of Jewish immigrants living in San Francisco, wrote a personal letter to Samuel Clemens of Hartford to express her admiration for *The Adventures of Tom Sawyer*. Fanny Fern's best-selling novel *Ruth Hall* (1855) is filled with fan mail to the title character once she becomes a successful author, though it is largely mediated through her pseudonym and her publisher.[47] Henry Wadsworth Longfellow, as the work of Jill Anderson has demonstrated, was a popular target for autograph seekers during the early years of cheap postage. Between 1844 and 1865, 410 separate requests for the poet's signature came to him through the mail. And though Longfellow, who wrote some four thousand letters during this period, complained of the burden of his ever-growing stack of unanswered mail ("as huge and inexhaustible as the guano on the odorous Chinchi Islands"), the inconvenience did not deter him from corresponding with people he did not know.[48]

Perhaps the best-known evidence of the growing practice of sending mail to famous strangers surfaced indirectly in the presidential election of 1848, when General Zachary Taylor's acceptance of the Whig nomination was delayed by his refusal to pay the postage on the rising tide of unsolicited mail sent to him in the period between the lowering of the postal rates and the mandating of prepayment. Since Taylor had instructed the Baton Rouge postmaster to dispose of all letters that came postage due, official notice of the nomination entered a substantial bundle of mail forwarded to the Dead Letter Office. Perplexed by Taylor's failure to reply, the chairman of the convention had to send a duplicate letter, much to the embarrassment of the party.[49]

Even beyond the emerging world of literary and political celebrity, postal users were growing accustomed to the accessibility of people they knew only by name and home town. After meeting his nephew for the first time and under remarkable circumstances, a character in E. D. E. N. Southworth's highly successful novel *The Hidden Hand* (1859) resolves to write him a letter as soon as he gets home. Once his identity comes fortuitously to light, the estranged relative becomes instantly accessible through the post.[50] The relationship between individual identity and postal address could work in the other direction as well. In John Rollin Ridge's popular 1854 narrative of the life of California outlaw Joaquín Murrieta, the protagonist is able to free one of his comrades from the clutches of the law by pretending to be a San Jose merchant named Samuel Harrington and testifying on behalf of the man in custody. To prove his identity to the court, Ridge recounts, Murrieta presented "five or six letters addressed in different hands to 'Mr. Samuel Harrington, San José,' and bearing the marks of various post offices in the State."[51] The new postal network introduced a system for mapping persons that was, at the same time, both anonymous and especially attached to the individual name.

By the 1870s, a great portion of the mail arriving daily in post offices was posted to parties whom the sender did not know. This development marked, in a superficial sense, a return to the first third of the century, when news and Congressional communications dominated the mails. But the new system was strikingly different. Before 1845, printed documents addressed to no one in particular comprised the bulk of postal transmission, but they were the special province of newspaper editors (who enjoyed subsidized rates) and government officials (who wielded franking privileges). After the mid-century reforms, the privilege became democratized, at least to the extent that the power to communicate with many unknown persons was available to anyone who could afford printing costs (or the burden of extensive copying) and radically reduced postal rates. A wide assortment of publishers, ideologues, schemers, fund-raisers, pranksters, entrepreneurs, solicitors, marriage-seekers, and others flooded the mails with the sort of correspondence that simultaneously exploited and eroded popular notions of the letter as a form of personal relationship across distance.

Less than a decade after the end of the Civil War, an unusual exhibit was staged before the U.S. Congress. In one of the more remarkable and famous scenes of nineteenth-century postal history, a young vice inspector named Anthony Comstock assembled for his distinguished audience a collection of obscene pamphlets, books, song lyrics, photographs, and novelty items—all of which had entered the mails. Comstock also shared some representative samples from a cache of fifteen thousand posted letters written by boys and girls in American boarding schools ordering such materials. Comstock's intention was to dramatize the alarming popularity of pornography, masturbation, and promiscuity among young Americans and to attach moral responsibility for the problem to a federal government whose postal service allowed the circulation of dangerous texts, images, and devices. Buffeted by an upsurge in organized evangelical activity and an expanded vision of the moral responsibility of Congress, Comstock famously succeeded in initiating a major government crusade against sexual vice.

In persuading legislators that the mail was serving the immoral purposes of many of its patrons, Comstock and his colleagues at the YMCA

— FIGURE 9 —

BACK OF THE NEW YORK POST OFFICE, WHERE OBSCENE MATERIALS ARE DEPOS-
ITED AND WITHDRAWN. FROM THE FRONTISPIECE TO ANTHONY COMSTOCK'S
FRAUDS EXPOSED (1880).

emphasized a very particular (though telling) dimension of this historical
transformation of the post. Calling Congressional attention to the volume of salacious literature, obscene photographs, and sexual paraphernalia that passed through the mail, Comstock's crusade reflected the new
power and priorities of an evangelical preoccupation with sexual vice.
The choice of the mail system as a target for this evangelical campaign
reflected, as historians have emphasized, a new attitude toward the use
of federal power to address social problems and a long-standing strategic
awareness among reformers that the post provided a singularly legitimate
and effective arena in which to exercise federal authority. But the post
may have attracted the scrutiny of vice crusaders and politicians for other
reasons as well. When Congress began considering the phenomenon of
obscene mail in 1865, it did so against the backdrop of the postal habits
of Civil War soldiers, whose correspondence had received such intense
publicity and had thrust the relationship between mail and moral influence so forcefully into national consciousness.[52] More important, by
the time Comstock's lobbying efforts bore major fruit in 1873 (when
Comstock himself was empowered as a special agent of the federal government to confiscate mail and arrest postal users), the tendency of the
post to bring strangers into contact was especially conspicuous. At once
public and private, anonymous and personal, the mail was a site of new
and recognizably disruptive forms of social and commercial connection.

The post "*goes everywhere*," Comstock would observe indignantly, even after he was granted special powers of surveillance, interdiction, and punishment, "and it is *secret*" (see fig. 9).[53] Both of these features of the modern mail network had of course been central to the charge of the United States Post Office since 1792, when the post was designed largely around the exigencies of long-distance political communication. But as Comstock's readers and supporters had come to recognize, a system that allowed strangers to communicate cheaply throughout the country could transform interpersonal relations as well.

EPILOGUE

By the 1870s America was a postal society. To live in (or visit) the United States at that time was to inhabit a world wired for interactive mail exchange, wired by habit and convention and not simply by bureaucratic administration and material infrastructure. Yet in many ways Americans stood at a communications crossroads. While the revolutionary implications of cheap postage in a mobile, literate society had been broadly realized, several developments and innovations pointed in unfamiliar directions.

Already in 1863, the introduction of free home delivery in America's largest cities portended a new relationship between mail and public space. A decade later the experiment was firmly entrenched, and the Post Office Department was employing one letter carrier for every 3,690 Americans. It would be several years before the post would systematically enter the domiciles of its users and provide, in effect, a standard amenity in the modern American home. Only with the expansion of the carrier system would postal participation become linked fundamentally to residence; and only then would a visit to the post office mark (as it does today) a departure from the ordinary conduct of postal business rather than its basic execution. But such a metamorphosis was clearly under way.

Other harbingers of change belong more squarely to the 1870s. Perhaps the most momentous came in 1874 at a meeting of the International Postal Congress in Bern, Switzerland. The treaty negotiated at that conference, which took effect the following year, established a World Postal Union (later titled the Universal Postal Union) in place of the bilateral postal agreements that had organized transnational mail exchange up to that point. Under the new system, the United States entered a shared postal space with all of Europe (including Russia) as well as Turkey and Egypt. Within two years Japan, Brazil, and Persia joined, along with European colonies on several continents. From this point on, correspondents in all of those places could post to one another for a single flat (and cheap) rate of international postage that did not depend either on distance or on the diplomatic relations between the countries of a letter's origin and destination.[1]

The World Postal Union was not a completely new idea in 1874. The American-born League of Universal Brotherhood (founded in 1847 by the pacifist Connecticut blacksmith Elihu Burritt) had from its inception advocated cheap ocean postage, a cause embraced during the Civil War by Postmaster General Montgomery Blair. And already at mid-century, the principle of postal districts that crossed several state jurisdictions was enacted in the German-Austrian Postal Union.[2] Seen from the perspective of administrative policy and ideology, the Bern agreement simply expanded the reach of the German-Austrian model (and even, one might argue, the federalist model of the U.S. Postal Act of 1792) and extended the logic of the cheap postage movements that had swept the West around mid-century. But seen from the perspective of American postal users, the union, though clearly consonant with the earlier strategies and priorities of Rowland Hill and like-minded American advocates of cheap postage, had a more ambiguous relationship to the reforms of 1845 and 1851. While cheap domestic postage had turned the United States into a single postal district, the international postal treaty established a postal zone without national borders. Between 1845 and 1875, in other words, part of what it meant to live in the United States was to have a special kind of access to other people living in the country, no matter how far away. Of course one could also use the same mail system to communicate with people outside the country, but to do so required special thinking about where those people were and what sorts of boundaries and costs stood in the way. Much as recent changes in the differentiated fee structure of long-distance phone communication have altered our perceptions of the proximity of friends, family, business associates, and hotel receptionists in foreign locales (or simply in other area codes), the World Postal Union reshuffled the categorical distinction between local and long distance that had been set up by the first postage reduction. For many American postal users this was probably a welcome development. In the years leading up to the signing of the treaty, international correspondence had become increasingly popular, rising at a much faster rate than domestic mail (in the decade after the Civil War, the number of letters posted between the United States and other countries nearly tripled, exceeding twenty-five million by 1875). But welcome or not, new international postal arrangements heralded the passing of an era.[3]

Like the standardization and simplification of international mail, the introduction of postcards both lowered participation costs even more and allowed a new experience of postal exchange. The earliest American postcards were issued in 1873 (Austria had inaugurated the age of the postcard in 1869, and Britain had followed shortly thereafter), and within two years they were bringing in more than a million dollars in annual revenue to the Post Office. For the first twenty-five years of their existence, postcards (as distinguished from private mailing cards, which did not qualify for the special one-cent postage rate) were nonpictorial and issued exclusively by the government. They had no appeal as visual souvenirs, as they would have in the twentieth century, nor were they in any direct sense descendants of the pictorial letter sheets that sold so well during the Gold Rush. Instead, the essence of the postcard innovation of the 1870s lay in its price, size, and transparency. There was from the start something elegant, not to mention convenient, about cards that bore their own one-cent postage and could travel anywhere in the country. And since postcards supplied a built-in excuse for being brief, they further lowered the threshold for mail exchange (the postcard, as one recent celebrant puts it, "justifies, from the outside, by means of the borders, the indigence of the discourse"). Before 1845 a correspondent assumed a heavy burden in deciding to send a letter. Over the next few decades that burden had lightened, but the cultural construction of the personal letter as a gesture of intimate connection tended to maintain some of the earlier pressures. Postcards, on the other had, accentuated the ease with which letters could be produced as well as transmitted, and were especially suited to brief, casual messages, such as those between an advertiser and a prospective consumer.[4]

But if in some respects postcards extended the logic and followed the momentum of the earlier reform movement, by other measures they reversed its course, signaling a break from mid-century understandings of the post. Cheap postage had introduced in the middle decades of the century a conception of mail as the undifferentiated, sealed contents of an envelope. But the advent of the prepaid card made it unnecessary to count pages or otherwise assess the contents of a postal exchange; it simply had to be weighed. Postcards recalled a time when users paid for a volume of words rather than for a half-ounce of miscellaneous enclosures. And if the postcard further democratized the exchange of interpersonal greetings, it fit uneasily into familiar constructions of epistolary intimacy. By emptying the personal letter of its enclosures, the tendency of the postcard was toward the reduction of correspondence to formal gestures. More obviously, postcards also exposed themselves to public view. Appearing the same year as the Comstock Act (which authorized inspection and interdiction of obscene materials), postcards belonged to a moment when the grounds of postal privacy were shifting perceptibly.

All of these innovations in the conduct and regulation of mail service during the 1870s changed the popular experience of the post. But the year of the national centennial brought a far more dramatic portent of the dissolution of the mid-century postal culture. Within a few years of its introduction, the telephone had entered the homes of sixty thousand subscribers, already providing more direct personal access to that medium than Americans had to the electromagnetic telegraph, which remained expensive to use on a regular basis (prohibitively so for those not engaged in high-value commercial exchanges), even three decades after its invention.[5] As the regular use of telephones spread during the ensuing decades, the mail network would lose its unique place as a popular medium of long-distance interaction. All of the forms of connection that different groups of Americans had cultivated through the mid-century post—among friends, relatives, consumers, and strangers—had emerged during a period when correspondence by mail was the dominant mechanism and model for both maintaining and imagining such connections. In a sense, the end of this period was now in plain view.

Phone contact did not of course render letter-writing obsolete in the twentieth century, though the forms of intimacy and connection that have grown up around the telephone over the last century are distinctive—something that is easier to discern now that new nonvocal media (some of them epistolary) have displaced phone use in a widening range of contexts. But the persistence of mail as a slower, seemingly more immanent form of communication in the age of instantaneous electronic exchange is potentially misleading. Despite all the changes that separate us from the postal culture of the mid-nineteenth century, our pervasive expectations of complete contact, of boundless accessibility, actually link us back to the cultural moment when ordinary Americans first experienced the mail in similar terms. The world we now inhabit belongs to the extended history of that moment.

NOTES

The archives housing the various collections of documents cited in these notes are identified in those citations by the following abbreviations.

AAS American Antiquarian Society, Worcester, MA
BANC Bancroft Library, University of California at Berkeley
CHS California Historical Society, San Francisco
NA National Archives, Washington, DC
NEW Newberry Library, Chicago, IL
N-YHS New-York Historical Society, New York, NY
SHC Southern Historical Collection, Louis Round Wilson Library, University of North Carolina, Chapel Hill

INTRODUCTION

1. Charles Emery Stevens, *Anthony Burns: A History* (Boston: John P. Jewett, 1856), 181–97. The text of Burns's letter to Dana appears in Albert J. Von Frank, *The Trials of Anthony Burns* (Cambridge, MA: Harvard University Press, 1998), 287–88.

2. Stevens, *Anthony Burns*, 194.

3. Ibid., 193.

4. Allan Pred, *Urban Growth and City Systems in the United States, 1840–1860* (Cambridge, MA: Harvard University Press, 1980), 224. Ronald Zboray claims that per capita correspondence more than quintupled during the same period, but he appears to have misread Pred's figures; see *A Fictive People: Antebellum Economic Development and the American Reading Public* (Oxford: Oxford University Press, 1993), 112. In an 1855 report, postal reformer Pliny Miles reported a higher figure for 1840 (almost 41 million), while Representative John Hutchins, in an 1862 congressional address, came up with a loftier figure for 1860 (more than 184 million). Gardiner Hubbard's 1875 analysis relied upon stamp sales to generate an even higher number of letters sent in 1860 (more than 245 million). By Hubbard's reckoning, the number of letters per capita reached 22 by the middle of the 1870s. See Pliny Miles, *Postal Reform: Its Urgent Necessity and Practicability* (New York: Stringer & Townsend, 1855), 26–27; *Speech of Hon. John Hutchins, of Ohio, in the House of Representatives, May 19th, 1862, on Low and Uniform Postage* (New York: D. Appleton, 1862), 17; Gardiner G. Hubbard, *Our Post Office* (Cambridge, MA: Riverside Press, 1875), 9.

5. James Holbrook, *Ten Years Among the Mail Bags: or, Notes from the Diary of a Special Agent of the Post-Office Department* (Philadelphia: H. Cowperthwait, 1855), 292–93.

6. *Proceedings of a Public Meeting of Citizens of Minnesota, in Favor of a Semi-Weekly Overland Mail from Saint Paul to Puget Sound. Held January 3, 1859.* (St. Paul, MN: Pioneer Printing, 1859), 10.

7. Junius Henri Browne, *The Great Metropolis: A Mirror of New York* (Hartford, CT: American Publishing, 1869), 417–18.

8. François Peyre-Ferry, *The Art of Epistolary Composition, or models of letters, billets, bills of exchange, bills of lading, invoices, &c. with preliminary instructions and notes. To which are added, a collection of fables intended as exercises for pupils learning the French language; a series of letters between a cadet and his father, describing the system pursued at the American, Literary, Scientific, and Military Academy, at Middletown* (Middletown, CT: E. & H. Clark, 1826); Samuel Kerl, *Elements of Composition* (1869), quoted in Lucille M. Schultz, "Letter-Writing Instruction in Nineteenth-Century Schools in the United States," in *Letter Writing as a Social Practice*, ed. David Barton and Nigel Hall (Amsterdam and Philadelphia: John Benjamins, 2000), 113. Earlier books asserted the popularity and importance of letter-writing, but typically in the context of genteel or bourgeois culture. See, for example, the frequently reprinted *Fashionable Letter Writer; Or, Art of Polite Correspondence* (New York: George Long, 1818), xi, xxiii. For an example somewhere between Peyre-Ferry's and Kerl's, see Richard Green Parker, *Aids to English Composition* (New York: Harper and Brothers, 1845), which claims somewhat tentatively that "a letter is, perhaps, one of the most common, as well as one of the most useful forms of composition, and there are few, who can read or write at all, who are not frequently called upon to perform it" (183–84).

9. Henry D. Thoreau, *Walden, Or Life in the Woods* (Boston: Houghton Mifflin, 1919), 104. By the time Thoreau published the book in 1854, he felt compelled to explain that his ungenerous assessment that he had "never received more than one or two letters . . . that were worth the postage" had been written "some years ago," that is, before the second postal reform. Thoreau reworked the text considerably between 1851 and 1854, and the disclaimer may have reflected some increasing dependence on the mail, even on the part of this famously reclusive author. Interestingly, at some even earlier point in his thinking about the post, Thoreau may not have associated it with letters at all. In the earliest notebook version of the post office passage (1846–1847), the central line about the dispensability of the mails appears to describe a news broadcast medium rather than a system of interpersonal correspondence: "I think that there are very few important communications made through the Post Office—and I never read any memorable news in a newspaper in my life." See J. Lyndon Stanley, *The Making of Walden, with the Text of the First Version* (Chicago: University of Chicago Press, 1957), 156.

10. Frances Webster to Lucien Webster, August 3, 1846, in *The Websters: Letters of an American Family in Peace and War, 1836–1853*, ed. Van R. Baker (Kent, OH: Kent State University Press, 2000), 94. Gardner's diary is quoted in Malcolm Rohrbough, *Days of Gold: The California Gold Rush and the American Nation* (Berkeley and Los Angeles: University of California Press, 1997), 233. Americans who lived outside of cities or in places without daily mail delivery grew increasingly attuned to delivery schedules. Emily Wharton Sinkler, an elite Philadelphian who had moved to South Carolina with her husband in 1842, recorded a detailed awareness of postal logistics in 1848: "There is a mail from Vances Ferry twice a week. A boy leaves The Eutaw [plantation] every Monday and Thursday at 3 pm for the Post Office with letters and returns the same evening with letters that have come from Charleston. The letters we send down to the office leave Vances Ferry early on the mornings of Tuesday and Friday and arrive in Charleston in time to go on the same afternoon in the Wilmington boat. Consequently the letters we send to the PO on Monday ought to arrive in Philadelphia on Friday afternoon." See Anne Sinkler Whaley LeClerq, *An Antebellum Plantation Household: Including the South Carolina Low Country Receipts and Remedies of Emily Wharton Sinkler* (Columbia: University of South Carolina Press, 1996), 27; see also Benjamin Wingate's admonitions to his wife about the timing of mail steamers to California: "By the way, the Steamers I think leave N. York on the 13th & 26th of each month. To reach them your letters should leave [Connecticut] about the 10th and 23rd. Will you please bear that in mind?" (Wingate Correspondence, Bancroft MSS 83/35c, BANC).

11. Charlotte Forten, *The Journal of Charlotte Forten: A Young Black Woman's Reactions to the White World of the Civil War Era,* ed. Ray Allen Billington (New York: W. W. Norton, 1981), 163.

12. H. Hastings Weld, "Some Thoughts on Letter Writing," *Godey's Lady's Book* 44 (April 1852), 250.

13. One clarification about terminology may be in order here. Most of the postal practices described in this book took place under the auspices of a state-sponsored bureaucracy, and it is surely an important feature of the American postal service that it was federally owned and operated—at a time when the imprint of the federal government on everyday life could be (otherwise) hard to detect. But for the purposes of understanding what was novel about the postal culture that emerged in the nineteenth century, the defining feature of a postal system is not whether letters are delivered by the state or by a private company. The crucial distinction is between the act of participating in a postal system of any kind and other epistolary exchanges (a note left for a neighbor, a letter sent via an individual traveler) that may require personal acquaintance or special identity and in any event do not involve a regular network of mail transmission. Postal systems such as Adams Express and Wells Fargo in 1850, much like Federal Express and UPS (and, to some extent, the semiprivatized United States Postal Service) in our own time, functioned as publicly accessible networks of communication, even if they were run for profit by private commercial interests. Private express companies do not form a large part of the story that unfolds in this book, but they do count as part of the postal culture within which users made sense of their place in the world.

CHAPTER ONE

1. Caroline Pettigrew to her mother, June 3, 1856, Pettigrew Family Papers, series 1.8 (folder 192), SHC.

2. Daniel R. Headrick, *When Information Came of Age: Technologies of Knowledge in the Age of Reason and Revolution, 1700–1850* (Oxford: Oxford University Press, 2000), 193–94.

3. Ibid., 193 (quoting the Center for the History of Electrical Engineering).

4. I have in mind here not so much the famous depictions of the Persian post in Xenophon and Herodotus, but the more fascinating account in the biblical Book of Esther, in which mail transports the absent body of an invisible king across a vast empire, extending a power capable of committing genocide, determining the outcome of war, and forging religious identity.

5. See Richard R. John, *Spreading the News: The American Postal System from Franklin to Morse* (Cambridge: Cambridge University Press, 1995). Konstantin Dierks has argued, on the basis of post office records in Newport in the middle of the eighteenth century, that the post was far more inclusive by the end of the colonial era than historians often suppose, and that "by the eve of the Revolution the Newport post office was being patronized by more middling and poorer people, more women, and more rural residents than ever before." But the Newport case still suggests that even in cities (which accounted for a negligible portion of the nation's population in the 1770s), those who used the post at all were a distinct minority (17 percent of white male adults and 2 percent of white female adults in 1774), and only a tiny elite used it with any frequency. No more than thirty-four people received mail even once a month in Rhode Island's largest city before the Revolution. See Konstantin Dierks, "'Let Me Chat a Little': Letter Writing in Rhode Island before the Revolution," *Rhode Island History* 53, no. 4 (1995): 120–33.

6. Richard D. Brown, *Knowledge Is Power: The Diffusion of Information in Early America, 1700–1865* (New York: Oxford University Press, 1989), 148–49. Even as late as the 1830s, letters sometimes carried special pleas for the postmaster to make sure that a letter found its way to its intended recipient. See, for example, Frances Crutchfield's note on the back of an 1835 letter to William Callaghan, in Harold H. Haines, *The Callaghan*

Mail, 1821–1859: A Book Featuring the Lives of William Callaghan, Missouri Pioneer, and His Slave Isaac Crawford (Hannibal, MO: Harold H. Haines, 1944), 39.

7. By 1854, the Portland/Savannah turnaround would be nine days, and the trip from New York to Canandaigua and back would take a single day; see "The United States Mail," *De Bow's Review* 16 (June 1854): 553–70.

8. As Konstantin Dierks has pointed out, "trusting that a letter would reach its intended recipient was, in the eighteenth century, something of a leap of faith" ("'Let Me Chat a Little,'" 123).

9. Susan Miller, *Assuming the Positions: Cultural Pedagogy and the Politics of Commonplace Writing* (Pittsburgh, PA: University of Pittsburgh Press, 1998), 238. Virginia physician Sextus Barbour, in his late twenties, wrote for his own benefit, a few years before the postal reform of 1845, "Directions for Writing," which included the admonition that "All letters should be enveloped but such as are sent by the post." At least for well-to-do Virginians during this era, the privately conveyed letter remained standard (ibid., 62). On the use of private conveyance during the late colonial era, see Dierks, "'Let Me Chat a Little,'" 124. On the particular dependence of international correspondence on the vagaries of individual travelers, see Sarah Marjorie Savage Pearsall, "'After All These Revolutions': Epistolary Identities in an Atlantic World, 1760–1815," PhD diss. (Harvard University, 2001), 94–99.

10. Pred, *Urban Growth*, 82; Wayne E. Fuller, *The American Mail: Enlarger of the Common Life* (Chicago: University of Chicago Press, 1972), 61. Expensive postage was not, of course, a new problem in the early national era. During colonial times, for example, the cost (to the recipient) of a simple letter was so prohibitive that Benjamin Franklin, scrupulous about extending his franking privileges to relatives, thought it reasonable that frugality had prevented his wife from sending a condolence to his sister Jane Mecom upon the death of a daughter in 1764; see Carl Van Doren, ed., *The Letters of Benjamin Franklin and Jane Mecom* (Princeton, NJ: Princeton University Press, 1950), 81. The incident is mentioned in William Merrill Decker, *Epistolary Practices: Letter Writing in America before Telecommunication* (Chapel Hill: University of North Carolina Press, 1998), 59.

11. Before 1845 the United States had no special arrangements with any European country for the exchange of mail; see George E. Hargest, *History of Letter Post Communication between the United States and Europe, 1845–1875* (Washington, DC: Smithsonian Institution Press, 1971).

12. John Pintard, *Letters from John Pintard to his Daughter, Eliza Pintard Davidson, 1816–1833* 4 vols. (New York: New-York Historical Society, 1841). For Pintard, the cost and the delays involved in sending letters through the post office were outweighed by the fact the post offered "more certainty & less trouble" (1:158, letter of February 24, 1817). For the postage bills of other well-to-do Americans during the Jacksonian era, see John, *Spreading the News*, 159–60.

13. Anna Briggs Bentley to "My dear friends," August 17, 1826, in *American Grit: A Woman's Letters from the Ohio Frontier*, ed. Emily Foster (Lexington, KY: University Press of Kentucky, 2002), 40. For other examples of letters sent by Bentley through private conveyance, see pp. 61, 73. Cross-writing was a popular practice that survived the arrival of penny postage. See the 1859 letter of Bessie Huntting reproduced in Ellen K. Rothman, *Hands and Hearts: A History of Courtship in America* (New York: Basic Books, 1984), 86. See also Jane E. Harrison, *Until Next Year: Letter Writing and the Mails in the Canadas, 1640–1830* (Hull, Quebec: Wilfrid Laurier University Press, 1997), 39. At least some correspondents (not to mention later historians) found the practice irritating. See Anne Sinkler Whaley LeClerq, ed., *Between North and South: The Letters of Emily Wharton Sinkler, 1842–1865* (Columbia: University of South Carolina Press, 2001), 20, 22, 40; David W. Blight, ed., *When This Cruel War Is Over: The Civil War Letters of Charles Harvey Brewster* (Amherst: University of Massachusetts Press, 1992), 91.

14. Letter of December 20, 1827, in *American Grit*, ed. Foster, 67. For other instances when Bentley took advantage of Stabler's frank, see ibid., 112, 118.

15. Letter of April 28, 1828, ibid., 80–81.

16. R. Watts to Mr. Hubbell S. Gregory, Jackson, MI, April 16, 1843, Rix and Walbridge Families Collection, MSS 1797A/1, CHS.

17. Kenneth R. de Lisle, *The W. L. L. Peltz Collection of Albany Postal History: The Hudson River Mail, 1804–1858* (Albany, NY: Albany Institute of History and Art, 1969), 11–12.

18. Haines, *Callaghan Mail*, 32–35. Even in the Northeast, where letter-writing was most popular during the first part of the nineteenth century, the cost of postage discouraged widespread, regular use of the mail. Looking back in 1909 at the postal history of her small Massachusetts town, Mary Anna Tarbell recalled a time when letters were an "expensive joy ... not to be lightly dispatched"; see Mary Anna Tarbell, *Stage Days in Brimfield: A Century of Mail and Coach* (Springfield, MA: F. A. Bassette, 1909), 17. On New England correspondence in the era of expensive postage, see William Gilmore, *Reading Becomes a Necessity of Life: Material and Cultural Life in Rural New England, 1780–1835* (Knoxville: University of Tennessee Press, 1989), 380–83; and John Robert Pankratz, "New Englanders, the Written Word, and the Errand into Ohio, 1788–1830," PhD diss., Cornell University, 1988.

19. "A Chapter upon Letters and Letter-Writers," *Ladies' Repository* 16 (February 1856), 70–71.

20. Elizabeth Keckley, *Behind the Scenes, or, Thirty Years a Slave, and Four Years in the White House*, ed. Frances Smith Foster (Chicago: Lakeside Press, 1998), 29.

21. John, *Spreading the News*; Richard B. Kielbowicz, *News in the Mail: The Press, Post Office, and Public Information, 1700–1860s* (New York: Greenwood Press, 1989). In 1832, for example, newspapers accounted for 95 percent of the total mail by weight, but generated less than 15 percent of revenues.

22. See editorial in *Harper's Monthly* (October, 1855), 697: "Strictly speaking, the transmission of correspondence is not a national concern." On the historical transformation of the post as an instrument of state power, see Bernhard Siegert, *Relays: Literature as an Epoch of the Postal System*, trans. Kevin Repp (Stanford, CA: Stanford University Press, 1999).

23. On the history of these enactments, see Kielbowicz, *News in the Mail*, 83–93; John, *Spreading the News*, 160–61.

24. David Vincent has pointed to the especially high correlation between railroad use and postal correspondence in Europe toward the end of the nineteenth century; see "The Progress of Literacy," *Victorian Studies* 45, no. 3 (2003): 405–31. On the interrelation of post, rail, and telegraph line in reinforcing new habits and expectations of punctuality, see Mark M. Smith, *Mastered by the Clock: Time, Slavery, and Freedom in the American South* (Chapel Hill: University of North Carolina Press, 1997), especially 73–89.

25. See Elliot Gorn, *The Manly Art: Bare-Knuckle Prize Fighting in Nineteenth-Century America* (Ithaca, NY: Cornell University Press, 1986), 94.

26. Kielbowicz, *News in the Mail*, 83–89. On the ideological relationship between cheap postage and liberal reform, see Siegert, *Relays*.

27. Historians of reading have recently begun to stress the uses of literacy rather than its simple acquisition and to question triumphalist accounts of the spread of writing and print in modern societies. See Harvey J. Graff, *The Literacy Myth: Literacy and Social Structure in the Nineteenth Century* (New York: Academic Press, 1979); Ruth Finnegan, *Literacy and Orality* (Oxford: Basil Blackwell, 1988). On the relationship between literacy and the rise of the cheap daily newspaper, see Michael Schudson, *Discovering the News: A Social History of American Newspapers* (New York: Basic Books, 1978), 35–39. See also David M. Henkin, *City Reading: Written Words and Public Spaces in Antebellum New York* (New York: Columbia University Press, 1998), 20–22.

28. Elijah P. Marrs, *Life and History of the Rev. Elijah P. Marrs* (Louisville, KY: Bradley and Gilbert, 1885), 12.

29. Letters had served these performative and pedagogical functions in earlier periods as well. What was new to mid-century postal culture was the extent to which masses of Americans participated in these rituals. For examples of parental evaluations of letters from the beginning of the nineteenth century, see Richard L. Bushman, *The Refinement of America: Persons, Houses, Cities* (New York: Knopf, 1992), 215–17; Miller, *Assuming the Positions*, 225, 228; Harvey J. Graff, *Conflicting Paths: Growing Up in America* (Cambridge, MA: Harvard University Press, 1995), 43. The most thorough discussion of the inculcation of letter-writing habits among children in late eighteenth-century America appears in Konstantin Dierks, "Letter Writing, Gender, and Class in America, 1750—1800" (PhD diss., Brown University, 1999), chap. 6.

30. Susan Winslow Hodge, ed., *The Elfreth Book of Letters* (Philadelphia: University of Pennsylvania Press, 1985), 29, 111. The Ridgely family in rural Delaware adopted a similar set of practices early in the century. Congressman Henry Moore Ridgely corresponded with his eight-year-old son, deliberately misspelling words for his son to locate and correct (Bushman, *Refinement of America*, 215–17).

31. E. Grey Dimond and Herman Hattaway, eds., *Letters from Forest Place: A Plantation Family's Correspondence, 1846–1881* (Jackson: University Press of Mississippi, 1993), 15, 17; Mary, Emily, Albert, and Lucy Wingate to Benjamin Wingate, April 15, 1851; Mary Wingate to Benjamin, February 4, 1852, both in Wingate Correspondence, Bancroft MSS 83/35c, BANC; unknown author to sister Mary, September 14, 1852, Bancroft MSS 83/35c, box 2, BANC. See also examples in Thomas E. Augst, *The Clerk's Tale: Young Men and Moral Life in Nineteenth-Century America* (Chicago: University of Chicago Press, 2003), 232–34. Recurrent affirmations of children's improved epistolary skills suggest the major role that letters played in the construction of family bonds, a topic explored further in a later chapter.

32. The surviving letters of German-born Peter Klein, for example, who settled first in Pennsylvania before joining the Gold Rush, appear in at least seven distinct hands. See Walter D. Kamphoefner, Wolfgang Helbich, and Ulrike Sommer, eds., *News from the Land of Freedom: German Immigrants Write Home*, trans. Susan Carter Vogel (Ithaca, NY: Cornell University Press, 1991), 383. For examples of illiterate Norwegian immigrants dictating letters or barely literate ones struggling to spell by ear, see Orm Øverland, "Learning to Read Immigrant Letters: Reflections towards a Textual Theory," in *Norwegian-American Essays, 1996*, ed. Øyvind T. Gullicksen, David C. Mauk, and Dina Tolfsby (Oslo: NAHA Norway, 1996), 218.

33. Randall M. Miller, ed., *"Dear Master": Letters of a Slave Family* (Ithaca, NY: Cornell University Press, 1978), 253.

34. Stephen Pembroke to his brother James W. C. Pennington, Sharpsburg, May 30, 1854, in *Slave Testimony: Two Centuries of Letters, Speeches, Interviews, and Autobiographies*, ed. John W. Blassingame (Baton Rouge: Louisiana State University Press, 1977), 108.

35. Solomon Northup, *Twelve Years a Slave. Narrative of Solomon Northup, a Citizen of New York* (Auburn, NY: Derby and Miller, 1853), 230.

36. *New Orleans Picayune*, July 11, 1841.

37. The diary entry was recorded on July 26, 1864, and printed a few months later in the *Liberator*. It appears in Edwin S. Redkey, ed., *A Grand Army of Black Men: Letters from African-American Soldiers in the Union Army, 1861–1865* (New York: Cambridge University Press, 1992), 69. Another former slave, Sarah Fitzpatrick, recalled that illiteracy exposed slaves' courtships to the unwelcome scrutiny of white neighbors. See Janet Duitsman Cornelius, *"When I Can Read My Title Clear": Literacy, Slavery, and Religion in the Antebellum South* (Columbia: University of South Carolina Press, 1991), 73.

38. William S. Pettigrew to Moses, June 24, 1856, Pettigrew Family Papers, series 1.8 (folders 173–97), SHC.

39. See, for examples, William S. Pettigrew to Moses, June 24, 1856; Lizzy, Henry, Moses, and Malica J. White to Pettigrew, July 5, 1856; Pettigrew to Moses, July 12, 1856; Malica J. White to Pettigrew, July 24, 1856; Henry and Moses to Pettigrew, August 2, 1856; in Pettigrew Family Papers, series 1.8 (folders 173–97), SHC. A few of these letters are excerpted in Robert S. Starobin, ed., *Blacks in Bondage: Letters of American Slaves* (New York: Viewpoints, 1974), 11–35.

40. Comparing mobility rates in the eighteenth and nineteenth centuries is complicated, given the different sorts of data available for various periods of American history. Recent work suggests that rates of demographic persistence (people staying in the same community for a significant period of time) in the second half of the eighteenth century were a bit lower than had been previously assumed. Persistence rates in the antebellum era may also need to be revised upward. Still, the best evidence supports the view that more people moved more often across far greater distances within the United States during the antebellum period than at any earlier time. Given the expansion of U.S. territorial sovereignty between 1783 and 1819, and given improvements in transportation during the first half of the nineteenth century, this point may be obvious, but its implications for the spread of the post are inestimable. The literature on mobility for both the colonial and the antebellum periods is considerable (less so for the early national era). On antebellum mobility, see especially, Michael B. Katz, Michael J. Doucet, and Mark J. Stern, "Migration and Social Order in Erie County, New York: 1855," *Journal of Interdisciplinary History* (Spring 1978): 669–701; Donald H. Parkerson, *The Agricultural Transition in New York State: Markets and Migration in Mid-Nineteenth-Century America* (Ames: Iowa State University Press, 1995); Kenneth J. Winkle, *The Politics of Community: Migration and Politics in Antebellum Ohio* (Cambridge: Cambridge University Press, 1988); Richard H. Steckel, "Household Migration, Urban Growth, and Industrialization: The United States, 1850–1860," National Bureau of Economic Research, Working Paper No. 2281, June 1987 (Cambridge, MA); Timothy R. Mahoney, *Provincial Lives: Middle-Class Experience in the Antebellum Middle West* (Cambridge: Cambridge University Press, 1999); James Davis, *Frontier America, 1800–1840: A Comparative Demographic Analysis* (Glendale, CA: Arthur H. Clark, 1977). For some representative revisions of the traditional picture of colonial America, see John W. Adams and Alice B. Kasakoff, "Migration and Family in Colonial New England: The View from Genealogies," *Journal of Family History* (Spring 1984): 24–43; and Georgia C. Villaflor and Kenneth C. Sokcloff, "Migration in Colonial America: Evidence from the Muster Rolls," *Social Science History* (1984): 539–70.

41. Peter Knights's study of demographic transition in Boston provides compelling evidence of population turnover (especially in the 1850s), even in one of America's oldest cities; see his "Population Turnover, Persistence, Residential Mobility in Boston, 1830–1860," in *Nineteenth-Century Cities: Essays in the New Urban History*, ed. Stephan Thernstrom and Richard Sennett (New Haven, CT: Yale University Press, 1969), 258–74. The rates of growth in New York, Philadelphia, Baltimore, and Cincinnati (to say nothing of new cities such as Chicago and San Francisco) guaranteed that at mid-century more than half the population had lived elsewhere twenty years earlier. Even among those who persisted from one decade to the next, residential mobility was quite high. This may not necessarily have produced dependence on long-distance contact, but it certainly enhanced the utility of a postal service that did not require users to identify the specific location of someone's residence. On intraurban mobility, see, for example, Kenneth A. Scherzer, *The Unbounded Community: Neighborhood Life and Social Structure in New York City, 1830–1875* (Durham, NC: Duke University Press, 1992), 19–48.

42. John Mack Faragher, *Sugar Creek: Life on the Illinois Prairie* (New Haven, CT: Yale University Press, 1986), 5–51; Lynn A. Bonfield and Mary C. Morrison, *Roxana's Children: The Biography of a Nineteenth-Century Vermont Family* (Amherst: University of Massachusetts Press, 1995), 23; Winkle, *Politics of Community*, 6. By 1860, only 30 percent of heads of household in Ohio were born in the state. The figure for Illinois was

only 8 percent. Only 29.2 percent of the white males living in Springfield, Illinois, in 1850 remained there for the rest of the decade. See Richard K. Vedder and Lowell E. Gallaway, "Migration and the Old Northwest," in *Essays in Nineteenth Century Economic History: The Old Northwest,* ed. David C. Klingaman and Richard K. Vedder (Athens: Ohio University Press, 1975), 170; and Kenneth J. Winkle, "The Votes of Lincoln's Springfield: Migration and Political Participation in an Antebellum City," *Journal of Social History* 25, no. 3 (Spring 1992): 596. Even in the South, which is often romanticized as premodern, mobility was extremely high, particularly among slaveholders and the human beings they claimed as property. Planters moved at staggering rates during the cotton boom of the late antebellum period: barely one in five of them stayed in the same place for twenty years. Slaves moved frequently even when their masters stayed put. The cumulative impact of runaways, inheritances, and the infamous slave trade (which broke up six hundred thousand slave marriages in the South between 1820 and 1860) was the formation of a highly mobile black population, especially by mid-century (though the steady westward flow of enslaved people actually peaked earlier, in the 1830s). By 1860, South Carolina was second to Vermont as the state with the highest proportion of its native population residing outside the state. See Paul W. Gates, *The Farmer's Age: Agriculture, 1815–1860* (New York: Holt, Rinehart and Winston, 1960), 122; Walter Johnson, *Soul by Soul: Life Inside the Antebellum Slave Market* (Cambridge, MA: Harvard University Press, 1999), 4–7; Peter D. McClelland and Richard J. Zeckhauser, *Demographic Dimensions of the New Republic: American Interregional Migration, Vital Statistics, and Manumissions, 1800–1860* (Cambridge: Cambridge University Press, 1982), 5–8, 50–53; Herbert Klein, *A Population History of the United States* (Cambridge: Cambridge University Press, 2004), 87–96.

43. "The Post-Office System, as an Element of Modern Civilization," *New Englander* 1 (1843): 22–23.

44. Pliny Miles, *Postal Reform: Its Urgent Necessity and Practicability* (New York: Stringer & Townsend, 1855), 66.

45. Hargest, *Letter Post Communication,* 1–5.

46. *Plough Boy,* December 30, 1820.

47. Anna Briggs Bentley to Sarah, Elizabeth, and Margaret, letter of July 14, 1827, in Foster ed., *American Grit,* 61. On the role of correspondence as both a consolation for the displaced and a recruitment device for chain migrations, see Jon Gjerde, *Minds of the West: Ethnocultural Evolution in the Rural Middle West, 1830–1917* (Chapel Hill: University of North Carolina Press, 1997), 86–88.

48. It is significant, however, that in Britain, use of the mails increased far more strikingly among correspondents in the same city than was true in the United States, where long-distance mail proved far more important. See Miles, *Postal Reform,* 33–35.

49. A. L. Stimson, *Express Office Hand-book and Directory, for the use of 1,200 express agents and their customers, being the History of the Express Business and the earlier rail-road enterprises in the United States. Together with some reminiscences of the old mail coaches and baggage wagons* (New York: John K. Stimson, 1860). In Stimson's view, the popularity of the private expresses "compelled" Congress to reduce letter rates in 1845 (82); Richard R. John argues that the Post Office was facing a major crisis in 1845 and had little choice but to lower rates or abandon the monopoly on mail transmission; see his "Private Enterprise, Public Good? Communications Deregulation as a National Political Issue, 1839–1851," in *Beyond the Founders: New Approaches to the Political History of the Early American Republic,* ed. Jeffrey L. Pasley, Andrew W. Robertson, and David Waldstreicher (Chapel Hill: University of North Carolina Press, 2004), especially 334–39; See also Richard R. John, "Recasting the Information Infrastructure for the Industrial Age," in *A Nation Transformed by Information: How Information Has Shaped the United States from Colonial Times to the Present,* ed. Alfred D. Chandler Jr. and James W. Cortada (New York: Oxford University Press, 2000), 70–71; Alvin F. Harlow, *Old Post Bags: The Story of Sending a Letter in Ancient and Modern Times* (New York: D. Appleton, 1928), 326–27.

50. "Report of George Plitt, Special Agent of the Post-Office Department, February 3, 1841," *New York Review* 9 (July 1841), 83.

51. "American Post Office," New York, January 20, 1844, broadside, N-YHS MSS.

52. Howard Robinson, *The British Post Office: A History* (Princeton, NJ: Princeton University Press, 1948); David Vincent, *Literacy and Popular Culture: England, 1750–1914* (Cambridge: Cambridge University Press, 1989), 32–49; Siegert, *Relays*, 100–107. British reform clearly reflected a new bureaucratic vision of the role of the state, the influence of which varied in the states that adopted British postal innovations.

53. For a detailed accounting of the immediate drop-off in postal revenues after the first reduction (and the Post Office Department's insistence that the reforms were not principally to blame), see the 1846 report of Postmaster General Cave Johnson, printed in *Niles' National Register*, December 19, 1846, 246.

54. Peter Gay, *The Naked Heart* (New York: W. W. Norton, 1995), 317; Pred, *Urban Growth*, 224–25; Zboray, *Fictive People*, 112; John, "Recasting the Information Infrastructure," 70.

55. New Englanders were in many respects in the vanguard of the postal culture that swept through the country in the later years, especially those who moved westward in the early decades of the century. For an interesting study of letter-writing among these Yankee migrants, see Pankratz, "New Englanders." On the differences between the epistolary habits of Southerners and Northerners as they moved west, see Richard Lyle Power, *Planting Corn Belt Culture: The Impress of the Upland Southerner and Yankee in the Old Northwest* (Indianapolis: Indiana Historical Society, 1953), 41–44.

56. Pred, *Urban Growth*, 147–49, 224–25; John, *Spreading the News*, 157–58; Miles, *Postal Reform*, 33; Pliny Miles, "History of the Post Office," pt. 2, *Bankers' Magazine and Statistical Register*, n.s., 7, no. 6 (December 1857): 444–46.

57. Caroline Kirkland, *A New Home, Who'll Follow?* ed. Sandra A. Zagarell (New Brunswick, NJ: Rutgers University Press, 1990), 177–78; Congressman quoted in Wayne E. Fuller, *Morality and the Mail in Nineteenth-Century America* (Champaign: University of Illinois Press, 2003), 60. In France, where an official government investigation gives us an unusually detailed picture of mail activity in 1847 (especially in rural areas), the link between postal participation and economic development is quite strong, supporting the view that the post was used heavily for business purposes. Note, however, that this survey was conducted two years before the postage reduction in that country made long-distance postal correspondence for social purposes a broadly affordable option. See Roger Chartier, Alain Boureau, and Cécile Dauphin, *Correspondence: Models of Letter-Writing from the Middle Ages to the Nineteenth Century*, trans. Christopher Woodall (Princeton, NJ: Princeton University Press, 1997), 12.

58. In his humorous portrayal of rural life during this era, Sherwood Bonner has his narrator explain that a particular character was bucking local custom in sending a boy to inquire for letters on a regular basis. "Most o' the folks on the perarer wuz mighty neglectful as to mail matter, trustin' usually to the chance of some neighbor inquirin' fur 'em, or lettin' it run on indefinite" (*Dialect Tales* [New York: Harper and Brothers, 1883], 42).

59. See the discussion of women's participation in chapter 3. The preponderance of male addressees in lists of uncollected mail is especially conspicuous in those mid-century newspapers (such as the *Chicago Tribune* and the *Philadelphia Ledger*) that divided their letter rolls into a "ladies" and a "gentlemen's" list. On gender disparities during the decades before cheap postage, see John, *Spreading the News*, 158. For a recent and blatant example of the crude identification of women with epistolary discourse, see Olga Kenyon's *800 Years of Women's Letters* (Boston: Faber and Faber, 1993), especially the foreword by P. D. James.

60. Starobin, *Blacks in Bondage*; Blassingame, *Slave Testimony*; Hebert Gutman, *The Black Family in Slavery and Freedom, 1750–1925* (New York: Pantheon, 1976), 5; David Brion Davis and Steven Mintz, eds., *The Boisterous Sea of Liberty: A Documentary History*

of America from Discovery through the Civil War (New York: Oxford University Press, 1998), 400; Keckley, *Behind the Scenes*, 14–15; John, *Spreading the News*, 158–59. A longer discussion of slave correspondence appears in Alejandra Dubcovsky, "Fighting the Storm: An Analysis of Letters from American Slaves," BA honors' thesis, University of California, Berkeley, 2005.

61. The most famous testimony on this point comes from Booker T. Washington's autobiographical recollections in *Up From Slavery: Three Negro Classics* (New York: Avon, 1965), 33. For other examples, see LeClerq, ed., *Between North and South*, 33; Mary Norcott Bryan, *A Grandmother's Recollection of Dixie* (New Bern, NC: O. G. Dunn, Printer, 1912[?]), 5 (digital version [1998] available at the Web site of the University of North Carolina: http://docsouth.unc.edu/bryan/menu.html); and Steven M. Stowe, *Intimacy and Power in the Old South: Ritual in the Lives of the Planters* (Baltimore, MD: Johns Hopkins University Press, 1987), 91. See also Sally E. Hadden, *Slave Patrols: Law and Violence in Virginia and the Carolinas* (Cambridge, MA: Harvard University Press, 2001), 150.

62. H. Mattison, *Louisa Picquet, the Octoroon: Or Inside Views of Southern Domestic Life* (New York: published by the author, 1861), 29–30. See also the earlier discussion of the regulation of slave access to the post.

63. Harriet Jacobs, *Incidents in the Life of a Slave Girl*, ed. Walter Teller (New York: Harcourt Brace Jovanovich, 1973), 130–31. An elaborate and insightful reading of the significance of letters and the post in Jacobs's text appears in Elizabeth Hewitt, *Correspondence and American Literature, 1770–1865* (Cambridge: Cambridge University Press, 2004), 119–41.

64. "A True Tale of Slavery," *The Leisure Hour: A Family Journal of Instruction and Recreation*, no. 476 (February 7, 1861), 85.

65. Henry Box Brown, *Narrative of the Life of Henry Box Brown* (New York: Oxford University Press, 2002).

66. Catherine Huntington to Joseph Huntington, July 16, 1845, Selden Huntington Family Papers, group 1064, box 1, folder 18, Yale University Manuscripts. Part of this letter is quoted in Gay, *Naked Heart*, 317; Mary Wingate to Benjamin Wingate, March 22, 1851, Wingate Correspondence, Bancroft MSS 83/35c, BANC. Cabinetmaker Edward Carpenter, discussed in chapter 2, noted the passage of the 1845 reform in his diary, just two days after remarking that his "postage bill counts up considerable." See entries for March 1 and March 3, 1845, in "The Diary of an Apprentice Cabinetmaker: Edward Jenner Carpenter's 'Journal' 1844–45," ed. Christopher Clark and Donald M. Scott, *Proceedings of the American Antiquarian Society* 98, pt, 2, 303–407.

67. Steve M. Stowe, ed., *A Southern Practice: The Diary and Autobiography of Charles A. Hentz, M.D.* (Charlottesville: University Press of Virginia, 2000), 163, 167; Weld, "Some Thoughts on Letter Writing," 250–51. Uncertainty over how to handle postage after 1845 surfaces in a letter from Edgar Allan Poe in which he instructs his correspondent, "Please write—and *do not* pay the postage"; see, John Ward Ostrom, ed., *The Letters of Edgar Allan Poe* (New York: Gordian Press, 1966), 2:333 (Poe to George Eveleth, December 15, 1846).

68. In the year before California was admitted to the Union, one diarist confided that she did not write to her friends because of the "enormous postage on letters between here and the United States"; see William Benemann, ed., *A Year of Mud and Gold: San Francisco in Letters and Diaries, 1849–1850* (Lincoln: University of Nebraska Press, 1999), 46. For other mentions of postage in Gold Rush correspondence, see David Jackson, ed., *Direct Your Letters to San Jose: The California Gold Rush Letters and Diary of James and David Lee Campbell, 1849–1852* (Kansas City, MO: Orderly Pack Rat, 2000), 211; R. W. G. Vail, ed., "California Letters of the Gold Rush Period: The Correspondence of John Ingalls, 1849–1851," *Proceedings of the American Antiquarian Society* 47 (April 1937): 166; Benjamin B. Richards, ed., *California Gold Rush Merchant: The Journal of Stephen Chapin Davis* (San Marino, CA: Huntington Library, 1956), 19; Harlow, *Old Post Bags*, 353.

69. Unknown author to sister Louisa, Rabbit Creek, Sierra County, February 9, 1856, California Gold Rush Letters, 1848–1859, Bancroft Library MSS, C-B 547, box 2, BANC; Franklin A. Buck, *A Yankee Trader in the Gold Rush: The Letters of Franklin A. Buck* (Boston, MA: Houghton Mifflin, 1930), 48; Enos Christman, *One Man's Gold: The Letters and Journal of a Forty-Niner* (New York: McGraw-Hill, 1930), 159–60, 210–11.

70. Øverland, "Immigrant Letters," 212; Theodore C. Blegen and Pauline Farseth, eds., *Frontier Mother: The Letters of Gro Svendson* (Northfield, MN: Norwegian-American Historical Association, 1950), 30; Hargest, *Letter Post Communication*.

71. Kamphoefner, Helbich, and Sommer, eds., *News from the Land of Freedom*, 341–42, 411.

72. Bell Irvin Wiley, ed., *Letters of Warren Akin Confederate Congressman* (Athens: University of Georgia Press, 1959), 59. See also, for examples, Linda Peavy and Ursula Smith, *The Gold Rush Widows of Little Falls* (St. Paul: Minnesota Historical Society Press, 1990), 43–44; Brian Roberts, *American Alchemy: The California Gold Rush and Middle-Class Culture* (Chapel Hill: University of North Carolina Press, 2000), 216.

73. In the collected correspondence of Henry Inman, his letters from New York to Cephas Grier Childs in Philadelphia appear on much smaller sheets after the postal reduction of 1845; see Henry Inman, letters, to Cephas Grier Childs, 1828—1845, in Henry Inman Letters, 1828–1845, AAS.

74. "Sending Letters Out of the Mail," reprinted in *Philadelphia Public Ledger*, August 27, 1851.

75. "Metropolitan Post-Offices: New York," *Illustrated Magazine of Art* 1 (1853): 268.

76. *Philadelphia Public Ledger*, September 3, 18, 1851.

77. Ibid., August 28, 1851.

78. Peter T. Rohrbach and Lowell S. Newman, *American Issue: The U.S. Postage Stamp, 1842–1896* (Washington, DC: Smithsonian Institution Press, 1984), 63.

79. LeClerq, ed., *Between North and South*, 165. Sinkler told her father of a friend who even used stamps when she sent letters by private conveyance, perhaps out of confusion, or more likely in an attempt not to appear to be either cheap or depriving the government of revenue. The major shift in the use of stamps took place after 1855, when prepayment was required. Between 1855 and 1856, postal revenue from stamps increased from $2.5 million to $4.24 million. For a discussion of similar shifts in stamp etiquette in France (where prepayment was not mandated until much later), see Chartier, Boureau, and Dauphin, *Correspondence*, 143–44.

80. Margaret Black Tatum, ed., "'Please Send Stamps': The Civil War Letters of William Allen Clark, Part 1," *Indiana Magazine of History* 91, no. 1 (1995): 96, 98. A longer discussion of the demand for postage stamps during the Civil War appears in chapter 5.

81. John J. Knox, *United States Notes: A History of the Various Issues of Paper Money by the Government of the United States* (New York: Charles Scribner's Sons, 1899), 100–105; Ernest A. McKay, *The Civil War and New York City* (Syracuse, NY: Syracuse University Press, 1990), 139–40; John T. Billings, *Hardtack and Coffee: The Unwritten Story of Army Life*, ed. Richard Harwell (1887; repr., Chicago: Lakeside, 1960), 55–56. See also chapter 2 of this book.

82. John K. Tiffany, R. R. Bogert, and Joseph Rechert, *The Stamped Envelopes, Wrappers and Sheets of the United States* (New York: Scott Stamp & Coin Co, 1892); John Murray Bartels, *Bartels Catalogue of the Stamped Envelopes and Wrappers of the United States and Possessions*, 5th ed. (Netcong, NJ: Prescott Holden Thorp, 1943), 1:1; Harlow, *Old Post Bags*, 349.

83. See, for example, the letter from Princeton student Theodore Cuyler to his aunt Charlotte Morrell on Tippecanoe letterhead, June 12, 1840, Morrell Family Papers, N-YHS; *Chronicle of the U.S. Classic Postal Issues*, 42, no. 2 (May, 1990): 101. See also James W. Milgram, *Abraham Lincoln Illustrated Envelopes and Letter Paper, 1860–1865* (Northbrook, IL: Northbrook Publishing, 1984).

84. See chapter 5 of this book.

85. For an important discussion of Cartesian cartography as a crucial blueprint for the American imagination of space during the early national era, see Philip Fisher, "Democratic Social Space: Whitman, Melville, and the Promise of American Transparency," in *The New American Studies: Essays from Representations*, ed. Philip Fisher (Berkeley and Los Angeles: University of California Press, 1991), 72–77; and Elizabeth Blackmar, *Manhattan for Rent, 1785–1850* (Ithaca, NY: Cornell University Press, 1989), 94–100. Of course, a postal system could have been organized spatially along the axes of a surveyor's map. A couple of decades ago a letter in Britain was successfully delivered on the basis of an address that consisted exclusively of longitude and latitude. See Georges Perec, *Species of Spaces and Other Pieces*, trans. John Sturrock (London: Penguin, 1987), 83.

86. Hawthorne, quoted in Decker, *Epistolary Practices*, 38; Carlyle's letter appears in Joseph Slater, ed., *The Correspondence of Emerson and Carlyle* (New York: Columbia University Press, 1964), 112–18. Fanny Fern, *Ruth Hall and Other Writings* ed. Joyce W. Warren (1855; repr., New Brunswick, NJ: Rutgers University Press, 1986), 145.

87. Walt Whitman, *Leaves of Grass and Selected Prose*, ed. Laurence Buell (New York: Modern Library, 1981), 73.

88. *The Post-office; or, An Illustration of Prayer* (Boston: Massachusetts Sabbath School Society, 1844), 9–21.

89. Rev. John Steele, *In Camp and Cabin, Mining Life and Adventure, in California During 1850 and Later* (Lodi, WI: J. Steele, 1901), reprinted in Milo Milton Quaife, ed., *Echoes of the Past . . . In Camp and Cabin* (Chicago: Lakeside Press, 1928), 306. For another juxtaposition of prayer and mail in descriptions of the Gold Rush post office, see William Taylor, *Seven Years' Street Preaching in San Francisco, California* (New York: Carlton and Porter, 1856), 289.

90. Harriet Prescott Spofford, "Six by Seven," in *The Moonstone Mass and Others*, ed. Jessica Amanda Salmonson (Ashcroft, British Columbia: Ash-Tree Press, 2000), 47–66. Originally printed in *Knickerbocker Magazine* (January 1860).

CHAPTER TWO

1. John, *Spreading the News*, 25–63.

2. Kielbowicz, *News in the Mail*, 63, 71; Solomon Henkel, "Post Office Book A in which are subscribed Names of the News Papers and Letter Accounts kept in New Market Shenandoah County Virginia begun in 1804," AAS; *New Orleans Picayune*, August 13, 1841.

3. Richard Henry Dana, *Two Years Before the Mast* (New York: Macmillan, 1911), 179; Forten, *Journal*, 156; LeClerq, *An Antebellum Plantation Household*, 20.

4. Foster, ed., *American Grit*, 86, 122, 158.

5. Quoted in Andie Tucher, *Froth and Scum: Truth, Beauty, Goodness, and the Ax Murder in America's First Mass Medium* (Chapel Hill: University of North Carolina Press, 1994), 90.

6. *New Orleans Picayune*, December 9, 1840.

7. "Edward Jenner Carpenter's 'Journal,' 1844–45," 303–407. *Proceedings of the American Antiquarian Society*, vol. 98, pt. 2.

8. Dana, *Two Years Before the Mast*, 276; Virginia Jeans Laas, ed., *Wartime Washington: The Civil War Letters of Elizabeth Blair Lee* (Urbana: University of Illinois Press, 1991), 75.

9. Forten, *Journal*, 203; entry for February 18, 1857, in *Journal of Anna May*, ed. George Robinson (Cambridge, MA: privately printed, 1941), 8.

10. Theodore Cuyler to Charlotte Morrell, June 12, 1840, N-YHS; Vail, ed., "Correspondence of John Ingalls," 180.

11. *Post-Office Law, Instructions and Forms, Published for the Regulation of the Post-Office* (Washington, DC: Way and Gideon, 1825), 8–9, 16–17; John B. McMaster, *History of the People of the United States*, 8 vols. (New York: D. Appleton, 1883–1913), 7:108; Fuller, *American Mail*, 62.

12. "Post Office Circular," *Daily National Intelligencer*, December 25, 1841; Postmaster General to a citizen of Kentucky, November 10, 1842, in unidentified newspaper clipping, *Scrapbook of Circulars, Notices, Instructions, Regulations, and Newspaper Clippings, 1823–1871*, Records of the Post Office Department, Record Group 28, Entry 3, 1 volume, NA (hereafter referred to as *Scrapbook*); *Commercial Journal and Lyford's Prices Current*, August 1843; Holbrook, *Ten Years Among the Mail Bags*, 392; "The Post-Office System, As an Element of Modern Civilization," *New Englander* 1 (1843): 22. By 1841 the *New York Herald* reported that "about fifty suits have been commenced against parties in this city" found guilty of "writing messages to their friends in newspapers" (February 19, 1841).

13. "A Milliner Cheating the Post Office," *New Orleans Picayune*, January 20, 1840. The *Picayune's* story reinforced a familiar Southern image of sharp Yankee trading practices and appealed to Southern fears of the antislavery uses of the mail. An anti-abolitionist story in the same newspaper two months later made this link explicit. "Some gray-haired baby in Boston sent us, through the post office, an antiquated abolition paper called 'Human Rights,' requesting us to read it and be edified, and give our support to the cause of anti-slavery! The hypocritical old swindler wrote this request upon a piece of paper, which he carefully enclosed in the newspaper, thereby cheating the post-office. This is a trifling circumstance, but how admirably does it display the knavish principles of abolitionism.—'A member of the Massachusetts Anti-Slavery Society', as he signs himself, whose benevolent mind would correct the constitution of the land, will in furthering his charitable scheme, cheat his beloved country out of twenty-five cents" (*New Orleans Picayune*, March 11, 1840). The rebus with the awl and the bucket is cited in Charles Wickliffe's 1842 letter to a citizen of Kentucky (*Scrapbook*). A different example of a rebus involving an awl and a well appears in Holbrook, *Ten Years Among the Mail Bags*, 393.

14. Charles Wickliffe to a citizen of Kentucky, 1842 (*Scrapbook*).

15. A Schenectady case from around the same time reaffirmed this principle as well; see "Post Office Law, Schenectady Justice's Court, Thomas L. Thompson vs. John Foster, David P. Forrest, Esquire, Justice," in *Scrapbook*.

16. For examples of the continued reposting of newspapers, see John Kent Folmar, ed., *"This State of Wonders": The Letters of an Iowa Frontier Family, 1858–1861* (Iowa City: University of Iowa Press, 1986), 29, 33, 129; "Letters of John and Sarah Everett, 1854–1864," *Kansas Historical Quarterly* 8, no. 1 (February 1939): 12–18; Robinson, ed., *Journal of Anna May*, 8, 9, 28, 30, 42–44, 56–57, 70, 84, 92; Laas, ed., *Wartime Washington*; Baker, ed., *The Websters*, 105; Thomas Dublin, ed., *Farm to Factory: Women's Letters, 1830–1860*, 2nd ed. (New York: Columbia University Press, 1993), 128. The Webster example also involved supplementary writing ("I have written a few words almost every mail on the papers I sent you that you might know how we were") a full year after the postage reform, and may have reflected a lingering habit of using newspapers for correspondence (whether or not military franking privileges were involved). Post Office investigator James Holbrook noted in 1855 that the "fine arts" of marking newspapers had become scarce "under the present low rates of postage," but exceptions to this rule persisted (*Ten Years Among the Mail Bags*, 393).

17. On the rise of the cheap daily press, see Schudson, *Discovering the News*; Gunther Barth, *City People: The Rise of Modern City Culture in Nineteenth-Century America* (New York: Oxford University Press, 1980).

18. Archer Butler Hulbert, ed., "Letters of an Overland Mail Agent in Utah," *Proceedings of the American Antiquarian Society at the Annual Meeting Held in Worcester*, 38, pt. 2 (October 17, 1928): 276–77.

19. *Plough Boy*, December 30, 1820. On the increasing fascination during the Jacksonian era with the post's ability to annihilate time and space, see John, *Spreading the News*, 7–14. This fascination anticipated much of the popular impact of the post on everyday life after the postage reductions of 1845.

20. William E. Channing, *The Works of William E. Channing, D.D.* (Boston, MA: American Unitarian Association, 1867), 1:353–54.

21. Mrs. John Farrar, *The Youth's Letter-Writer; or, the epistolary art made plain and easy to beginners, through the example of Henry Moreton* (New York: H. & S. Raynor, 1840), 3.

22. Newspapers and transient printed documents continued to be assessed at a different rate from letters, but in those mail classes as well weight became the principal consideration.

23. Holbrook, *Ten Years Among the Mail Bags*, 136–37.

24. Miles, *Postal Reform*, vi.

25. *New Englander* 1 (1843): 20.

26. Foster, ed., *American Grit*, 49.

27. Twenty years later, for example, Nicholas Hentz mailed two halves of different hundred-dollar banknotes to his son Charles. A week later, the other halves arrived; see Stowe, ed., *A Southern Practice*, 140, 143.

28. Foster, ed., *American Grit*, 84.

29. Holbrook, *Ten Years Among the Mail Bags*, 382.

30. [Louis Bagger], "The Dead-Letter Office," *Appleton's Journal* 10, no. 422 (November 8, 1873): 594. Postal reformer Pliny Miles estimated in 1855 that merchants put $100 million worth of negotiable currency into the mail every year. Cited in John, *Spreading the News*, 54.

31. *National Intelligencer*, July, 5, 1845; Knox, *United States Notes*, 100–105; [Bagger], "Dead-Letter Office," 594.

32. Michael Warner, *Letters of the Republic: Publication and the Public Sphere in Eighteenth-Century America* (Cambridge, MA: Harvard University Press, 1990); Tamara P. Thornton, *Handwriting in America* (New Haven, CT: Yale University Press, 1996), especially 26–29.

33. Miron Winslow, *Memoir of Mrs. Harriet L. Winslow* (New York: American Tract Society, 1840), 210; Susan Leigh Blackford and Charles Minor Blackford, *Letters from Lee's Army* (Lincoln, NE: University of Nebraska Press, 1998), 24; Theodore Tilton to Elizabeth, January 1 and January 30, 1867, in "The Tilton Letters," *Chicago Tribune*, August 13, 1874; Enos Christman to Ellen Apple, May 24, 1850, in Christman, *One Man's Gold*, 163; James H. Hammond to Emily H. Cumming, quoted in Stowe, *Intimacy and Power in the Old South*, 118. Confederate Army surgeon Junius Bragg resisted his wife's request that he destroy her letters, insisting that "anything that has ever been touched by her fingers is dear to me"; see Mrs. T. J. Gaughan, *Letters of a Confederate Surgeon, 1861–65* (Camden, AK: Hurley, 1960), 146. For an insightful interpretation of handwriting as a form of embodiment in the correspondence of Emerson and Dickinson, see Decker, *Epistolary Practices*, 40–41.

34. Thornton, *Handwriting in America*, 86–88. As early as 1837, John Quincy Adams noted the "recent fashion" of strangers sending requests for autographs. Those seeking signatures of famous people prior to 1845 may have favored those who, like Adams, enjoyed the benefits of free postage. See Allan Nevins, ed., *The Diary of John Quincy Adams, 1794–1845* (New York: F. Unger, 1951), 480.

35. Forten, *Journal*, 115; Alden's letter to Longfellow is quoted in Jill Anderson, "'Send Me a Nice Little Letter All to Myself': Henry Wadsworth Longfellow's Fan Mail and Antebellum Poetic Culture," paper delivered to the University of Virginia Early American Seminar, January 2004, quoted with permission of the author; Harriet Lane Levy, *920 O'Farrell Street: A Jewish Girlhood in Old San Francisco* (Berkeley, CA: Heyday Books, 1996), 14. Novelist Fanny Fern reported receiving letters from readers writing for the sole purpose of obtaining her autograph (Fern, *Ruth Hall*, 268–69).

36. Josephine Clifford, "Down Among the Dead Letters," *Overland Monthly* 3 (December 1869), 521. The utility of postal exchanges in securing autographs was not lost among forgers, who would sometimes initiate a bogus correspondence in order to obtain

handwriting samples from bankers or merchants. See, for example, *Life and Adventures of the Accomplished Forger and Swindler, Colonel Monroe Edwards* (New York: H. Long and Brother, 1848), 86.

37. Alan Trachtenberg, *Reading American Photographs: Images as History, Mathew Brady to Walker Evans* (New York: Hill and Wang, 1989).

38. See, for example, *Report of the Postmaster General*, 38th Cong., 1st sess., House Executive Documents 5:1 (Washington, DC: Government Printing Office, 1863). For some examples of the postal exchange of photographs, in addition to those mentioned in what follows, see Julia A. Drake, *The Mail Goes Through: Or, the Civil War Letters of George Drake* (San Angelo, TX: Anchor, 1964), 19; William Allen to "Dear Brother," February 16, 1868, Letters from William and Charles Allen, 1853–1878, Bancroft MSS 88/129c, BANC; Paul Fatout, ed., *Letters of a Civil War Surgeon* (West Lafayette, IN: Purdue University Studies, 1961), 12, 18; Hiram Rumfield to his wife Frank, December 4, 1865, Hiram S. Rumfield Letters, 1849–1866, AAS; Lillian Schlissel, Byrd Gibbens, and Elizabeth Hampstein, *Far from Home: Families of the Westward Journey* (New York: Schocken, 1989), 31, 34; Dublin, *Farm to Factory*, 150–51; Judy Nolte Lensink, ed., *"A Secret to be Burried": The Diary and Life of Emily Hawley Gillespie* (Iowa City: University of Iowa Press, 1989), 65; Nina Silber and Mary Beth Sievens, eds., *Yankee Correspondence: Civil War Letters between New England Soldiers and the Home Front* (Charlottesville: University Press of Virginia, 1996), 150, 159; Folmar, ed., *Letters of an Iowa Frontier Family*, 108; Keckley, *Behind the Scenes*, 230–31; E. D. E. N. Southworth, *The Hidden Hand, Or, Capitola the Madcap*, ed. Joanne Dobson (New Brunswick, NJ: Rutgers University Press, 1998), 347.

39. For another example of the fetishization of the photographic portrait, see Robert Manson Myers, ed., *The Children of Pride: A True Story of Georgia and the Civil War* (New Haven, CT: Yale University Press, 1972), 1:447.

40. Folmar, ed., *Letters of an Iowa Frontier Family*, 80; Sabrina Swain to William Swain, April 15, 1849, in J. S. Holliday, *The World Rushed In: The California Gold Rush Experience* (New York: Simon and Schuster, 1981), 80.

41. Mary Wingate to Benjamin Wingate, April 1, 1853, Wingate Correspondence, Bancroft MSS 83/35c, BANC.

42. For examples of mailing locks of hair, see John Rozier, ed., *The Granite Farm Letters: The Civil War Correspondence of Edgeworth and Sallie Bird* (Athens: University of Georgia Press, 1988), 50; Richards, ed., *Journal of Stephen Chapin Davis*, 20; Frances D. Gage, "A Lock of Hair," *Ladies' Repository* 23 (November 1863), 691–92; Mary Wingate to Benjamin Wingate, April 15, 1851, Wingate Correspondence, Bancroft MSS 83/35c, BANC; Mary Everett to her sisters, June 1, 1855, in "Letters of John and Sarah Everett, 1854–1864," *Kansas Historical Quarterly* 8, no. 1 (February 1939), 10; and Schlissel, Gibbens, and Hampstein, *Far From Home*, 28. When a Scandinavian immigrant to Iowa died, her husband mailed a lock of her hair back to Norway; see Theodore C. Blegen and Pauline Farseth, eds., *Frontier Mother: The Letters of Gro Svendson* (Northfield, MN: Norwegian-American Historical Association, 1950), xii.

43. Elizabeth Tilton to Theodore Tilton, February 11, 1867, in "The Tilton Letters," *Chicago Daily Tribune*, August 13, 1874; Buck, *Yankee Trader in the Gold Rush*, 131.

44. William to "Dear Brother," February 16, 1868, Letters from William and Charles Allen, 1853–1878, Bancroft MSS, 88/129c, BANC.

45. Ellen Horton to husband Edwin, May 6, 1864, in Silber and Sievens, *Yankee Correspondence*, 150.

46. Trachtenberg, *Reading American Photographs*, 21–33; on the flourishing of photography in Gold Rush San Francisco, see George Robinson Fardon, *San Francisco Album: Photographs, 1854–1856* (San Francisco: Chronicle Books, 1999), 11–24.

47. Stevens to his brother, August 2, 1858, in *War Letters: Extraordinary Correspondence from American Wars*, ed. Andrew Carroll (New York: Charles Scribner's Sons, 2001), 44.

48. LeClerq, *An Antebellum Plantation Household*, 13; Joan D. Hedrick, *Harriet Beecher Stowe: A Life* (New York: Oxford University Press, 1994), 80; Baker, ed., *The Websters*, 45, 122; Drake, *Mail Goes Through*, 121; Buck, *Yankee Trader in the Gold Rush*, 132; Stephen Wing to "Old Gent" and Mina, April 1, [?], 1853, Stephen Wing Correspondence, Bancroft MSS, BANC; Benjamin Wingate, San Francisco, April 16, 1853; Mary Wingate, Meriden, March 3, 1852, both in Wingate Correspondence, Bancroft MSS 83/35c, BANC; Annette Kolodny, *The Land Before Her: Fantasy and Experience of the American Frontiers, 1630–1860* (Chapel Hill: University of North Carolina Press, 1984), 146, 237; Alfred Charles True, *A History of Agricultural Experimentation and Research in the United States, 1607–1925*, United States Department of Agriculture Miscellaneous Publication No. 251, July 1937 (Washington, DC: Government Printing Office, 1937), 24–25; John, *Spreading the News*, 123. Interestingly, seeds figured in the famous 1844 Mazzini mail affair in Great Britain, as Mazzini enclosed seeds in his letter as a way of detecting the opening of his seal; see David Vincent, *The Culture of Secrecy: Britain, 1832–1998* (New York: Oxford University Press, 1998), 1–9.

49. Schlissel, Gibbens, and Hampstein, *Far from Home*, 29; "Letters of John and Sarah Everett, 1854–1864," 29; Myers, ed., *Children of Pride*, 42; Kolodny, *Land Before Her*, 237–38; Buck, *Yankee Trader in the Gold Rush*, 132; Mary Wingate to Benjamin, March 3, 1852, and Benjamin Wingate to Mary, April 16, 1853, Wingate Correspondence, Bancroft MSS 83/35c, BANC. For an early example of a westerly request for seeds to be brought, not mailed, see the 1818 letter from Illinois to Connecticut quoted in Power, *Planting Corn Belt Culture*, 31.

50. Kamphoefner, Helbich, and Sommer, eds., *News from the Land of Freedom*, 77.

51. Myers, ed., *Children of Pride*, 49.

52. Quoted in Decker, *Epistolary Practices*, 46.

53. For an earlier example of epidemiological fears of mail in connection with the 1793 Philadelphia yellow fever epidemic, see the report of the practice of disinfecting letters posted from the city in Matthew Carey, *A Short Account of the Malignant Fever, Lately Prevalent in Philadelphia* (Philadelphia, PA: printed by the author, 1973), 93. The eminent physician Benjamin Rush dismissed such fears, affirming the immunity of texts to the disease. See David Paul Nord, *Communities of Journalism: A History of American Newspapers and Their Readers* (Urbana: University of Illinois Press, 2001), 216, 224. Fears of the transmission of disease through the mail survived the shift in epidemiological thinking from miasma to germ. See, for example, Khaled J. Bloom, *The Mississippi Valley's Great Yellow Fever Epidemic of 1878* (Baton Rouge: Louisiana State University Press, 1993), 17.

54. Quoted in Karen Lystra, *Searching the Heart: Women, Men, and Romantic Love in Nineteenth-Century America* (New York: Oxford University Press, 1989), 23.

55. Wiley, ed., *Letters of Warren Akin, Confederate Congressman*, 22; Lucy Breckinridge, *Lucy Breckinridge of Grove Hill: The Journal of a Virginia Girl, 1862–1864*, ed. Mary D. Robertson (Kent, OH: Kent State University Press, 1979), 89. For an additional reference to sending quinine during the war, see the letter from Hattie to his daughter Emmie, February, 1865, in Elliott and Gonzales Family Papers, Personal Correspondence, 1861–1865, electronic edition available at the University of North Carolina Web site, among the pages for "Documenting the American South": http://docsouth.unc.edu/imls/gonzales/gonzales.html.

56. Blegen and Farseth, eds., *Frontier Mother*, 54, 57.

CHAPTER THREE

1. "Women and Children in America" *The Ladies' Repository* 27 (May 1867): 294–98. The article appeared originally in a January, 1867 issue of *Blackwood's Magazine*.

2. In 1851, the year of the second postage reduction, 19,796 post offices were in operation, most of them in the interior of the country. The state of Ohio alone was home to more than 1,700 post offices, Tennessee had more than 800. A complete list of offices and

routes appears in Eli Bowen, *The United States Post-Office Guide* (1851; repr., New York: Arno Press, 1976). By the end of the Civil War the total had reached 30,000, including 1,000 in the lightly inhabited state of Iowa alone. See J. Disturnell, *Post-Office Directory for 1867* (New York: American News Company, 1867), 227–30.

3. Tarbell, *Stage Days in Brimfield*, 16; Frederick Calvin Norton, *A Yankee Post Office: Its History and Its Postmasters* (New Haven, CT: Tuttle, Morehouse & Taylor, 1935), 71; J. L. M. Curry, *The South in the Olden Time* (Harrisburg, PA: Harrisburg Publishing, 1901), 5; Benjamin P. Thomas, *Lincoln's New Salem* (New York: Alfred A. Knopf, 1954), 97–98; "Interesting and Affecting Tale," *Rural Repository Devoted to Polite Literature*, January 7, 1846.

4. "New York City Post Office," *Harper's New Monthly Magazine* (October 1871): 645–63; Harrison Adreon, *A Brief History of the Baltimore Post Office, from 1775 to 1882, with statistics* (Baltimore, MD: White and Graham, 1882); Madison Davis, *A History of the Washington City Post-Office. From 1795 to 1903* (Lancaster, PA: New Era Printing, 1903); Sister Marciana Hennig, SSJ, ed., *Post Offices of Michigan* (Washington, DC: U.S. Postal Service, 1976), 246; James H. Bruns, *Great American Post Offices* (New York: John Wiley & Sons, 1998), 13–16.

5. *San Francisco Daily Evening News*, November 8, 1853. For indications of the use of the post office as a city center, see the *Salt Lake City Deseret News*, June 29, 1850, September 14, 1850, January 11, 1851, and February 22, 1851.

6. Quoted in *New Orleans Picayune*, September 11, 1841.

7. "The New York Post-Office," *Appleton's Journal* 5, no. 3 (September 1878): 194–95. If post offices had continued to function primarily as broadcast sites for nonlocal news by the time the telegraph came into commercial use, they might have become focal points for popular reception of up-to-the-minute information during events of special interest, but by the 1850s that function had shifted to the offices of various big-city newspapers.

8. Miles, *Postal Reform*, 33, 45; "The New York Post-Office," 193. On the rise of cheap dailies that circulated in city streets rather than post offices, see Schudson, *Discovering the News*, 12–60; Tucher, *Froth and Scum*; Henkin, *City Reading*, 101–135. For a critical discussion of the standard account of the penny press (especially of its applicability beyond the borders of the very largest cities), see John C. Nerone, "The Mythology of the Penny Press," *Critical Studies in Mass Communication* 4 (1987): 376–422.

9. *New Orleans Picayune*, January 9, 1841. For other reports of pickpockets at the New Orleans post office, see the *Picayune*, February 5, 6, 1840.

10. Bates Lowry, *Building a National Image: Architectural Drawings for the American Democracy, 1789–1912* (Washington, DC: National Building Museum, 1985), 48–57; Geoffrey P. Moran, "The Post Office and Custom House at Portsmouth, New Hampshire, and Its Architect, Ammi Burnham Young," *Old-Time New England* 57, no. 4 (April–June 1967): 85–102; Lois Craig, *The Federal Presence: Architecture, Politics, and Symbols in United States Government Building* (Cambridge, MA: MIT Press, 1984); *History, Organization, and Functions of the Office of the Supervising Architect of the Treasury Department* (Washington, DC: Government Printing Office, 1886); *A History of Public Buildings Under the Control of the Treasury Department* (Washington, DC: Government Printing Office, 1901).

11. See the image, based on a photograph, in *Frank Leslie's Illustrated Newspaper*, May 21, 1859.

12. *Plans of Public Buildings in Course of Construction... Under the Direction of the Secretary of the Treasury* (1855), Records of the Public Building Service, Record Group 121, nos. 7, 8, 9, 10, 11, 12, NA.

13. Lowry, *Building a National Image*; Bruns, *Great American Post Offices*, 55–69.

14. Rev. B. F. Tefft, "A Sweet Home," *The Ladies' Repository* 6 (1846): 241; Taylor, quoted in Harlow, *Old Post Bags*, 351; James Rees, *Foot-prints of a Letter-Carrier* (Philadelphia: J. P. Lippincott, 1866), 241. For another portrait of the heterogeneity of the crowds at the San Francisco post, see *The Mysteries and Miseries of San Francisco* (New York: Garrett, 1853), 74–75.

15. The Krimmel and Woodville images appear conveniently juxtaposed in Alfred D. Chandler Jr. and James W. Cortada, eds., *A Nation Transformed by Information* (New York: Oxford University Press, 2000), 66–67.

16. Tomkins Harrison Matteson (1813–1884), best known for such classics as *Washington Crossing the Delaware* and *Last of the Race*, produced two images of post offices, one rural and one urban, which fit better into the Krimmel/Woodville tradition of seeing the post as a site of collective communal engagement. His *Justice's Court in the Backwoods* (1852), which depicts country court life in a building that doubled as a tavern and a post office, stands in vivid contrast to the emerging urban post office of the period. The image is reproduced opposite p. 279 of Alan Taylor, *William Cooper's Town: Power and Persuasion on the Frontier of the Early American Republic* (New York: Vintage, 1995). Matteson's other relevant work, *Post Office in Philadelphia*, shows a family gathered anxiously and somberly in front of the letterboxes as a male figure reads a freshly arrived letter. No other figures appear, but the presence of advertisements, posters, and boxes subtly frames the otherwise domestic scene within the context of an explosive urban culture of reading and writing.

17. Exterior views of urban post offices appeared frequently in *Frank Leslie's Illustrated Newspaper*. See, for example, images of foot and horse traffic outside the post offices in New York (January 3, 1857, 73); Milwaukee (May 21, 1859, 386); Boston (November 30, 1872, 193); and Cincinnati (June 17, 1876, 245). See also the Currier & Ives lithograph, "U.S. Post Office, New York" ca. 1872, AAS.

18. See, for additional examples, "Scene at the San Francisco Post Office," engraving by Anthony and Baker, letter sheet published by Leland & McCombe (San Francisco, 1854), BANC; William Taylor, *California Life Illustrated* (New York: Carlton and Porter, 1858), 203 ("Scene at the San Francisco Post"). An analogous image of lines outside the express office in Denver around the time of the Civil War (without the same emphasis on jubilant letter recipients), F. Webb's "Waiting for Letters," appears in Albert D. Richardson, *Beyond the Mississippi: From the Great River to the Great Ocean* (Hartford: American Publishing, 1867), 298.

19. Frank J. Webb, *The Garies and Their Friends*, ed. Robert Reid-Pharr (Baltimore, MD: Johns Hopkins University Press, 1997), 288.

20. Holbrook, *Ten Years Among the Mail Bags*, xv.

21. Prof. L. C. Loomis, A.M., "Development of Woman," *The Ladies' Repository* 27 (November 1867). In Harriet Prescott Spofford's short story, "Six by Seven" (1860), the first-person female narrator inquires for letters at the post office, something "she scarcely ever" did. "Tim, our man," she explained, "always went" (55). See also Sherwood Bonner, *Dialect Tales* (New York: Harper and Brothers, 1883), 42. For evidence of enslaved men being assigned the task of visiting the post office, see LeClerq, *Between North and South*, 33; Bryan, *Grandmother's Recollection of Dixie*, 5; Stowe, *Intimacy and Power in the Old South*, 91. See also Hadden, *Slave Patrol*, 150. For another example of women depending upon men to deliver their letters (beyond those discussed here), see Rohrbough, *Days of Gold*, 233.

22. Benjamin Brown French, *Witness to the Young Republic: A Yankee's Journal, 1828–1870*, ed. Donald B. Cole and John J. McDonough (Hanover, NH: University Press of New England, 1989), 280–81.

23. Miles, *Postal Reform*, 45.

24. John, *Spreading the News*, 164–66. In many cities even lists of letters held at the post office were divided by gender; see, for example, letter lists in the *Chicago Daily Tribune*, the *Philadelphia Public Ledger*, and the *San Francisco Golden Era*.

25. *Plans of Public Buildings in Course of Construction... Under the Direction of the Secretary of the Treasury* (1861), Records of the Public Building Service, Record Group 121, NA. Even after Young stepped down, gender segregation continued to appear in the post office buildings designed under the auspices of the supervising architect.

26. Mary P. Ryan, *Women in Public: Between Banners and Ballots, 1825–1880* (Baltimore, MD: Johns Hopkins Press, 1990), 58–94, quotation at 78; Amy G. Richter, *Home on the*

Rails: Women, the Railroad, and the Rise of Public Domesticity (Chapel Hill: University of North Carolina Press, 2005); Diane Shaw, *City Building on the Eastern Frontier: Sorting the New Nineteenth-Century City* (Baltimore, MD: Johns Hopkins University Press, 2004), 96–102; Katherine C. Grier, *Culture and Comfort: People, Parlors, and Upholstery, 1850–1930* (Amherst: University of Massachusetts Press, 1988), 19–58; Abigail A. Van Slyck, "The Lady and the Library Loafer: Gender and Public Space in Victorian America," *Winterthur Portfolio* 31, no. 4 (Winter 1996): 222–42. Van Slyck's account of the movement to separate the sexes at the library underscores many of the same anxieties about heterosocial intermingling associated with the post office. Both projects merged cultural investments in women's reading and writing habits with concerns about the interaction of men and women in public space. The cultural construction of the library as a domestic space, however, may have dulled the threat posed by female users. Van Slyck, pursuing a suggestion by Kathleen James, even speculates that domestic conceptions of reading may account for the absence of sex-segregated spaces in the designs of Massachusetts libraries in the 1870s and '80s (29).

27. Clifford, "Down Among the Dead Letters," 517–22.

28. See, for example, "New York City Post-Office," *Harper's New Monthly Magazine* 43 (October 1871), 659, which includes both a description and an image of the ladies' window in New York.

29. *Alta California*, December 29, 1855, in *Papers, Documents, and Correspondence in Relation to the Case of Charles L. Weller, Deputy Postmaster at San Francisco, CAL* (Washington, DC: William A. Harris, 1859), 86; Charles Weller, "The History of a Letter," *Hutchings' California Magazine*, January, 1858. In the early days of the Gold Rush, women collected their letters at a postal counter shared with French, Spanish, Chinese, the military, and the clergy; see William Taylor, *Street Preaching in San Francisco*, 283.

30. Fern, *Ruth Hall*, 281, 313–14.

31. Alice Carey [sic], "Annie Heaton," *Ladies' Repository* 11 (May 1851): 169–77.

32. Virginia Penny, *How Women Make Money, Married or Single* (Philadelphia, D. E. Fisk, 1870), 407; *List of Letters Remaining in the Post Office Chicago and Vicinity, January 1834–July 1836* (Chicago: Chicago Genealogical Society, 1970), iii.

33. Mrs. A. Marquam (Lafayette, IN) to Mrs. Mary J. Bass (Columbus, IN), February 5, 1856, quoted in Lewis Saum, *The Popular Mood of Pre-Civil War America* (Westport, CT: Greenwood Press, 1980), 130; "Interesting Postal Decision," *Scientific American*, December 17, 1859, 398.

34. Southworth, *Hidden Hand*, 297; Harriet E. Wilson, *Our Nig; or, Sketches of the Life of a Free Black* (1859; repr., New York: Vintage, 1983), 114–15; Maria Cummins, *The Lamplighter* (New Brunswick, NJ: Rutgers University Press, 1988), 239.

35. Laas, ed., *Wartime Washington*, 73; C. Vann Woodward, ed., *Mary Chesnut's Civil War* (New Haven, CT: Yale University Press, 1981); Lensink, ed., *The Diary and Life of Emily Hawley Gillespie*, 27.

36. Polly Welts Kaufman, ed., *Apron Full of Gold: The Letters of Mary Jane Megquier from San Francisco, 1849–1856* (Albuquerque: University of New Mexico Press, 1994), 162.

37. Penny, *How Women Make Money*, 407.

38. Patricia Cline Cohen, *The Murder of Helen Jewett: The Life and Death of a Prostitute in Nineteenth-Century New York* (New York: Alfred A. Knopf, 1998), 115–28. Cohen describes Jewett's visits to the Post Office as a defiant and public "invasion of male space" (125).

39. Browne, *The Great Metropolis*, 423; Dell Upton, ed., *Madaline: Love and Survival in Antebellum New Orleans* (Athens: University of Georgia Press, 1996), 315.

40. *New York Herald*, May 8, 1855. For other examples, see the section of personal ads in the *Herald* for almost any day that month. On personal advertisements, see Henkin, *City Reading*, 125–26.

41. *Congressional Globe, Containing the Debates and Proceedings, 1833–1873*, 109 vols. (Washington, DC: Government Printing Office, 1833–1873), 37th Cong., 2nd sess., 161.

42. Kamphoefner, Helbich, and Sommer, eds., *News from the Land of Freedom*, 349. An 1851 post office guide instructed users "inquiring for letters addressed in foreign language (or other than English), . . . to give the address in *writing*. Mistakes in pronunciation of names, as well as in spelling, are known to be frequent, and sometimes really unfortunate in their results" (Bowen, *United States Post-Office Guide*, 71).

43. Browne, *Great Metropolis*, 420. For other complaints about postal workers, see Helen Jewett's letter to Richard Robinson, quoted in Cohen, *Murder of Helen Jewett*, 125; Stephen Wing to brother, sister, and mother, Red Hill, April 30 (no year), BANC.

44. Kate Harrington, "A Half-Hour in the Post-Office," *Genius of the West* 2, no. 1 (January 1854): 100—101. For other examples of public mockery of inexperienced postal users, see "A New Wrinkle at the Post Office," *Chicago Daily Tribune*, August 12, 1860, which recounts the attempt of a "butternut colored and apparelled stranger" to put hay into the mails; "A Knowing Boy," *New Orleans Picayune* August 10, 1840, which tells of a boy who sticks his letter into a mail slot at the post office without paying the postage.

45. *San Francisco Daily Evening News*, November 7, 1853; Horatio Alger, *Ragged Dick and Struggling Upward* (1867; repr., New York: Penguin, 1985), 124–35.

46. Browne, *The Great Metropolis*, 421–22. Rees, *Foot-prints*, 24–49. Elsewhere in Rees's dramatic description of the Philadelphia post office, the author treats the expressions of postal patrons as more opaque and the nature of the mail they carry as more safely concealed, but he is clearly playing with the tension between secrecy and exposure: "There you see an old lady carefully depositing a letter: she glances down the opening, takes one last look, and sighing, silently moves away. What are the contents of that letter? It is her secret" (241). See also "New York City Post-Office," which includes both a description and an image of the ladies' window in New York.

47. Taylor, *California Life Illustrated*, 203; Taylor, *Seven Years' Street Preaching*, 283.

48. "Editor's Drawer," *Harper's Monthly* (April 1857). For other examples of interest in the legibility of private emotion at the post office during the Gold Rush, see Hubert Howe Bancroft, *California Inter Pocula* (San Francisco: History Company, 1888), 273–74; Gage, "A Lock of Hair," 691–92; "Scene at the San Francisco Post Office," (see n. 18 above); B. E. Lloyd, *Lights and Shades in San Francisco* (San Francisco: A. L. Bancroft, 1876), 523.

49. John G. Palfrey, quoted in *Speech of Hon. John Hutchins, of Ohio, in the House of Representatives, May 19th, 1862, on Low and Uniform Postage* (New York: D. Appleton, 1862), 26.

50. Pliny Miles, "History of the Post Office," pt. 2, *Bankers' Magazine and Statistical Register* n.s., 7, no. 6 (December, 1857), 433–48, quotation at 437. See also Miles, *Postal Reform*; New York Postal Reform Committee, *Postal Reform: Proceedings of a Public Meeting held in the City of New York, March 24th, 1856* (New York: New York Postal Reform Committee, 1856).

51. The leading congressional supporter of free delivery pointed out in 1862 that as of 1860 the British had sent more letters in the last five years than had been posted in the United States since 1776 (*Speech of Hon. John Hutchins*, 18–19).

52. Miles, *Postal Reform*, 43. Frequent controversies erupted over the box system, most notably in San Francisco, where the long lines awaiting infrequent steamer arrivals heightened the demand for preferential access. See the voluminous documents surrounding the battles (at times bordering on violence) between Postmaster Charles Weller and the Penny Post Company during the 1850s: *Statement Including Correspondence and Documents Relating to the Allegations Made Against the San Francisco Post Office and Charles L. Weller, Post Master* (Sacramento, CA: S. W. Raveley, 1858); *Papers, Documents, and Correspondence in Relation to the Case of Charles L. Weller, Deputy Postmaster at San Francisco, Cal.* (Washington, DC: William A. Harris, 1859); "Copy of the notes taken by the Hon. D. O. Shattuck presiding Judge, in the suit brought in the Superior Court of the City of San Francisco by the Penny Post Co. against Charles L. Weller, the Post Master at San Francisco," David Shatttuck Papers, AAS.

53. Miles, "History of the Post Office," pt.2, 439. See also John, *Spreading the News*, 153.

54. Miles, "History of the Post Office," pt.2, 439.

55. Hennig, SSJ, ed., *Post Offices of Michigan*, v; "The Street Post-Office," *Scientific American*, July 9, 1859, 24.; *New York Times*, March 13, 1860. Pliny Miles complained in 1855 of the inadequacy of the tin boxes, which he claimed were unsafe, inaccessible, and objects of widespread confusion. Urban patrons were often misled, Miles added, by "seeing signs and announcements all over a city, of 'POST OFFICE,' and 'LETTER BOX,'" which were presumably put up by private companies (*Postal Reform*, 39–40, 42). Potts's Philadelphia boxes bore the inscription "Philada. P.O. U.S.M. Letter Box, G.G. Westcott. P.M."; see Nicholas B. Wainwright, *Philadelphia in the Romantic Age of Lithography* (Philadelphia: Historical Society of Pennsylvania, 1958), 119.

56. Anecdotes about English letterboxes circulated frequently in the United States. *The Post-office; or, An Illustration of Prayer* (Boston: Massachusetts Sabbath School Society, 1844), a reprint of an English edition, told of a young boy, who, having seen his mother put letters in an outdoor box and claim she had put them in the post, assumed he could mail a letter by placing it in "an old wooden post in a shady lane" (6). The mistake amused the boy's mother, but a report from the English postmaster general in 1877 indicated that such errors were neither uncommon nor limited to children: "There is hardly any opening onto the street that is not occasionally mistaken for the slot of a mailbox by some uninformed person," he noted; see Bernhard Siegert, *Relays: Literature as an Epoch of the Postal System*, trans. Kevin Repp (Stanford, CA: Stanford University Press, 1999), 111–12. A character in Anthony Trollope's *He Knew He Was Right* (1868–69) errs in the opposite direction, disdaining the practice of "chucking" letters into "an iron stump," and disclaiming the "faintest belief that any letter put into one of them would ever reach its destination"; see Nigel Hall, "The Materiality of Letter Writing: A Nineteenth-Century Perspective," in *Letter Writing as a Social Practice*, ed. David Barton and Nigel Hall (Amsterdam and Philadelphia, PA: John Benjamins, 2000), 103.

57. "Report of John A. Dix," appended to the *Annual Report of the Postmaster General*, 36th Cong., 2nd sess., December 1860 (1080), Senate Document 1, 515; Rees, *Foot-prints*, 251; Lloyd, *Lights and Shades in San Francisco*, 399. As late as 1865 a New Yorker could treat as a novelty the fact that "there are iron boxes put up on different parts of the city to accommodate people at a distance from the Post-office" (Alexander Anderson to Julia Anderson Halsey, New York City, May 1865, quoted in Brown, *Knowledge Is Power*, 306).

58. Miles, *Postal Reform*, 44; "Report of John A. Dix," 518. Ferocious battles over the box system in San Francisco erupted during the 1850s, both in the press and in the courts, between Postmaster Charles Weller and a local private delivery firm. See the sources cited in note 51 above.

59. Home delivery of mail was legally established in 1825, and letter carriers were familiar enough in New York by the mid-1830s that the *New York Sun* could accuse the editor of the rival *Transcript* of walking "on both sides of the street, like a two-penny postman"; see Frank M. O'Brien, *The Story of the Sun: New York, 1833–1928* (New York: D. Appleton, 1928), 31.

60. John, *Spreading the News*, 152–54; Robert Meyersburg, "New York: An Overview of Its Carrier Operations between 1825 and June 30, 1863," *Chronicle of the U.S. Classic Postal Issues* 40, no. 4 (1988): 242–47, and 41, no. 1 (1989), 28–31; *Annual Report of the Postmaster General*, 36th Cong., 1st sess., December 1859 (1025), Senate Document 2, 1399–1400; *Annual Report of the Postmaster General*, December 1860, 443–45, 515–20; *Congressional Globe*, 37th Cong., 2nd sess., 158–61.

61. *House Journal*, 37th Cong., 3rd sess., February 21, 1863, 450. The bill was approved by the Senate without a vote; see *Senate Journal*, 37th Cong., 3rd sess., February 10, 1863, 225.

62. Browne, *The Great Metropolis*, 417–18; L. W. Bacon, "City Postal Service in the United States," *Putnam's Magazine* 1 (January–June 1868): 348–54. As Bacon reminded readers, the persistent habit of going to the post office for letters would have appeared

absurd in London. "The Londoner no more thinks of sending to the Post-office for his letters, than the New Yorker thinks of sending to the printing-office for his newspaper."

63. *Congressional Globe*, 37th Congress, 2nd Session, 161.

64. Daniel Bluestone, "Civic and Aesthetic Reserve: Ammi Burnham Young's 1850 Federal Customhouse Designs," *Winterthur Portfolio*, 25, nos. 2–3 (Summer–Autumn 1990): 154; "New Boston Post-Office Building," *Ballou's Pictorial*, July 31, 1858.

65. "The Proposed New York Post-Office," *Putnam's Magazine* 2, July–December 1868, 372.

66. Bruns, *Great American Post Offices*, 18. The documentary basis for this interpretation is not identified. Richard R. John characterizes home delivery, along with the introduction of outdoor mailboxes, as the logical culmination of efforts to improve women's access to the post (John, *Spreading the News*, 164–67).

67. Charles White, *The United States Mail: A Farce in One Scene*, Dewitt's Ethiopian and Comic Drama, no. 156 (New York: Dewitt, n.d.).

68. Significantly, post office design from the 1870s on appears to emphasize the regulation of postal workers rather than the managing of crowds; see Anna Vemer Andrzejewski, "Architecture and the Ideology of Surveillance in Modern America, 1850–1950," (PhD diss., University of Delaware, 2000), 62–96.

CHAPTER FOUR

1. Frederick and Sarah Clapp to John Clapp, April 1, 1845. Clapp Family Letters, 1836–1856, AAS. Hereafter cited as Clapp Family Letters.

2. Benjamin Wingate to Charles, March 1, 1854, Wingate Correspondence, Bancroft MSS 83/35c, BANC.

3. See Katherine Gee Hornbeak, *The Complete Letter-Writer in English, 1568–1800*, Smith College Studies in Modern Languages, vol. 15, nos. 3–4 (April–July, 1934): 3.

4. Folmar, ed., *Letters of an Iowa Frontier Family*, 26.

5. Frederick and Sarah Clapp to John Clapp, April 1, 1845, Clapp Family Letters; "The Postal System of the U.S.A.," *Massachusetts Quarterly Review* (March, 1850): 276.

6. I am indebted to Dell Upton for sharing a draft of his forthcoming work on office design in the nineteenth century, in which he shows how the antebellum merchant organized space on the model of pigeonhole subdivisions in which he stored his correspondence. On the classic mercantile desk of the antebellum period, see Deborah Cooper, "The Evolution of Wooton Patent Desks," in *Wooton Patent Desks: A Place for Everything and Everything in its Place*, ed. J. Camille Showalter and Janice Driesbach (Bloomington: Indiana University Press, 1983), 57. For a description of the importance of correspondence and the prominence of compartmentalized desks in the mercantile offices of eighteenth-century London, see David Hancock, *Citizens of the World: London Merchants and the Integration of the British Atlantic Economy, 1735–1785* (Cambridge: Cambridge University Press, 1995), 101–4.

7. Sam Bass Warner, *The Private City* (Philadelphia: University of Pennsylvania Press, 1968), 83.

8. On the relationship of nonmanual labor to middle-class identity, see Stuart M. Blumin, *The Emergence of the Middle Class* (Cambridge: Cambridge University Press, 1989); and Augst, *Clerk's Tale*.

9. Lewis G. Welsh, *A Practical Guide to Business; Being a Handbook for the American Farmer, Merchant, Mechanic, Investor, and all Concerned in Earning or Saving Money* (Philadelphia, PA: J. G. Fergus, 1872), 34. Welsh observes that writing qualities "are rightly considered to indicate the general tenor of the mind and habits." For a larger discussion of the cultural meanings attached to handwriting, see Thornton, *Handwriting in America*.

10. Alger, *Ragged Dick and Struggling Upward*, 124–35.

11. John, *Spreading the News*, chap. 5, especially 190–93.

12. Morse's letter of April 15, 1855, is cited in Augst, *Clerk's Tale*, 72.

13. Breckinridge, *Lucy Breckinridge of Grove Hill*, 57. Interestingly, a contemporary list of Sabbath prohibitions appears to exempt personal correspondence from a list of closely related activities. Reverend Thomas Scott proscribes "buying and selling, paying wages, settling accounts, writing letters of business, reading books on ordinary subjects, trifling visits, journeys, excursions, dissipation, or conversation which serves only for amusement" (Rees, *Foot-prints*, 302–3). An intriguing, though ambiguous, document of shifting attitudes toward correspondence on the Sabbath appears in the writings of the eminent Cincinnati physician and civic leader Daniel Drake, who recorded his early memories and personal history in a series of letters to his children in the late 1840s. Drake concluded an 1847 letter to his son-in-law, Alexander Hamilton McGuffey, with the remark that "It's after 1 oc'k: I'm in the Sabbath—so good night!" but when his son Charles Drake prepared the letters for publication in 1870, he deleted the reference to the Sabbath, either because the implied concern about writing letters on the Sabbath no longer made sense or because Charles wished (as he did elsewhere) to downplay his father's lax or heterodox religious stances. See Daniel Drake, *Pioneer Life in Kentucky*, ed. Emmet Field Horine (New York: Henry Schuman, 1948), ix, 50.

14. Apparently, Clark had been taught to write letters on Sunday at his Sabbath school in Indiana. See Tatum, ed., "Civil War Letters of William Allen Clark," 105.

15. Bancroft, *California Inter Pocula*, 270.

16. Alexis McCrossen, *Holy Day, Holiday: The American Sunday* (Ithaca, NY: Cornell University Press, 2000), 39–41, 47, 124. Charles Stanton, member of the ill-fated Donner Party, wrote to his bother Sidney that "we are laying by to keep the Sabbath, and I am keeping it as I did the last Sunday, in writing to you, with the hope that I may meet with an opportunity, while travelling along, of forwarding it on"; see Dale Morgan, *Overland in 1846: Diaries and Letters of the California-Oregon Trail* (Lincoln: University of Nebraska Press, 1993), 1:611. For other examples of correspondents describing letter-writing as an appropriate Sabbath activity, see Miriam Doody, ed., *Yours in Love: Joseph Manson's Letters from the War of the Rebellion, 1864–1865* (Mill Valley, CA: TracPress, 1996), 38, 52; Stowe, ed., *Southern Practice*, 116; Mary Wingate to Benjamin Wingate, November 13, 1853, Wingate Correspondence, Bancroft MSS 83/35c BANC; Dublin, ed., *Farm to Factory*, 62.

17. Welsh, *Practical Guide*, 36; Weld, "Some Thoughts on Letter Writing," 250; "A Chapter upon Letters and Letter-Writers," *Ladies' Repository* 16 (February 1856): 71; Bancroft, *California Inter Pocula*, 278; Henry R. Dewitt to his mother, July 31, 1849, in Benemann, ed., *Year of Mud and Gold*, 62–63.

18. For a related discussion of letters between Gold Rush migrants and their spouses, see chapter 5. The second example appears in Miller, ed., *Letters of a Slave Family*, 211.

19. Augst, *Clerk's Tale*, 76–80. An 1852 report on the activities of the Dead Letter Office in Washington observed that "banker's clerks … generally seem to vie with each other, in writing with brevity and illegibility, and it is actually easier, in many cases, to decipher the pot-hooks and trammels of the poor Irish servants, than the hieroglyphics of these 'beautiful writers'" ("Dead Letters," *New York Times*, September 24, 1852).

20. Warner, *Private City*, 83.

21. Concerns over intrusion upon the privacy of letters figured in the Thomas Hutchinson affair prior to the American Revolution. See Warner, *Letters of the Republic* (Cambridge, MA: Harvard University Press, 1990), 91–92. On the Mazzini affair, see Vincent, *Culture of Secrecy*, 1–9.

22. On the decision of the United States to guarantee the privacy of posted correspondence, see John, *Spreading the News*, 42; and Paul Starr, *Creation of the Media: Political Origins of Modern Communications* (New York: Basic Books, 2004), 94–96. On the problem of postal theft, see Holbrook, *Ten Years Among the Mail Bags*. See also David

J. Seipp, *The Right to Privacy in American History* (Cambridge, MA: Harvard University Program on Information Resources Policy, 1978), 2–24. In a recent book, literary scholar Milette Shamir identifies the middle of the nineteenth century as the period when the right to privacy began to acquire its modern implication of a right to have one's domestic and intimate affairs shielded from public scrutiny. Significantly, Shamir notes, the early articulations of this right by the courts emphasized the intellectual property rights of the authors of personal correspondence. See *Inexpressible Privacy: The Interior Life of Antebellum American Literature* (Philadelphia: University of Pennsylvania Press, 2006), 157–62.

23. Elizabeth Heckendorn Cook, *Epistolary Bodies: Gender and Genre in the Eighteenth-Century Republic of Letters* (Stanford, CA: Stanford University Press, 1996), 13.

24. Johann Ludwig Kluber, quoted in Siegert, *Relays*, 38. Letters continue to enjoy this association with concealed truths, even in sophisticated and self-conscious academic writing. See, for example, literary scholar Nancy Walker's claim that letters (and diaries) allow readers to glimpse the "invisible presences" in a writer's life (the phrase comes from Virginia Woolf), in "'Wider Than the Sky': Public Presence and Private Self in Dickinson, James, and Woolf," in *The Private Self: Theory and Practice of Women's Autobiographical Writings*, ed. Shari Benstock (Chapel Hill: University of North Carolina Press, 1988), 275.

25. Ik Marvel [Donald G. Mitchell], *Reveries of a Bachelor* (1850; repr., Philadelphia, PA: H. Altemus, 1893), 53–54; Theodore Tilton, to wife Elizabeth, December 22, 1866, reprinted in "The Tilton Letters," *Chicago Daily Tribune*, August 13, 1874. That Tilton's letters resurfaced eight years later in the columns of a Chicago daily newspaper was not simply an ironic commentary on the nature of epistolary privacy but also a testament to the enormous weight attributed to letters as evidence of the emotional states of their authors (see below).

26. Carrie Carlton, *Carrie Carlton's popular letter-writer: A valuable assistant to those engaged in epistolary correspondence, and peculiarly adapted to the requirements of California* (San Francisco: A. Roman, 1868), 7–8.

27. Bancroft, *California Inter Pocula*, 278.

28. John Frost, *Easy Exercises in Composition: Designed for the Use of Beginners* (Philadelphia, PA: Marshall, Williams & Butler, 1841; see, for instance, Arthur Martine, *Martine's Sensible Letter Writer for the Use of Ladies' [sic] and Gentlemen* (New York: Dick & Fitzgerald, 1866), 15. For other examples of this trope, which appeared in virtually every published pedagogical description of letter-writing, see *The New Universal Letter-Writer; or, Complete Art of Polite Correspondence* (1834; repr., Philadelphia, PA: Lippincott, Grambo, 1854), 12; H. T. Tuckerman, "Letter-Writing and Madame de Sevigne," pt. 2, *Godey's Lady's Book*, March 1850; Lucy Fountain, "Letter-Writing," *Putnam's Magazine*, January–June 1870), 236; Farrar, *Youth's Letter-Writer*, 6; *The Letter Writer, containing a great variety of letters on the following subjects: Relationship, business, love, courtship, and marriage* (Boston, MA: Charles Gaylord, 1832), 111; *The Letter-Writer's Own Book: or, the Art of Polite Correspondence* (New York: N. C. Nafis, 1846), xiv; Carlton, *Carrie Carlton's popular letter-writer*, 14; Gay *Naked Heart*, 323; Decker, *Epistolary Practices*, 40. The model of letter-writing as long-distance conversation was common in French epistolary manuals and received authoritative endorsement in Anglo-American culture in the writings of Hugh Blair, the influential Scottish professor of rhetoric. See Decker, *Epistolary Practices*, 40; Bruce Redford, *The Converse of the Pen: Acts of Intimacy in the Eighteenth-Century Familiar Letter* (Chicago: University of Chicago Press, 1986), 5; Cécile Dauphin, "Letter-Writing Manuals in the Nineteenth Century," in *Correspondence*, ed. Chartier, Boureau, and Dauphin, 132–34. For a detailed discussion of the elaboration of this epistolary ideal in Anglo-American letter-writing manuals of the second half of the eighteenth century, see Dierks, "Letter Writing, Gender, and Class in America," especially 81–85.

29. Alger, *Ragged Dick and Struggling Upward*, 122. When Dick's friend Fosdick reads over his letter, he pronounces it good enough to send: "Yes; it seems to me to be quite

a good letter. It is written just as you talk." The *locus classicus* of this trope in American literature appears in J. Hector St. John de Crèvecoeur, *Letters from an American Farmer* (1782; repr., New York: E. P. Dutton, 1957). The difference between this text and Alger's is telling, however. Crèvecoeur's farmer uses the analogy between correspondence and conversation to legitimate an act of vernacular publication. Reluctant to pick up a pen and enter into polite discourse (to "pretend to send epistles to a great European man," in the words of his skeptical wife), the farmer is encouraged by his aristocratic correspondent's insistence that "writing letters is nothing more than talking on paper," a proposition that strikes the farmer at first as "quite a new thought." Faith in this new thought emboldens the farmer and underwrites a declaration of authorial legitimacy that is central to this foundational text in American literature. A century later, what is enabled is not the participation of hard-working, literate American farmers in the public sphere of letters but the admission of ordinary young men into the daily rituals of middle-class literate respectability.

30. Keckley, *Behind the Scenes*, 6–7. On the larger saga, see Jennifer Fleischner, *Mrs. Lincoln and Mrs. Keckly: The Remarkable Story of the Friendship between a First Lady and a Former Slave* (New York: Broadway Books, 2003), 285–325.

31. "The Tilton Letters," *Chicago Daily Tribune*, August 13, 1874. On the scandal, see Richard Wightman Fox, *Trials of Intimacy: Love and Loss in the Beecher-Tilton Scandal* (Chicago: University of Chicago Press, 1999).

32. Fox, *Trials of Intimacy*, especially 53–87, 251–54. Tilton charged at one point that he had seen "from one of [Beecher's] sisters a private letter" proving that Beecher's marriage was unhappy and loveless (60). In a similar but less famous scandal, spiritualist medium Margaret Fox published her romantic correspondence with the late Arctic explorer Elisha Kane in 1865 after Kane's brother withheld a bequest to her. See David Chapin, *Exploring Other Worlds: Margaret Fox, Elisha Kent Kane, and the Culture of Curiosity* (Amherst: University of Massachusetts Press, 2004). For two other mid-century controversies over published correspondence, both of which went to trial, see Shamir, *Inexpressible Privacy*, 159–60. In the later case, *James W. Woolsey v. Owen B. Judd* (1855), the New York State Court of Appeals cited the exclusive property right of letter-writers to the contents of their correspondence in order to prevent the publication of letters that were designed to remain forever inviolable secrets."

33. Cohen, *Murder of Helen Jewett*, 128.

34. Dublin, ed., *Farm to Factory*, 132–34.

35. Kenneth L. Holmes, ed., *Covered Wagon Women: Diaries and Letters from the Western Trails, 1862–1865*, 10 vols. (Lincoln: University of Nebraska Press, 1989), 8:38. Cornelia Hancock, stationed in a military hospital during the Civil War, would ask her sister to forward letters to their mother, "for I hate to take the time to write often"; see Henrietta Stratton Jaquette, ed., *Letters of a Civil War Nurse: Cornelia Hancock, 1863–1865* (Lincoln: University of Nebraska Press, 1998), 16, 100; see also Stephen Wing's letter to his brother, sister, and mother, April 30, [no year], in which he writes "Please tell F. that I hope she will excuse my not writing to her this mail.... You will please let her see this—May do better than *none*" (Stephen Wing Correspondence, BANC). Writers from California may have been especially conscious of the larger audience for their letters. For other examples of friends and family members sharing forty-niners' letters, see Rohrbough, *Days of Gold*, 233–34; Roberts, *American Alchemy*, 173; Augst, *Clerk's Tale*, 72. On the sharing of intimate correspondence among women in mid-century Michigan, see Marilyn Ferris Motz, *True Sisterhood: Michigan Women and Their Kin, 1820–1920* (Albany: State University of New York Press, 1983), 59. On letter-writing as a kind of literary performance, see Hedrick, *Harriet Beecher Stowe*, 77.

36. Buck, *Yankee Trader in the Gold Rush*, 13. This letter was written before Buck sailed to California.

37. Even enthusiastic devotees of the cult of epistolary privacy recognized that letters from settlers to their communities of origin were occasions for public reading. An 1831

article in the *Ladies' Magazine and Literary Gazette*, after commenting on the power and sincerity of "private letters, . . . those quiet rills of affection from domestic springs, gliding so calmly on in the deepest shades of retired life," touts the role of migrants' mail and imagines a community at the other end of the correspondence: "Let a single member of a New England family settle at the South or West, and how soon will the State to which the wanderer has gone become familiar to his friends at home! How eagerly they con every scrap of intelligence his letters impart, and how solicitous they feel for the prosperity of the place where *he*, still their own, has fixed his abode!" See "Letter Writing, in its Effects on National Character," *Ladies' Magazine and Literary Gazette*, June, 1831, 241–42.

38. The classic contribution to the study of this genre of immigrant letters came from Theodore C. Blegen. See David A. Gerber, "The Immigrant Letter between Positivism and Populism: The Uses of Immigrant Personal Correspondence in Twentieth-Century American Scholarship," *Journal of American Ethnic History* 16, no. 4 (1997): esp. 3–6; Øverland, "Immigrant Letters," 212–15. Elsewhere, Gerber draws a clear distinction between the personal correspondence of European immigrants to the United States in the nineteenth century and those letters studied by Blegen, but the line between intimate letters and those designed for communal readership is difficult to identify. Most posted correspondence between immigrants and home communities straddles the divide, containing expressions of intimacy and details of personal life while betraying an awareness that letters from America might be read by potential migrants who were not explicitly addressed. See, for example, the letters of Norwegian immigrant Gro Svendson to her parents, which Blegen classifies as "America letters" despite their inclusion of intimate details about the family, in Blegen and Farseth, eds., *Frontier Mother*. See also David A. Gerber, "Epistolary Ethics: Personal Correspondence and the Culture of Emigration in the Nineteenth Century," *Journal of American Ethnic History* 19, no. 4 (2000), 10.

39. Unknown author to sister Mary, September 14, 1852, San Francisco, Bancroft Letters, box 2, BANC.

40. Peavy and Smith, *Gold Rush Widows*, 92–93.

41. Theodore Tilton to Elizabeth, January 30, 1867; Elizabeth to Theodore, January 9, 1867, both in "The Tilton Letters," *Chicago Daily Tribune*, August 13, 1874; Louisa Cook to Mother and Sisters, June 20, 1862, in Holmes, *Covered Wagon Women*, 8: 38. Fergus is quoted and discussed in Peavy and Smith, *Gold Rush Widows*, 39, 247. As the next chapter discusses, injunctions to save the letters during Civil War were especially common.

42. Welsh, *Practical Guide to Business*, 207; Jay Fliegelman, *Declaring Independence: Jefferson, Natural Language, and the Culture of Performance* (Stanford, CA: Stanford University Press, 1993). For examples of the practice of copying personal mail, see Henry Southworth's letter to his grandmother, March 4, 1853, Henry C. Southworth papers, N-YHS; Hector Dulany to his brother, October 16, 1849, Dulany Family Collection, Bancroft MSS C-B 727, BANC; Fred Worth, *Private Letter Book*, BANC.

43. Øverland, "Immigrant Letters," 212.

44. Schlissel, Gibbens, and Hampstein, *Far From Home*, 34; Michael O'Brien, ed., *An Evening When Alone: Four Journals of Single Women in the South, 1827–1867* (Charlottesville: University Press of Virginia, 1993), 33; Silber and Sievens, eds., *Yankee Correspondence*, 152; For another example, see Motz, *True Sisterhood*, 59.

45. Richard D. Brown notes that references to letter-burning "were almost so common as to be a typical ritual" (Brown, *Knowledge Is Power*, 180); "George" to Mrs. Mary A. Hindee, Pittsford Vermont, February 27, 1848, author's private collection; Gaughan, *Letters of a Confederate Surgeon*, 146. For other examples, see Dublin, ed., *Farm to Factory*, 42–47; Breckinridge, *Lucy Breckinridge of Grove Hill*, 123; Cohen, *Murder of Helen Jewett*, 121. For an excellent discussion of the relationship between private letters and publication, especially among the literary figures of the American Renaissance, see Decker, *Epistolary Practices*, 18–56.

46. Eliza Leslie, *Behaviour Book; A Guide and Manual for Ladies as Regards Their Conversation, Manners, Dress, . . . etc.* (Philadelphia, PA: T. B. Peterson and Brothers, 1859), 162–63.

47. Farrar, *Youth's Letter-Writer*, 103–4.

48. Morse quoted in Gay, *Naked Heart*, 320–21.

49. Pankratz, "New Englanders," 286.

50. Woodward, ed., *Mary Chesnut's Civil War*, 166 (entry for August 27, 1861). For another example of a parent infringing upon the privacy of his daughter's mail, see Breckinridge, *Lucy Breckinridge of Grove Hill*, 96.

51. Wiley, ed., *Letters of Warren Akin, Confederate Congressman*, 130. For another example, of struggles between mothers and daughters over correspondence, see the January 14, 1860, diary entry of twenty-two-year-old Emily Hawley, who was then living at her parents' home in rural Michigan: "Mother does not approve of letters from strangers," Hawley noted upon the arrival of a letter from a man. "[P]erhaps a stranger is as good as some acquaintances," she added. See Lensink, ed., *Diary and Life of Emily Hawley Gillespie*, 27. In an 1855 Alice Cary story, a young girl makes a point of promising a boy that she will correspond with him without telling her parents; see "The Boys and the Men," *Ladies' Repository* 15 (August, 1855), 484.

52. *The Young Lady's Friend* (Boston, 1837), 281; North Carolina paper quoted in Louis R. Wilson, ed., *Selected Papers of Cornelia Phillips Spencer* (Chapel Hill: University of North Carolina Press, 1953), 382. See also Barbara Maria Zaczek, *Censored Sentiments: Letters and Censorship in Epistolary Novels and Conduct Material* (Newark: University of Delaware Press, 1997); Mary A. Favret, *Romantic Correspondence: Women, Politics and the Fiction of Letters* (Cambridge: Cambridge University Press, 1993); Hornbeak, *Complete Letter-Writer in English*. Women's correspondence, like women's reading more generally, had been stigmatized within Anglo-American art and literature for some time as a practice of absorption into sexual fantasy and stealthy abdication of familial or conjugal duties. The letter-writer withdraws from public view into secret relationships that leave but a faint trace. Donald G. Mitchell's narrator in his popular mid-century fiction *Reveries of a Bachelor*, imagining a less-than-devoted wife, reinforces this association: "She is not sluttish," he muses "unless a *negligé* till three o'clock, and an ink stain on the forefinger be sluttish" (27). Hidden excesses of the pen, indulged within the secluded spaces of the middle-class bedroom, connoted multiple intimacy and promiscuous sociability.

53. Caroline Loomis Edwards to her brother Elias, January 25, 1841, quoted in Pankratz, "New Englanders," 286. See longer discussion of husbands' access to their wives' letters in the previous chapter.

54. On the Ladies Epistolary, see Thornton, *Handwriting in America*, 56–59; Fountain, "Letter-Writing," 236; *A New Letter-Writer, for the Use of Ladies* (Philadelphia, PA: n.p., ca. 1860), excerpted in Decker, *Epistolary Practices*, 98; "Thoughts on Letter-writing," reprinted in John Pierpont, *The American First Class Book; or, Exercises in Reading and Recitation* (Boston: Carter, Hendee, 1835), 341; Tuckerman, "Letter-Writing and Madame de Sevigne." One letter-writing manual published originally in 1834 but reprinted through the antebellum era noted that "ladies have been accused, probably with some reason, of reserving the most important part of a letter for the postscript," a practice derided as "needless, and in bad taste" (*New Universal Letter-Writer*, 11). For a parody of the excessive use of postscripts in women's letters, see for example "A Western Love Letter" in the *New Orleans Picayune*, April 19, 1841.

55. Motz, *True Sisterhood*, 53–81. Carroll Smith-Rosenberg's landmark article on friendships between women in the nineteenth century implies some similar claims about their distinctive brand of epistolary intimacy; see Carroll Smith-Rosenberg, "The Female World of Love and Ritual: Relations Between Women in Nineteenth-Century America," in *Disorderly Conduct: Visions of Gender in Victorian America* (New York: Oxford

University Press, 1985), 53–76. Lillian Schlissel glosses a particular line in an 1850 letter from an Oregon correspondent by citing "a masculine discomfort with letter writing," reinforcing the identification between the personal letter and femininity; see Schlissel, Gibbens, and Hampstein, *Far From Home*, 24. For an alternative view, see Zboray, *Fictive People*, 239–40.

56. Fred Worth to his grandmother, January 19, 1859, in Worth, *Private Letter Book*, Bancroft Library MSS, BANC.

57. The word *conversation* had not always referred exclusively to oral communication. In the eighteenth century one might speak of having conversation with the sea, and the phrase *criminal conversation* might denote nonverbal forms of contact and interaction. Still, the uses of term in the nineteenth-century sources cited here appear to be employing *conversation* in a new, more restrictive sense. David Hancock, "Commerce and Conversation in the Eighteenth-Century Atlantic: The Invention of Madeira Wine," *Journal of Interdisciplinary History* 29, no. 2 (Autumn, 1998), 197–219.

58. Motz, *True Sisterhood*, 62; Abigail Malick, quoted in Schlissel, Gibbens, and Hampstein, *Far From Home*, 52; Wiley, ed., *Letters of Warren Akin, Confederate Congressman*, 34–35; Starobin, ed., *Blacks in Bondage*, 76. Samuel Birney of Georgia, serving in the Confederate Army, apologized to his wife for "very dull letters," but explained that "what I write springs from my heart with no study of arrangement." Then, as if to add a literary assessment, he observed that "these honest hearted letters written in plain language, tell of a soldier's strong love for his wife and little one." Nat S. Turner III, *A Southern Soldier's Letters Home: The Civil War Letters of Samuel A. Birney, Cobb's Georgia Legion, Army of Northern Virginia* (Macon, GA: Mercer University Press, 2002), 93–94.

59. Benemann, ed., *Year of Mud and Gold*, 43–44; Samuel Adams, quoted in Roberts, *American Alchemy*, 160; Mary Wingate, Meriden, December 23, 1850; Wiley, ed., *Letters of Warren Akin, Confederate Congressman*, 63. For other uses of "talk" or "chat" by correspondents to describe their personal letters, see Elizabeth Tilton to Theodore Tilton, February 24, 1868, in "The Tilton Letters," *Chicago Daily Tribune*, August 13, 1874; Laas, ed., *Wartime Washington*, 35; Doody, ed., *Yours in Love*, 73; Buck, *Yankee Trader in the Gold Rush*, 2; Rozier, ed., *Granite Farm Letters*, 139; Decker, *Epistolary Practices*, 40, 249; Lystra, *Searching the Heart*, 21–22.

60. Holliday, *The World Rushed In*, 83. The inadequacy of the letter as a form of contact was, of course, a more widespread trope. See for example Emma Randolph's letter to her wounded cousin in the Union Army, in which she longs "to greet you this morning with something besides the pen," or the assurances of an ardent lover thirty years earlier that his next epistle would be "written not with ink," in Judith A. Bailey and Robert I. Cottom, eds., *After Chancellorsville: Letters from the Heart: The Civil Letters of Private Walter G. Dunn and Emma Randolph* (Baltimore: Maryland Historical Society, 1998), 143; Lystra, *Searching the Heart*, 23. For a related discussion of the centrality of Emily Dickinson's interest in the paradoxical relationship between intimate correspondence and corporeal presence, see Hewitt, *Correspondence and American Literature*, 158.

61. Myers, ed., *Children of Pride*, 106. There was, on the other hand, some reason to suppose that physical absence facilitated intimacy. In an 1826 letter to a woman he was courting, Robert Conrad of Virginia observed that he "should be rather more at ease, here, in my office, with pen, ink and paper—than if we were full face to face; . . . I can hold freer converse with you in this way than in another." Quoted in Brenda Stevenson, *Life in Black and White: Family and Community in the Slave South* (New York: Oxford University Press, 1996), 57.

62. Charles F. Larimer, ed., *Love and Valor: Intimate Civil War Letters between Captain Jacob and Emeline Ritner* (Western Spring, IL: Sigourney Press, 2000), 234; Buck, *Yankee Trader in the Gold Rush*, 1.

63. Peter Gay, *The Bourgeois Experience, Victoria to Freud*, vol. 1, *Education of the Senses* (New York: Oxford University Press, 1984), 125.

64. Vail, ed., "Correspondence of John Ingalls," 149; Wiley, ed., *Letters of Warren Akin, Confederate Congressman,* 48; Donald F. Danker, ed., *Mollie: The Journal of Mollie Dorsey Sanford in Nebraska and Colorado Territories, 1857–1866* (Lincoln: University of Nebraska Press, 1959), 143–44. See also Bayard Taylor's 1847 letter to John B. Phillips in Paul C. Wermuth, ed., *Selected Letters of Bayard Taylor* (Lewisburg, PA: Bucknell University Press, 1997), 66.

65. Decker, *Epistolary Practices,* 57–103. The phrase about enduring presence in quotation marks appears on p. 60 and then, in slightly contracted form, on p. 95.

66. Silber and Sievens, eds., *Yankee Correspondence,* 85; Drake, *The Mail Goes Through,* 40; Judith Lee Hallock, ed., *The Civil War Letters of Joshua K. Calloway* (Athens: University of Georgia Press, 1997), 77; Myers, ed., *Children of Pride,* 1:434. Civil War soldiers appear to have been especially fond of this standard opening, as these examples (and countless others in Silber and Sievens) attest, but the formulaic opening of a letter with a dated acknowledgment of postal receipt appears in letter collections of writers of every social description by mid-century. The letters of artist Henry Inman present an interesting example of a writer who turned to this formula with increasing regularity in the 1840s; see Henry Inman letters, AAS. On the codes of epistolary reciprocity that underlay this formula, see Gerber, "Epistolary Ethics."

67. Fatout, ed., *Letters of a Civil War Surgeon,* 17; Jonathan F. Locke to his wife, March 27, 1850, in Benemann, ed., *Year of Mud and Gold,* 157. On affirmations of reciprocity in immigrant letters, see Gerber, "Epistolary Ethics."

68. Examples are taken from Samuel V. Tripp Correspondence, 1849–1850, NEW. For a few others that adhere quite closely to the model, see Drake, *The Mail Goes Through,* 53, 59, 134; letters of James Gipson, Bella DeRosset, and Sara Boon in Starobin, ed., *Blacks in Bondage,* 59, 78, 91; several letters in Blassingame, ed., *Slave Testimony,* 37, 38, 40, 41; letter of Phoebe Stanton in Holmes, ed., *Covered Wagon Women,* 1:87; letters of Walter Birket and William Corlett in Charlotte Erickson, *Invisible Immigrants: The Adaptation of English and Scottish Immigrants in Nineteenth-Century America* (London: Wiedenfield and Nicholson, 1972), 85, 106, 107; letter of John D. Biles to Rachel Malick in Schlissel, Gibbens, and Hampstein, eds., *Far from Home,* 18; letter to Jacob Blauvelt from his father, April 1, 1862, in John D. Kohlepp, "The Blauvelt Correspondence," *Chronicle of the U.S. Classic Postal Issues* (August, 1975): 162–63; letter of David C. Clark to his son, William A. Clark, December 10, 1862, in Tatum, ed., "Civil War Letters of William Allen Clark," 104; letter of Thomas Josephus Moore to Martha Barron, September 20, 1861, in Ray Mathis, *In the Land of the Living: Wartime Letters by Confederates from the Chattahoochee Valley of Alabama and Georgia* (Troy, AL: Troy State University Press, 1981), 14; letter of T. E. E. Jackson to Micajah B. Stinson, September, 1863, in Thomas Cutrer, ed., *Oh, What a Loansome* [sic] *Time I Had: The Civil War Letters of Major William Morel Moxley, Eighteenth Alabama Infantry, and Emily Beck Moxley* (Tuscaloosa: University of Alabama Press, 2002), 150; letter of Richard Gould to Hannah Thomas, December 26, 1862, in Robert F. Harris and John Niflot, eds., *Dear Sister: The Civil War Letters of the Brothers Gould* (Westport, CT: Praeger, 1998), 49; letter of J. W. Tomberlinson to Amanda E. Mastin, from captured Confederate post office, transcribed in Elvira J. Powers, *Hospital Pencillings: Being a Diary While in Jefferson General Hospital, Jeffersonville, Indiana and Others at Nashville, Tennessee, as Matron and Visitor* (Boston: E. L. Mitchell, 1866), 150–51. Virginia Reed's letter to her cousin in 1847 opens with a slight variant of this model, even though the letter proceeds to provide a firsthand account of the gruesome fate of the Donner Party; see Holmes, ed., *Covered Wagon Women,* 1:80–81.

69. Decker, *Epistolary Practices,* 58. For an eighteenth-century instance of this usage, see Dierks, "'Let Me Chat a Little,'" 124. By the antebellum period, the opportunity embraced was far less likely to be an unexpected private conveyance. A letter from gold miner John Allan of Nevada City in 1850 illustrates the change nicely: "I embrace the opportunity of again writing to you, through the medium of a post office that is now

established in our shingle city"; see *California Gold Rush Letters, 1848–1859*, BANC-MSS C-B 547, box 1, BANC.

70. See, for example, the 1850 courtship letter of John D. Biles to westward migrant Rachel Malick, in Schlissel, Gibbens, and Hampstein, eds., *Far from Home*, 18.

71. In addition to the examples referred to above, see Dublin, *Farm to Factory*; Theodore Blegen, ed., *Land of Their Choice: The Immigrants Write Home* (St. Paul: University of Minnesota Press, 1955); H. Arnold Barton, *Letters from the Promised Land: Swedes in America, 1840–1914* (Minneapolis, MN: University of Minnesota Press, 1975); Kamphoefner, Helbich, and Sommer, eds., *News from the Land of Freedom*.

72. Jackson, ed., *Direct Your Letters to San Jose*, 74, also 91 and 93.

73. Ibid., 145, 210; see also 146, 215.

74. Ibid., 76, 127. David's sole use of the formula appears on p. 188. An intriguing parallel case to the Campbell brothers appears in the wartime letters home of Daniel and Alexander Chisholm, two young Pennsylvania brothers who fought in the Union Army. There too, the correspondence of the slightly younger sibling routinely begins, "I take this opportunity of writing to let you know I am well, and hoping you are the same" (or some close approximation), while the older son typically began with a direct acknowledgement of the receipt of his parent's letters; see W. Springer Menge and J. August Shimrak, eds., *The Civil War Notebook of Daniel Chisholm: A Chronicle of Daily Life in the Union Army 1864–1865* (New York: Ballantine Books, 1989), 103–65.

75. *New Orleans Picayune*, April 19, 1841; Webb, *The Garies and Their Friends*, 264–65.

76. "A Bundle of Old Letters," *Southern Illustrated News*, August 1, 1863, 30; Farrar, *Youth's Letter-Writer*, 67, 153.

77. Weld, "Some Thoughts on Letter Writing," 251; Dublin, *Farm to Factory*, 187. For another instance of self-consciousness about formulaic openings, see Emily Sinkler's expression of concern that acknowledgments of receiving mail tend to degenerate into "small talk" in LeClerq, ed., *Between North and South*, 71.

78. John Kenedy, *The American Polite Letter Writer, Containing About Sixty Letters, Written in the most fashionable style* (New York: N. C. Nafis, [1839]), 44, 46. Another letter from "a young milliner to her parents" (38) offers a slight variant on the same opening.

79. Karen Lystra suggests that middle-class readers probably did not often borrow language from the guides, which valorized individual self-expression (*Searching the Heart*, 14). Roger Chartier argues that epistolary manuals in France had little practical value for ordinary readers through the early part of the nineteenth century and that the appeal of eighteenth-century guides owed more to their status as guides to lost or exotic worlds of courtly manners or as an embryonic form of epistolary fiction than to their practicality. Even when the French guidebooks began addressing the practical needs of ordinary correspondents, many of them continued to reprint letters from earlier models; see Roger Chartier, "*Secrétaires* for the People? Model Letters of the Ancien Régime: Between Court Literature and Popular Chapbooks," in Chartier, Boureau, and Dauphin, *Correspondence*, 59–111. Dauphin's contribution to this volume offers some scant evidence that epistolary manuals might have been used to compose letters in mid-nineteenth-century France (a disclaimer by one man who "never cop[ies] out a letter," for example, is unconvincingly interpreted as an indication that he imagined the practice of borrowing letters from published guides to be common), but she too doubts that the *secrétaire* was suited to straightforward application. See Dauphin, "Letter-Writing Manuals in the Nineteenth Century," in Chartier, Boureau, and Dauphin, *Correspondence*, 148–50. However uncertain the utility of letter-writing guides, the richness of this popular genre cannot be denied, especially in the American context. For a catalogue of titles published in the United States, see Harry B. Weiss, "American Letter-Writers, 1698–1943," pt. 2, *Bulletin of the New York Public Library* 49, no. 1 (1945): 33–61. A majority of these are from the nineteenth century. See also Weiss's discussion of the genre in "American Letter-Writers, 1698–1943," *Bulletin of the New York Public Library* 48, no. 12 (1944): 959–82; and Hornbeak, *Complete Letter-Writer in English*, 105–16.

80. Samuel Richardson, *Familiar Letters on Important Occasions* (1741; repr., London: George Routledge and Sons, 1928); *The Complete Letter Writer; containing a great variety of letters . . . selected from judicious and eminent writers* (San Francisco: Marion and Hitchcock, 1853). Occasionally, some minor modification was in order. Richardson's Letter 9, for example, "An elder to a younger Brother, who is in Love with a young Lady of great Gaiety, &c.," reappeared in San Francisco as Letter 40, "From an elder to a younger Brother, cautioning him in the choice of a wife." Richardson's letters appeared as well in guides published in other cities. See the letter from a daughter to a father on behalf of her sister in *The Fashionable American Letter Writer: Or, the art of polite correspondence. Containing a variety of plain and elegant letters on business, love courtship, marriage, relationship, friendship, &c* (Hartford, CT: Ezra Strong, n.d.), 86–89; *The Fashionable American Letter Writer: Or, the art of polite correspondence. Containing a variety of plain and elegant letters on business, love courtship, marriage, relationship, friendship, &c* (Boston: James Loring, 1823), 111–12; *The Letter-Writer's Own Book: or, the Art of Polite Correspondence. Containing a variety of plain and elegant letters, on business, love, courtship, marriage, relationship, friendship, &c. with forms of complimentary cards, and directions for letter writing* (Philadelphia, PA: John B. Perry, 1846), 102–5.

81. Lucille M. Schultz, "Letter-Writing Instruction in Nineteenth-Century Schools in the United States," in *Letter Writing as a Social Practice*, ed. Barton and Hall, 114. On the role of letter-writing in nineteenth-century composition instruction, see Miller, *Assuming the Positions*, 89.

82. Charles Morley, *A Practical Guide to Composition, with progressive exercises in prose and poetry* (Hartford, CT: R. White, 1839), 46–48. The formulaic opening to the letter to the brother ("Although it is several years since I saw you, yet time has not at all lessened, but rather increased my affection for you.") exactly mimics a line from a sample letter appearing a few pages earlier in a letter from a niece to her uncle (41).

83. Dierks, "Letter Writing, Gender, and Class in America."

CHAPTER FIVE

1. Letter from Philip V. R. Stanton (Brooklyn NY) to George McKistry (Sutter's Fort, CA), February 14, 1848, McKistry Papers, BANC. The letter is printed in Morgan, *Overland in 1846*, 2: 466–69. For some samples of Charles's letters to his siblings, see ibid., 531–33, 611–20.

2. For another example of the use of maps to track migrating family members, see the letter of John Everett to his brother Robert, October 21, 1854, in "Letters of John and Sarah Everett, 1854–1864," 4. Writing from Kansas City, Missouri (a temporary stop on his westward journey), John instructs his brother to look up the county name of his provisional residence on a map in order to address a reply.

3. Elizabeth Tilton to Theodore Tilton, February 7, 1869, in "The Tilton Letters," *Chicago Daily Tribune*, August 13, 1874.

4. See O'Brien, *An Evening When Alone*; Stowe, ed., *A Southern Practice*, 118.

5. LeClerq, *An Antebellum Plantation Household*, 27, 47.

6. Roxana Brown Walbridge Watts to Augusta Gregory, may 29, 1853; Dustan Walbridge to his sister Sarah Walbridge Way, March 14, 1863, both quotations appear on the epigraph page in Bonfield and Morrison, *Roxana's Children*.

7. Colton Storm, ed., *"A Pretty Fair View of the Eliphent" Or, Ten Letters by Charles G. Hinman Written during his Trip Overland from Groveland, Illinois, to California in 1849 and his Adventures in the Gold Fields in 1849 and 1850* (Chicago: Gordon Martin, 1960), 13.

8. Peavy and Smith, *Gold Rush Widows*, 42; Julia Ann Archibald to Lydia Sayer, in Holmes, ed., *Covered Wagon Women*, 7:209.

9. Storm, ed., *View of the Eliphent*, 17, 23.

10. Williams's letter appears in Holmes, ed., *Covered Wagon Women*, 3:133; Cook's letter appears in Holmes, *Covered Wagon Women*, 8: 45; Delano is quoted in Richard T. Stillson, "Golden Words: Communications and Information Dispersal in the California

Gold Rush," PhD diss., Johns Hopkins University (2003), 134–35; Putnam's letter appears in Morgan, *Overland in 1846*, 1:632; Harlow, *Old Post Bags*, 342–43. For other examples of migrants entrusting mail to eastward travelers, see Morgan, *Overland in 1846*, 1:278, 522, 559, 564, 611; Peavy and Smith, *Gold Rush Widows*, 118; Stillson, "Golden Words," 134–39.

11. "A Nebraska Post Office," *Frank Leslie's Illustrated Weekly*, October 26, 1867.

12. Danker (ed.), *Journal of Mollie Dorsey Sanford*, 133. To put this cost in some perspective, Mollie's family had been lured westward by the rumor that her father could earn $8–10 a day at his trade.

13. Storm, ed., *View of the Eliphent*, 36, 39; Richards, ed., *Journal of Stephen Chapin Davis*, 19. See also Christman, *One Man's Gold*, 125.

14. Buck, *Yankee Trader in the Gold Rush*, 57; David Dustin to John K. Dustin, August 14, 1850, California Gold Rush Letters, 1848–1859 Bancroft MSS C-B 547, BANC. Another reference to the miscarriage of letters sent to forty-niners by private conveyance appears in D. B. Stillman, "Seeking the Golden Fleece," *Overland Monthly* (March, 1874), 254. Miners appeared to have relied upon private couriers mostly in the first year of the Gold Rush. See, for example, Storm, ed., *View of the Eliphent*, 36, 39; Oscar Bennet to his brother, July 15, 1849, Oscar Bennet Letters, California Historical Society MS 143, CHS; John Ingalls to Jonathan Trumbull Smith, September 24, 1849, in Vail, ed., "Correspondence of John Ingalls," 158.

15. Benjamin Wingate to Mary Wingate, March 1, 1851, Wingate Correspondence, Bancroft MSS 83/35c, BANC.

16. For references to faulty mails, see Vail, ed., "Correspondence of John Ingalls," 157, 166; Benjamin Wingate to Mary Wingate, Feb. 1, 1851 and Mary Wingate to Benjamin Wingate, April 18, 1852, both in Wingate Correspondence, Bancroft MSS 83/35c, BANC; Charles Dulany to Elizabeth (sister). Sacramento, February 26, 1850 [misdated 1849], Dulany Family Collection, Bancroft MSS, C-B 727, BANC; Kaufman, ed., *Apron Full of Gold*, 58–61.

17. For an example of sending gold or money in the mail during the Gold Rush, see the entry for May 18, 1852, in "Daily Journal of Alfred and Chastina W. Rix," Rix and Walbridge Families Collection, CHS.

18. Benjamin Wingate to Mary Wingate, January 15, 1854, Wingate Correspondence, Bancroft MSS 83/35c, BANC.

19. Thomas L. Megquier to his son-in-law Charles, November 30, 1852, in Kaufman, *Apron Full of Gold*, 102.

20. Mary Wingate to Benjamin Wingate, March 17, 1852; Benjamin Wingate to Mary Wingate, May 1, 1851, Wingate Correspondence, Bancroft MSS 83/35c, BANC.

21. See, for example Thomas and Mary Jane Megquier's 1849 letter to their son Arthur, in Kaufman, *Apron Full of Gold*, 33.

22. Benjamin Wingate to Mary Wingate, June 1, 1852, Wingate Correspondence, Bancroft MSS 83/35c, BANC.

23. Buck, *Yankee Trader in the Gold Rush*, 57, 103, 118–19.

24. Amy Lippert, "Consuming Identities: Visual Culture and Celebrity in Antebellum San Francisco," unpublished paper, 2004 (cited with permission of author); Peter E. Palmquist and Thomas R. Kailbourn, eds., *Pioneer Photographers of the Far West: a Biographical Dictionary, 1840–1865* (Stanford, CA: Stanford University Press, 2000). For examples of the postal exchange of daguerreotype portraits during the early years of the Gold Rush, see Christman, *One Man's Gold*, 244, 249, 250, 252; July 16, 1852, entry in "Daily Journal of Alfred and Chastina W. Rix," Rix and Walbridge Families Collection, CHS.

25. Christman, *One Man's Gold*, 244, 250; Jonathan F. Locke to his wife, in Benemann, ed., *Year of Mud and Gold*, 157–58. As with correspondence more generally, daguerreotypes could strike their recipients as tokens of absence as much as presence, a point raised in chapter 2. In the particular case of the Gold Rush, the longer someone stayed in California, the more easily he could be reduced, in the mind of his correspondent, to a pictorial

representation. Mary Wingate emphasized this point to her husband through the perspective of their young daughter, who asked her mother whether her absent father had feet. "A new idea seemed to strike her that her dear father was a man, not a picture." Some months later, Mary reiterated the concern. "Ella talks a great deal about *Pa* and her *own* father but has some doubts as to whether he is a real man or a picture." See Mary Wingate to Benjamin, November 1, 1852, and June 16, 1853, Wingate Correspondence, Bancroft MSS 83/35c, BANC.

26. Mary Wingate to Benjamin, July 10, 1853, Wingate Correspondence, Bancroft MSS 83/35c, BANC; Buck, *Yankee Trader in the Gold Rush*, 131. John McCracken to his sister Lottie in Benemann, ed., *Year of Mud and Gold*, 215; Paschal Mack to "Dear Sister," December 13, 1852. Bancroft MSS C-B 547:61, BANC. The recurrence of brother-sister correspondence among these examples (and throughout this chapter) is not coincidental. Affectionate letters between siblings of the opposite sex were paradigms of epistolary intimacy.

27. Benemann, ed., *Year of Mud and Gold*, 215.

28. Henry Perry to his parents, April 18, 1849, Henry Perry Letters, NEW. Franklin Buck also details his weight to his sister (Buck, *Yankee Trader in the Gold Rush*, 131).

29. See, for example, Bonfield and Morrison, *Roxana's Children*, 76; April 24, 1852, entry in "Daily Journal of Alfred and Chastina W. Rix" Rix and Walbridge Families Collection, CHS. One letter in the Bancroft Library collection includes four drawings of Chinese miners; see "Anonymous to Dear Sister," San Francisco, September 14, 1852, BANC.

30. Joseph Armstrong Baird Jr., *California's Pictorial Letter Sheets, 1849–1869* (San Francisco: D. Magee, 1967), 11.

31. Ibid., 26. Baird even suggests that the relative absence of "true letters" among the surviving pictorial sheets "suggests that most letter sheets were intended for the semi-literate or the lazy." That conclusion may not be warranted, especially since the few surviving sheets may not be representative (they may include a disproportionate number that were purchased but not mailed, or were mailed purely for their pictorial value), and given the unreasonable standard of literary effort that Baird may be applying (he expresses surprise and disappointment that "a dismal refrain of loneliness, of hopes high but unfulfilled, of plans to return to the native hearth, recurs in many of them"). Yet the phenomenon he observes certainly indicates the centrality of images and visual access to the postal impulses of new Californians in the 1850s; see p. 16.

32. Baird, *Pictorial Letter Sheets*, 11–26; Jesse L. Coburn, *Letters of Gold: California Postal History through 1869* (Canton, OH: Philatelic Foundation, 1984), 266–90. My thinking about the visual component of Gold Rush correspondence has benefited from reading an unpublished paper by Amy Lippert (see n. 24 above).

33. Mary Wingate to Benjamin Wingate, February 4, 1852; March 15, 1853; April 15, 1851, Wingate Correspondence, Bancroft MSS 83/35c, BANC.

34. "Daily Journal of Alfred and Chastina W. Rix," Rix and Walbridge Families Collection, CHS.

35. Bayard Taylor, *Eldorado, or Adventures in the Path of Empire* (Lincoln: University of Nebraska Press, 1988), 157; Reverend William Taylor, quoted in Harlow, *Old Post Bags*, 351; Bancroft, *California Inter Pocula*, 270, 275; Lloyd, *Lights and Shades in San Francisco*, 521; See also Weller, "The History of a Letter."

36. Taylor, *Eldorado*, 156; Bancroft, *California Inter Pocula*, 272, 278–79; Frank Soulé, John H. Gihon, and James Nisbet, *The Annals of San Francisco* (1855; repr., Berkeley, CA: Berkeley Hills Books, 1999), 260. An 1853 novel set in San Francisco describes a line at the post office "as extensive as that of Banquo's issue which flitted before the eyes of the Scottish regicide" (*The Mysteries and Miseries of San Francisco* [New York: Garrett, 1853], 74). Benjamin Lloyd told of men standing in lines for hours, or sitting down in the line, drinking, smoking, and playing cards (*Lights and Shades in San Francisco*, 523). See also

the account of the post office in a letter of young clerk Brady Morse, quoted and discussed in Augst, *Clerk's Tale*, 75.

37. Taylor, *Eldorado*, 159; Soulé, Gihon, and Nisbet, *Annals of San Francisco*, 260; Steele, *In Camp and Cabin*, 207. See also Taylor, *Seven Years' Street Preaching*, 284; Lloyd, *Lights and Shades in San Francisco*, 523. In a letter to his wife, one forty-niner cited the practice of selling places on the post office line as an illustration of the remarkable orderliness and civility of public life in San Francisco, see John S. Way to Sarah Walbridge Way, February 21, 1850, quoted in Bonfield and Morrison, *Roxana's Children*, 45.

38. Hilda Rosenblatt, "For Three Weeks," *Overland Monthly* 3 (December 1869), 557.

39. Benemann, ed., *Year of Mud and Gold*, 40, 52–53.

40. Ibid., 51; Alexander, quoted in Roberts, *American Alchemy*, 90; Kaufman, ed., *Apron Full of Gold*, 40; Mulford's letter appeared in a 2002 exhibit in the National Postal Museum and is part of the Rensselaerville Correspondence, The Frances Long Collection, New York. Correspondents in the eastern states offered reciprocal expressions, as in Mary Wingate's epistolary avowal that she "would give a mine of gold if I could see and speak with you even for a short time. Write me ever thing you can think of for every word is a treasure to *me*." Mary Wingate to Benjamin Wingate, December 1, 1850, Wingate Correspondence, Bancroft MSS 83/35c, BANC (emphasis in original).

41. *San Francisco Daily Evening News*, November 22, 1853. The anecdote is repeated in Bancroft, *California Inter Pocula*, 278.

42. Bancroft, *California Inter Pocula*, 278.

43. Soulé, Gihon, and Nisbet, *Annals of San Francisco*, 260.

44. Bancroft, *California Inter Pocula*, 274, 275, 278. See also Soulé, Gihon, and Nisbet, *Annals of San Francisco*, 260. An interesting parallel expression of this belief in the power of letters to exert a monitory moral influence appears in the view among antebellum asylum reformers that patients needed to be sequestered from personal mail. Though newspapers and periodicals were available in the new institutions that emerged in the Northeast during the 1840s, the authorities discouraged mail out of concern that, in the words of David J. Rothman, "news from home might intrude on the calm and regular routine of the asylum and upset the patients' stability." An Ohio superintendent justified the suppression of mail with the observation that "long and tender letters, containing some ill-timed news . . . may destroy weeks and months of favorable progress"; see David J. Rothman, *The Discovery of the Asylum: Social Order and Disorder in the New Republic* (Boston: Little, Brown, 1971), 143.

45. Christman, *One Man's Gold*, 187, 233.

46. Charles Thompson to his uncle, September 10, 1851, California Gold Rush Letters, 1848–1859 Bancroft MSS C-B 547, BANC.

47. Bancroft, *California Inter Pocula*, 274; Soulé, Gihon, and Nisbet, *Annals of San Francisco*, 260. Bancroft's text appeared decades after the *Annals* was first published.

48. Christman, *One Man's Gold*, 186–87.

49. Steele, *In Camp and Cabin*, 350; Stephen Chapin Davis, *California Gold Rush Merchant: The Journal of Stephen Chapin Davis*, ed. Benjamin B. Richards (San Marino, CA: Huntington Library, 1956), 20. See also Benemann, ed., *Year of Mud and Gold*, 48.

50. Frederick P. Tracy to wife, Emily, SF, August 26, 1849, California Gold Rush Letters, 1848–1859, Bancroft MSS C-B 547, box 2, BANC; Buck, *Yankee Trader in the Gold Rush*, 24.

51. Mary A. Livermore, *My Story of the War: A Woman's Narrative of Four Years Personal Experience as Nurse in the Union Army* (Hartford, CT: A. D. Worthington, 1889), 141. One indication of the increase in correspondence during the war is the rise in postal revenue in the North. In states that did not secede, postal receipts for the year ending on June 30, 1864, were more than a third higher than they had been three years earlier; see D. D. T. Leech, *The Post Office Department of the United States of America*, completed by W. L. Nicholson (Washington, DC: Judd & Detweiler, 1879), 52. For a general discussion of Civil War letters, see James M. McPherson, *For Cause and Comrades: Why Men Fought in the Civil*

War (New York: Oxford University Press, 1997), 11–12. The best estimates suggest that 80–90 percent of soldiers were literate, and even some who could not read or write managed to correspond through intermediaries. See, for example, the case of a Confederate soldier who composed and received correspondence for his friends, mentioned in Bell Irvin Wiley, *The Life of Johnny Reb: The Common Soldier of the Confederacy* (Indianapolis, IN: Bobbs-Merrill, 1943), 284.

52. Livermore, *My Story of the War*, 140–41. Massachusetts Artilleryman John Billings recalled that "all wrote letters more or less, [and] there were a few men who seemed to spend the *most* of their spare time in this occupation," especially in the early period of their service; see Billings, *Hardtack and Coffee*, 55.

53. James M. Greiner, Janet L. Coryell, and James R. Smither, eds., *A Surgeon's Civil War: The Letters and Diary of Daniel M. Holt, M.D.* (Kent, OH: Kent State University Press, 1994), 106. See also Reid Mitchell, "The Northern Soldier and His Community," in Maris A. Vinovskis, *Toward a Social History of the American Civil War: Exploratory Essays* (Cambridge: Cambridge University Press, 1990), 78–92.

54. Silber and Sievens, eds., *Yankee Correspondence*, 120, 121.

55. Drake, *The Mail Goes Through*, 73, 96.

56. Tatum, ed., "Civil War Letters of William Allen Clark," 85.

57. Richard B. Graham, "Lossing's Civil War in America" *Chronicle of the U.S. Classic Postal Issues* 30, no 1 (1978): 44–45. The words in quotation marks are Benjamin Lossing's. Part of the reason the Post Office Department issued these new envelopes was to invalidate extant issues that were held in the South; see John Murray Bartels, *Bartels Catalogue of the Stamped Envelopes and Wrappers of the United States and Possessions*, vol. 1, 5th ed. (Netcong, NJ: Prescott Holden Thorp, 1943), 13. For another description of some of these envelopes, see Billings, *Hardtack and Coffee*, 57. Patriotic envelopes appeared on the Confederate side as well, though in smaller numbers; see Patricia Kaufmann, "The Rebel Post," *Scott's Monthly Stamp Journal* (April, 1976), available online at http://www.webuystamps.com/rebpost.htm.

58. Sarah Emma Edmonds, *Unsexed: or the Female Soldier. The thrilling adventures, experiences and escapes of a woman as nurse, spy and scout, in hospitals, camps and battle-fields* (Philadelphia, PA: Philadelphia Publishing Co., 1864), 36; Katherine S. Holland, ed., *Keep All My Letters: The Civil War Letters of Richard Henry Brooks, 51st Georgia Infantry* (Macon, GA: Mercer University Press, 2003), 36; Billings, *Hardtack and Coffee*, 55–56; Livermore, *My Story of the War*, 139–41.

59. Wiley, ed., *Letters of Warren Akin, Confederate Congressman*, 96.

60. Eunice Snow to Henry Snow, February 21, 1864, in Silber and Sievens, eds., *Yankee Correspondence*, 148; see also Billings, *Hardtack and Coffee*, 55–56. For other discussions of using an officer's frank, see Larimer, ed., *Love and Valor*, 257; Tatum, ed., "Civil War Letters of William Allen Clark," 96, 98; Frank M. Lee, Letter to Henry H. Hadley, June 23, 1864, in *Letters of William Wheeler of the Class of 1855, Y.C.* (privately published, 1875), 467, published online by Alexander Street Press, *The American Civil War: Letters and Diaries*, http://alexanderstreet.com/products/cwld.htm; Oliver Wilcox Norton, Letter of October 4, 1861, in *Army Letters, 1861–1865: Being Extracts from Private Letters to Relatives and Friends from a Soldier in the Field during the Late Civil War, with an Appendix Containing Copies of Some Official Documents, Papers and Addresses of Later Date* (Chicago, IL: O. L. Deming, 1903), 25–26. Charles Gould of New York State was able to use the frank of his congressman when writing from Camp Caldwell in Washington, D.C.; see Harris and Niflot, eds., *Dear Sister*, 5. Mary Chesnut's famous diary refers to some letters from "a Yankee soldier's portfolio ... franked by Senator Harlan"; see Woodward, ed., *Mary Chesnut's Civil War*, 108. Stampless letters not endorsed by an officer but identified as the correspondence of a soldier could also travel postage due. See Alan Hiebert, "With Love from Nashville," *EnRoute* 4:4 (Oct.—Dec. 1995); For other references to these practices, see Morgan Ebenezer Wescott, Letter of May 20, 1864, in *Civil War Letters, 1861 to 1865: Written by a Boy in Blue to His Mother*. (Mora, MN: privately published,

1909), 20, http://alexanderstreet.com/products/cwld.htm; Alonzo Miller, Letter to Sarah Miller, September 9, 1864, in Alonzo Miller, *Diaries and Letters, 1864–1865* (Prescott, WI: privately published, 1958), 31, http://alexanderstreet.com/products/cwld.htm.

61. Paul Fatout, ed., *Letters of a Civil War Surgeon* (West Lafayette, IN: Purdue University Studies, 1961), 45. Requests for stamps by Union soldiers persisted to very late dates in the war. See for example Robert F. Harris and John Niflot (eds.), *Dear Sister: The Civil War Letters of the Brothers Gould* (Westport, 1998), 132 [9/9/64]. For other complaints about scarcity of stamps see Drake, *The Mail Goes Through*, 19, 42–43, 74; Doody, ed., *Yours in Love*, 73; Harris and Niflot, eds., *Dear Sister*, 46, 47, 53, 132; Tatum, ed., "Civil War Letters of William Allen Clark," 92, 94, 98, 107; Julia Johnson Fisher, "Diary," entry for February 6, 1864, transcript of the manuscript available online at the University of North Carolina Web site, in "Documenting the American South": http://docsouth.unc.edu/fisherjulia/menu.html; Alonzo Miller, Letter of August 11, 1864, in Miller, *Diaries and Letters, 1864–1865*, 29; Spencer Kellogg Brown, Letter to Cora Brown, March 8, 1861, in George Gardner Smith, ed., *Spencer Kellogg Brown, His Life in Kansas and His Death as a Spy, 1842–1863, As Disclosed in His Diary* (New York: D. Appleton, 1903), 184. Mary Livermore remarked that "most of the letters sent to the army contained stamped envelopes, and paper, for the men were without money so much of the time" (Livermore, *My Story of the War*, 140). Especially in the South, such complaints also appeared in the letters of those at home. See, for example, Cutrer, ed., *Oh, What a Loansome* [*sic*] *Time I Had*, 87. Paper became scarce throughout the South during the War, forcing correspondents to use old envelopes, tax receipts, flyleaves of bound books, and even wallpaper. Stamp collectors refer to these unusual postal materials, some of which have survived, as "adversity covers"; see Patricia Kaufmann, "The Rebel Post."

62. Tatum, "Civil War Letters of William Allen Clark," 86; Gaughan, *Letters of a Confederate Surgeon*, 179; Walker quoted in Silber and Sievens, eds., *Yankee Correspondence*, 61; Boyle quoted in ibid., 103; Dekle to his wife, August 16, 1862, in John K. Mahon, "Peter Dekle's Letters," *Civil War History* (March, 1958), 17; Greiner, Coryell, and Smither, eds., *Surgeon's Civil War*, 116. Testimony about the unusual physical circumstances under which letters were composed appears frequently in the correspondence of soldiers. Pennsylvanian Daniel Chisholm explained to his father on one occasion, that "most of this letter was wrote by putting the paper up against" the back of his brother Alex, having complained in an earlier missive of having "to use Alex [*sic*] back for a writing desk"; see Menge and Shimrak, eds., *Civil War Notebook of Daniel Chisholm*, 106, 113. Charles Harvey Brewster recounted to his sister in 1862 that "I am writing in what you would consider a very uncomfortable position, lying flat on my side, with my Woolen Blankets folded up for a table to write on"; see Blight, ed., *When This Cruel War Is Over*, 131.

63. Tatum, ed., "Civil War Letters of William Allen Clark," 91; Sam Evans to Andrew Evans, June 7, 1863, in Robert F. Engs and Corey M. Brooks, eds., *Their Patriotic Duty: The Civil War Letters of the Evans Family of Brown County, Ohio*, original transcription by Joseph Evans Jr. (New York: Fordham University Press, forthcoming [2007]). I am indebted to Corey Brooks for making this text available to me in advance of publication. The wartime letters of Sam, John, and Will Evans are held in the Evans Collection, Ohio State Archives, Columbus, Ohio.

64. Donald C. Elder III, ed., *Love Amid the Turmoil: The Civil War Letters of William and Mary Vermilion* (Iowa City: University of Iowa Press, 2003), 91; James J. Higginson to Henry Lee Higginson, September 4, 1863, in *Life and Letters of Henry Lee Higginson*, ed. Bliss Perry (Boston, MA: Atlantic Monthly Press, 1921), 207; Livermore, *My Story of the War*, 690. For a discussion of prisoners' letters and the obstacles they encountered see John L. Kimbrough, M.D., "A Prisoner's Story: Lt. William A. Smith, Company J 50th Virginia Regiment," in *Confederate Philatelist* (January–February 1997). James M. McPherson makes much of the absence of censorship during the war in his *For Cause and Comrades*, 12.

65. This trend is especially evident in the letters collected by Silber and Sievens in *Yankee Correspondence.*

66. Jaquette, ed., *Letters of a Civil War Nurse,* 29–30. For other striking expressions of anxiety about miscarried mail, see Fatout, *Letters of a Civil War Surgeon,* 73; Green Berry Samuels, Letter to Kathleen Boone Samuels, June 3, 1863, in Carrie Esther Samuels Spencer and Kathleen Boone Samuels, comps., *A Civil War Marriage in Virginia: Reminiscences and Letters* (Boyce, VA: Carr, 1956), 183, online at http://alexanderstreet.com/products/cwld.htm.

67. On the association between death and letter-writing, see Decker, *Epistolary Practices,* esp. 95–99.

68. Elder, *Love Amid the Turmoil,* 125; Rozier, ed., *Granite Farm Letters,* 157; Mills Lane, *Dear Mother: Don't Grieve About Me: If I Get Killed, I'll Only Be Dead: Letters from Georgia Soldiers in the Civil War* (Savannah, GA: Beehive Press, 1977), 90. For other examples see Cutrer, ed., *Oh, What a Loansome [sic]Time I Had,* 36, 87; Robert Partin, "'The Money Matters' of a Confederate Soldier," *Alabama Historical Quarterly* 25 (1963): 49–69; John Bratton, Letter to Bettie Bratton, October 3, 1863, in *Letters of John Bratton to his Wife,* comp. Elizabeth Porcher Bratton (privately published, 1942), 113, online at http://alexanderstreet.com/products/cwld.htm.

69. Letter of John H. W. N. Collins, in Edwin S. Redkey, ed., *A Grand Army of Black Men: Letters from African-American Soldiers in the Union Army, 1861–1865* (New York: Cambridge University Press, 1992), 69–70.

70. Letter of "E. G." in Livermore, *My Story of the War,* 646–47. See also Union soldier Charles Harvey Brewster's description of his mother's letters as "angels' visits," the same term used by Enos Christman to convey the appeal and effect of letters to California during the Gold Rush (*One Man's Gold*). "You do not realize how everything that savors of home relishes with us," Brewster explained. See Blight, *When This Cruel War Is Over,* 148.

71. Greiner, Coryell, and Smither, eds., *Surgeon's Civil War,* 80; Oliver Wilcox Norton, Letter of January 28, 1862, in *Army Letters, 1861–1865: Being Extracts from Private Letters to Relatives and Friends from a Soldier in the Field during the Late Civil War, with an Appendix Containing Copies of Some Official Documents, Papers and Addresses of Later Date* (Chicago, IL: O. L. Deming, 1903), 43.

72. Jane Evans to Sam Evans, April 28, 1862, in Engs and Brooks, eds., *Their Patriotic Duty,* Mitchell, "The Northern Soldier and His Community," 84. For two examples of officers having to answer charges of sexual misconduct circulated by those under their command, see pp. 78 and 87. Of course the surveillance worked in the other direction as well. As Peter Dekle of Georgia wrote to his spouse, "[Y]ou do not noe what sorter talk there are here about soldiers wifes about the wifes and the men that are left behind I do not want to here no such talk about you being intimate with the men." See Mahon, "Peter Dekle's Letters," 17. See also the letter of Ellen Horton to husband Edwin, May 6, 1864, in Silber and Sievens, eds., *Yankee Correspondence,* 150.

73. Silas W. Browning to his wife, December 10, 1862, quoted in Mitchell, "The Northern Soldier and His Community," 83; Letter of "G. T.," in Livermore, *My Story of the War,* 660–61.

74. Livermore, *My Story of the War,* 613–16. For a more conventional example of the circulation of a dead soldier's correspondence, see the offer of Amanda Willson, the bereaved fiancée of fallen Confederate infantryman Alexander Spence, to share his penultimate letter with his sister in Mark K. Christ, ed., *Getting Used to Being Shot At: The Spence Family Civil War Letters* (Fayetteville: University of Arkansas Press, 2002), 120. See also Blight, *When This Cruel War Is Over,* 9.

75. Woodward, ed., *Mary Chesnut's Civil War,* 108. Elvira J. Powers took special interest in captured "Rebel Love Letters" in her 1864 diary. See her *Hospital Pencilling,* 147–52; Oliver Wendell Holmes, "My Hunt After The Captain," *Atlantic Monthly,* December 1862, 749.

76. Alf Burnett, *Incidents of the War: Humorous, Pathetic, and Descriptive* (Cincinnati, OH: Rickey & Carroll, 1863), 296–97. Andrew Evans showed his son's correspondence to neighbors and assured him that "letters from soldiers of known reputation & stamina, have a happy influence on our elections." Andrew Evans to Sam Evans, October 23, 1864, in Engs and Brooks, eds., *Their Patriotic Duty*.

77. Blackford and Blackford, *Letters from Lee's Army*, 196. Much mail from the front reflects self-consciousness about the destiny of letters as historical documents. See, for example, James Williams's letter of July 9, 1862 to his wife Lizzy, in John Kent Folmar, ed., *From That Terrible Field: Civil War Letters of James M. Williams, Twenty-First Alabama Infantry Volunteers*, (University, AL: University of Alabama Press, 1981), 99.

78. See especially Stephanie Coontz, *The Social Origins of Private Life: A History of American Families, 1600–1900* (New York: Verso, 1988), 161–209; Mary P. Ryan, *Cradle of the Middle Class: The Family in Oneida County, New York, 1790–1865* (Cambridge: Cambridge University Press, 1981).

79. Motz, *True Sisterhood*, 58.

80. Rozier, ed., *Granite Farm Letters*, 57.

81. Stowe, ed., *A Southern Practice*, 112–13; Theodore Tilton to Elizabeth, January 3, 1867, in "The Tilton Letters," *Chicago Daily Tribune*, August 13, 1874. For a related argument about the centrality of letter-writing to the discharge of family obligations in the antebellum middle class, see Augst, *Clerk's Tale*, 71–79.

CHAPTER SIX

1. Diary of William Quesenbury Claytor, February, 1851, in *Diary of William Claytor, 1849–1896*, vol. 1 (Alexandria, VA: Alexander Street Press, 2002), 46–47; available on line at http://www.alexanderstreet4.com.

2. Leigh Eric Schmidt, *Consumer Rites: The Buying and Selling of American Holidays* (Princeton, NJ: Princeton University Press, 1995), 49.

3. *New Orleans Picayune*, March 3, 1840; Schmidt, *Consumer Rites*, 50; "St. Valentine and Valentines," *Harper's Weekly*, February 13, 1858, 105. By the time of the Civil War, a Confederate officer would imagine "young lovers, all over the loving lands of Christendom" celebrating the day "sacred to love's sweet correspondence"; see Folmar, ed., *From That Terrible Field*, 35.

4. Schmidt, *Consumer Rites*, 50; *Daily San Francisco Times*, February 14, 1860; "A New Fashion for Valentines," *Godey's Lady's Book* (February, 1849), 73–74; Bowen, *United States Post-Office Guide*, 19; "Metropolitan Post-Offices, New York," *Illustrated Magazine of Art* 1 (1853): 269; "St. Valentine's Day," *Harper's Weekly*, February 19, 1859; *San Francisco Daily Evening News*, February 14, 1855.

5. *New Orleans Picayune*, March 3, 1840.

6. Harry Sunderland, "Kate's Valentine," *Godey's Lady's Book*, February, 1850.

7. *New Orleans Picayune*, March 3, 1840. The *San Francisco Daily Evening News* offered the following account of the holiday rituals: "How the mysterious characters are pored over, in the search after some sign to reveal the author! How hand-writing, however disguised, is penetrated—and how the wishes of the heart often assists [*sic*] deception, by fixing the authorship upon some favorite. All these things are familiar" (February 14, 1855).

8. *The Caricature Valentine Writer, Containing an Entirely New and Original Collection of Epistolary Sketches, ridiculous, witty, and severe* (New York: C. P. Huestis, 1848), 28. According to *Harper's*, fully one half of the printed valentines were of the "comic" type; see "St. Valentine and Valentines," 104. On mock valentines, see Schmidt, *Consumer Rites*, 72–85.

9. Harlow, *Old Post Bags*, 333; "St. Valentine and Valentines," 104. An 1850 story in *Godey's* tells of the firing of a village postmistress for revealing the name of the sender of a valentine; see "Our Post-Mistress; or, Why she was turned out," *Godey's Lady's Book* (February, 1850).

10. *New Orleans Picayune*, March 3, 1840; Bowen, *United States Post-Office Guide*, 19.

11. "A New Fashion for Valentines," 73–74; "St. Valentine's Day," *Harper's Weekly*, February 19, 1859.

12. See John, *Spreading the News*, 257–72.

13. The case of the Lynn postmaster is reported in the *New Orleans Picayune*, August 18, 1841. *Harper's* figured that more than 1.5 million comic valentines were sold annually in the United States by 1858 ("St. Valentine and Valentines," 105).

14. Holbrook, *Ten Years Among the Mail Bags*, 388. Without a named addressee, however, the letter would probably not arrive at its destination.

15. "A Chapter upon Letters and Letter-Writers," *Ladies Repository* 16 (Feb. 1856), 70. Begging letters are referred to in another magazine article as well, where they are counted among those "which are not letters any more than backgammon boards and patent-office reports are books" (Fountain, "Letter-Writing," 236–37).

16. "A Chapter upon Letters and Letter-Writers," 70–71.

17. Fuller, *Morality and the Mail*, 169; John, *Spreading the News*, 161. Rohrbach and Newman, *American Issue*, 85. On circulars and junk mail in the British post immediately following the institution of penny postage, see Vincent, *Culture of Secrecy*, 68–70.

18. Henry W. Bellows, "Seven Sittings with Powers the Sculptor, Part 7," *Appleton's Journal* (September 11, 1869): 106.

19. LeClerq, *An Antebellum Plantation Household*, 41. For another invidious comparison between circulars and "letters . . . of value," see Reverend Robert Mallard's 1856 letter to his fiancée Mary Sharpe Jones, in Myers, ed., *Children of Pride*, 280.

20. See Henkin, *City Reading*.

21. Holbrook, *Ten Years Among the Mail Bags*, 244–54.

22. Ibid., 254–58. Many more anecdotes of postal fraud appear in Anthony Comstock's *Frauds Exposed; or, How the People are Deceived and Robbed, and Youth Corrupted* (New York: J. Howard Brown, 1880). A fascinating account of the role of fraudulent letters and postmarks in the earlier and celebrated case of the prolific forger Monroe Edwards (to whom Melville alludes in "Bartleby") appears in *Life and Adventures of the Accomplished Forger and Swindler, Colonel Monroe Edwards* (New York: H. Long and Brother, 1848).

23. See John F. Kasson, *Rudeness and Civility: Manners in Nineteenth-Century Urban America* (New York: Hill and Wang, 1990) 70–111; Karen Halttunen, *Confidence Men and Painted Women* (New Haven, CT: Yale University Press, 1982); Paul J. Erickson, "Welcome to Sodom: The Cultural Work of City-Mysteries Fiction in Antebellum America" (PhD diss., University of Texas, 2005); Stuart M. Blumin, "George G. Foster and the Emerging Metropolis," in *New York by Gas-light and Other Urban Sketches*, by George G. Foster, ed. Stuart M. Blumin (Berkeley and Los Angeles: University of California Press, 1990), 1–61.

24. Mathew Hale Smith, *Sunshine and Shadow in New York*, 694–705; Edward Crapsey, "The Nether Side of New York," *Galaxy* 11 (May 1871): 652–60.

25. Smith, *Sunshine and Shadow*, 695; Crapsey, 655; Anthony Comstock, *Traps for the Young* (New York: Funk and Wagnall's, 1884), 134. Comstock charged that publishers of sexually explicit material would send "circulars to postal clerks and others through the country, offering prizes for a list of the names of youth of both sexes under twenty-one years of age."

26. Crapsey, "Nether Side," 652–54.

27. "Table-Talk," *Appleton's Journal* 7 (March 30, 1872): 358–60.

28. Leech, *Post Office Department of the United States of America*, 46–49; *Post-Office Law, Instructions and Forms, Published for the Regulation of the Post-Office* (Washington, DC: Government Printing Office, 1825), 15.

29. "Dead Letters," *New York Times* September 24, 1852. The article appeared originally in the *Albany Register*. Some time after the war, the Post Office began selling the paper on which dead letters had been written, rather than burning them, adding about

four thousand dollars per year to the treasury; see Mary Clemmer Ames, *Ten Years in Washington: Life and Scenes in the National Capital* (Hartford: A. D. Worthington, 1874), 399.

30. Miles, *Postal Reform*, 71; Herman Melville, *Great Short Works of Herman Melville*, ed. Warner Berthoff (New York: Harper, 1969), 73–74. An account of the dead letter repository in San Francisco, published the same year as Miles's text and just two years after Melville's, places similar emphasis on the death metaphors. "Here the poet could find themes for his muse, . . . and he who gathers from the warm ashes of the departed material to bring to life again in newer beauty the 'forms of the departed,' might immortalize himself" (*Alta California*, December 29, 1855).

31. Richard R. John, "The Lost World of Bartleby, the Ex-Officeholder: Variations on a Venerable Literary Form," *New England Quarterly* 70 (December 1997): 637–38.

32. "Dead Letters, Opened and Burned by the Postmaster-General, Revived and Published by Timothy Quicksand," *New-England Magazine* 1 (1831): 505.

33. On urban sensationalism from this period, see Kasson, *Rudeness and Civility*; Blumin, "George G. Foster and the Emerging Metropolis"; and David S. Reynolds, *Beneath the American Renaissance: The Subversive Imagination in the Age of Emerson and Melville* (Cambridge, MA: Harvard University Press, 1988).

34. "Dead Letters."

35. [Bagger], "Dead-Letter Office," 593; Clifford, "Down Among the Dead Letters," 517.

36. Ames, *Ten Years in Washington*, 398; Clifford, "Down Among the Dead Letters," 519; "Dead-Letter Office," 594.

37. Clifford, "Down Among the Dead Letters," 520; Ames, *Ten Years in Washington*, 402; "Dead-Letter Office," 594.

38. "Dead-Letter Office," 594; Clifford, "Down Among the Dead Letters," 518.

39. "Dead Letters"; Mary Clemmer Ames offered her own list of "patchwork quilts, under garments, and outer garments; hats, caps, and bonnets; shoes and stockings; with no end of nicknacks and keepsakes; 'sets' of embroidery, baby-wardrobes, watches, and jewels of every description" (*Ten Years in Washington*, 402). Postal clerk James Rees enumerated tobacco, obscene literature, "gaffs for game-fowls" and "ladies' slippers *half worn*," among the mixed multitude of errant postal matter. See "Pandora's Mail-Box Opened," in Rees, *Foot-prints*, 313–14.

40. "Dead Letters"; "Dead-Letter Office," 593.

41. Melville's choice of the Dead Letter Office as Bartleby the scrivener's previous employment makes perfect sense in this context. Identifying an alienated urban stranger with the dead letter, Melville offered an astute reading of the culture of the post in the late antebellum period.

42. "Editor's Drawer," *Harper's Monthly* 11 (September 1855): 570; Holbrook, *Ten Years Among the Mail Bags*, 387; *Scientific American*, July 9, 1859. In Horatio Alger's *Ragged Dick* (1867), the title character is told of a letter waiting for him at the post office addressed to his nickname, which no longer applies now that he has turned respectable. He reclaims his old outfit and dresses the part in order to persuade the clerk that he is the intended recipient (*Ragged Dick and Struggling Upward* [New York: Penguin, 1985], 117–19).

43. LeClerq, ed., *Between North and South*, 57. On Alfred Huger, see John, *Spreading the News*, 257–80; *New Universal Letter-Writer*, 33.

44. *New Orleans Picayune*, September 21, 1840; Charles Allen to brother William, February 14, 1854, Letters from William and Charles Allen, 1853–1878, Bancroft MSS 88/129c, BANC; James Harris Ham to Charlie, San Francisco, January 22, 1853, California Gold Rush Letters, Bancroft MSS C-B 547, part 1, box 2, BANC; Rees, *Foot-prints*, 308; Mary Wingate to husband Benjamin, August 26, 1851, Wingate Correspondence, Bancroft MSS 83/35c, BANC.

45. Bowen, *United States Post-Office Guide*, 71.

46. Gail Hamilton, "A Business Letter," *Our Young Folks: An Illustrated Magazine for Boys and Girls* 1 (1865): 368–72.

47. Starkey's letter appears in Blassingame, *Slave Testimony*, 86; Levy, *Jewish Girlhood in Old San Francisco*, 14. For Fern's reflections on her own fan mail, see her February 9, 1856, article in the *New York Ledger*, printed in Fern, *Ruth Hall*, 268–69.

48. Jill Anderson, "'Send Me a Nice Little Letter All to Myself.'"

49. The incident is described in all of the Taylor biographies. See K. Jack Bauer, *Zachary Taylor: Soldier, Planter, Statesman of the Old Southwest* (Baton Rouge: Louisiana State University Press, 1985), 237–38; Holman Hamilton, *Zachary Taylor: Soldier in the White House* (Indianapolis, IN: Bobbs-Merrill, 1951), 117–18; Brainerd Dyer, *Zachary Taylor* (Baton Rouge: Louisiana State University Press, 1946), 284–85.

50. Southworth, *Hidden Hand*, 59.

51. Yellow Bird [John Rollin Ridge], *The Lives and Adventures of Joaquín Murieta* (Norman: University of Oklahoma Press, 1955), 95.

52. The senator who introduced the 1865 bill that sought (unsuccessfully) to authorize the destruction of all obscene publications deposited in the mail explained that "it is said that our mails are made the vehicle for the conveyance of great numbers and quantities of obscene books and pictures, which are sent to the Army, and sent here and there and everywhere. . . ."; quoted in Helen Lefkowitz Horowitz, *Rereading Sex: Battles over Sexual Knowledge and Suppression in Nineteenth-Century America* (New York: Vintage, 2002), 313.

53. Comstock, *Frauds Exposed*, 391.

EPILOGUE

1. Vincent, "Progress of Literacy"; Siegert, *Relays*, 136–45.

2. Siegert, *Relays*, 136–42.

3. Leech, *Post Office Department of the United States of America*, 33. One might compare the symbolic significance of the 1874 treaty for Americans with that of the initial laying of the transatlantic telegraph cable in 1858, since from the U.S. perspective the World Postal Union was about bridging continents and not just countries. For Europeans, on the other hand, the railroad had already familiarized the concept—and the experience—of transnational space.

4. Siegert, *Relays*, 146–64; Robinson, *British Post Office*, 368–75; Vincent, *Literacy and Popular Culture*, 46–51. The quotation is from Jacques Derrida, *The Post Card: From Socrates to Freud and Beyond*, trans. Alan Bass (Chicago: University of Chicago Press, 1987), 22.

5. Claude S. Fischer, *America Calling: A Social History of the Telephone to 1940* (Berkeley and Los Angeles: University of California Press, 1992), 1–59.

INDEX

African Americans, 33–34. *See also* slavery
Alger, Horatio: *Ragged Dick*, 81, 96,
    100
Anderson, Jill, 168
anonymity, 150–51, 165. *See also* names
Augst, Thomas, 98
autographs, 56, 168, 190n34, 191n36

Beecher, Henry Ward, 100, 102
Blythe, David, 69–70
Bowman, Alexander, 67
Brown, Henry "Box," 34
Brown, Richard D., 17
Bruns, James, 88–89
Burns, Anthony, 1–2, 33, 166
business letters, 31, 95–99, 105,
    199n19

Carlyle, Thomas, 39
cartography, postal, 38–39, 173, 188n85
Channing, William Ellery, 50–51
Chartier, Roger, 206n79
cheap postage. *See* postage rates
Chesnut, Mary, 77, 107, 144
circulars, 154–58
Civil War, American, 4, 11, 26, 38, 46,
    57–59, 105–6, 113, 137–46; mail
    censorship during, 141
clerks. *See* business letters
Cohen, Patricia Cline, 79
Comstock, Anthony, 157, 169–71
Comstock Act, 174–75
confidentiality. *See* privacy
conversation (letters compared to), 10,
    100–101, 109–11, 200–201n29
Cooke, Jay, 95, 98
Crevecoeur, J. Hector St. John de: *Letters
    from an American Farmer*, 200–201n29
cross-writing, 19, 180n13
Cummins, Maria: *The Lamplighter*, 77

daguerreotypes. *See* photography
Dana, Richard Henry, 1, 43, 46, 166
Dead Letter Office, 11, 52, 56, 75, 158–65
dead letters, 32, 158–65
Decker, William Merrill, 112
Dierks, Konstantin, 179, 180n8
disease, 61–62, 192n53
Donner Party, 119, 121

Emerson, Ralph Waldo, 39, 61
epistolary novels, 99

family, 136–37, 142, 146–47
Farrar, Mrs. John, 51, 106
Fern, Fanny, 75–76, 190n35; *Ruth Hall*, 39,
    168
France, 31, 185n57, 206n79
franking privileges, 19, 20, 37, 140

Garrison, William Lloyd, 43
gender, 72; disparities in postal use, 32, 72–74,
    108. *See also under* women
Gold Rush, 4, 11, 35, 36, 38, 40, 57–58, 69, 71,
    81, 113–14, 123–37, 142, 146–47, 186n68,
    195n29
Great Britain, 20, 29–31, 59, 63, 83, 84, 87, 99

handwriting, 55–56, 98, 162
Hawthorne, Nathaniel, 39
Headrick, Dan, 5
Hewitt, Elizabeth, 186n63
Hill, Rowland, 30–31, 82, 173
Holbrook, James, 3, 52–53, 72,
Holmes, Oliver Wendell, 145
home delivery, 82–90

immigrants, 35, 60–61, 80, 103–5, 113,
    202n38
international mail, 29, 35, 172–73
intimacy. *See* privacy

219